Read On . . . Science Fiction

Read On . . . Science Fiction

Reading Lists for Every Taste

Steven A. Torres-Roman

Read On Series
Barry Trott, Series Editor

AN IMPRINT OF ABC-CLIO, LLC
Santa Barbara, California • Denver, Colorado • Oxford, England

Library of Congress Cataloging-in-Publication Data

Torres-Roman, Steven A.
  Read on— science fiction : reading lists for every taste / Steven A. Torres-Roman.
    p. cm. — (Read on series)
  Includes bibliographical references and index.
  ISBN 978-1-59158-769-9 (pbk : acid-free paper) 1. Science fiction, American—Bibliography. 2. Science fiction, English—Bibliography.
3. Science fiction—Bibliography. 4. Fiction in libraries—United States.
5. Readers' advisory services—United States. 6. Public libraries—United States—Book lists. I. Title. II. Title: Science fiction.
Z1231.S38T76 2010
[PS374.S35]
016.813'0876208—dc22   2010024075

ISBN: 978-1-59158-769-9

14 13 12 11 10   1 2 3 4 5

This book is also available on the World Wide Web as an eBook.
Visit www.abc-clio.com for details.

Libraries Unlimited
An Imprint of ABC-CLIO, LLC

ABC-CLIO, LLC
130 Cremona Drive, P.O. Box 1911
Santa Barbara, California 93116-1911

This book is printed on acid-free paper ∞
Manufactured in the United States of America

This book is the result of a long and fruitful endeavor. I would be remiss if I didn't thank the people who helped me through this process:

Karen, for all her patience. This book is dedicated to her.

Dee Coover, director of the DeKalb Public Library, for giving me a chance and good advice.

Barbara Ittner and Barry Trott, for giving me this opportunity.

My coworkers, for their support and for putting up with me talking to myself.

My proofreaders: Jonathan Burke, Angela Camp, Danika Duvall, Joseph Merrit, Leif Mogren, Angela Moloney, Sarah Ott, Cason Snow, and Andrew Weckerly, for listening to me babble, donating their time, and flattering me by finding these entries useful in their own literary explorations.

The DeKalb Public Library's Destination Wonder speculative fiction book discussion group, Teen Advisory Group, and Anime Alliance, for being my guinea pigs.

Tony Rakittke, my ideological partner in crime.

My friends and family, for their understanding and support.

Catherine Asaro (she writes SF!), for her kind interest.

Roger Zelazny, whose work repeatedly renews my sense of wonder.

Contents

Series Foreword

Welcome to Libraries Unlimited's Read On series of fiction and nonfiction genre guides for readers' advisors and for readers. The Read On series introduces readers and those who work with them to new ways of looking at books, genres, and reading interests.

Over the past decade, readers' advisory services have become vital in public libraries. A quick glance at the schedule of any library conference at the state or national level will reveal a wealth of programs on various aspects of connecting readers to books they will enjoy. Working with unfamiliar genres or types of reading can be a challenge, particularly for those new to the field. Equally, readers may find it a bit overwhelming to look for books outside their favorite authors and preferred reading interests. The titles in the Read On series offer you a new way to approach reading:

- they introduce you to a broad sampling of materials available in a given genre;

- they offer you new directions to explore in a genre—through appeal features and unconventional topics;

- they help readers' advisors better understand and navigate genres with which they are less familiar;

- and they provide reading lists that you can use to create quick displays, include on your library Web sites and in the library newsletter, or hand out to readers.

The lists in the Read On series are arranged in sections based on appeal characteristics—story, character, setting, and language (as described in Joyce Saricks' *Reader's Advisory Services in the Public Library*, 3d ed., ALA Editions, 2005), with a fifth section on mood. These are hidden elements of a book that attract readers. Remember that a book can have multiple appeal factors; and sometimes readers are drawn to a particular book for several factors, while other times for only one. In the Read On lists, titles are placed according to their primary appeal characteristics, and then put into a list that reflects common reading interests. So if you are working with a reader who loves fantasy that features quests for magical objects or a reader who is interested in memoirs with a strong sense of place you will be able to find a list of titles whose main appeal centers around this search. Each list indicates a title that is an especially good starting place for readers, an exemplar of that appeal characteristic.

Story is perhaps the most basic appeal characteristic. It relates to the plot of the book – what are the elements of the tale? Is the emphasis more on the people or the situations? Is the story action focused or more interior? Is it funny? Scary?

Many readers are drawn to the books they love by the characters. The Character appeal reflects such aspects as whether there are lots of characters or only a single main character; are the characters easily recognizable types? Do the characters grow and change over the course of the story? What are the characters' occupations?

Setting covers a range of elements that might appeal to readers. What is the time period or geographic locale of the tale? How much does the author describe the surroundings of the story? Does the reader feel as though he or she is "there," when reading the book? Are there special features such as the monastic location of Ellis Peters' Brother Cadfael mysteries or the small town setting of Jan Karon's Mitford series?

Although not traditionally considered an appeal characteristic, mood is important to readers as well. It relates to how the author uses the tools of narrative – language, pacing, story, and character – to create a feeling for the work. Mood can be difficult to quantify because the reader brings his or her own feelings to the story as well. Mood really asks how does the book make the reader feel? Creepy? Refreshed? Joyful? Sad?

Finally, the Language appeal brings together titles where the author's writing style draws the reader. This can be anything from a lyrical prose style with lots of flourishes to a spare use of language ala Hemingway. Humor, snappy dialog, word-play, recipes and other language elements all have the potential to attract readers.

Dig into these lists. Use them to find new titles and authors in a genre that you love, or as a guide to expand your knowledge of a new type of writing. Above all, read, enjoy , and remember—never apologize for your reading tastes!

Barry Trott
Series Editor

Introduction

Don't Panic

If you're the kind of person who actually reads introductions, welcome, and thank you for picking up this book. Let me be the first to assure you, in case there is any doubt, that you may already be a science fiction fan—even if you don't know it yet.

Curiosity is the cornerstone of exploration and discovery after all, and the origin of many an adventure as well. It is my hope that *Read On . . . Science Fiction* will act as a signpost, a trusty guide if you will, for seasoned explorers and hapless hitchhikers alike on their intergalactic journeys.

SF in a Nutshell: What Is Science Fiction?

So what is science fiction (SF for short)? When I'm asked that question, I usually use the ostensive definition: to quote author Damon Knight, "the term science fiction . . . means what we point to when we say it" (Damon Knight, *In Search of Wonder: Essays on Modern Science Fiction*, 3rd ed. [Chicago: Advent Publishers, 1996], 11).

I'm only half-joking, you know.

As you may guess, there are a few problems in giving a hard and fast definition for something as amorphous as a fiction genre. Science fiction creators are as varied in their tastes and interests as anyone else, and the work they produce will inevitably be just as varied. Moreover, creators and consumers of SF are also as contentious as anyone else, so agreement on any definition will be tentative at best and will include many caveats.

Most important, though, any but the most inclusive definition of science fiction will inevitably exclude works that have been generally accepted within the genre to date. For example, if I assert that the term "science fiction" should refer only to those works in which the authors demonstrate only the most rigorous adherence to scientific detail in both presentation and extrapolation, then this guidebook quickly becomes a lot shorter. Perhaps I can grandfather in the books in which the science is a bit out of date or has since proven false. But what do I do with all those galactic empires that use faster-than-light technology for travel and communication, or the telepaths, or the aliens with funny foreheads that we've never encountered (and aren't likely to)? Do the books containing these elements simply disappear in a puff of logic? I sure hope not, and I suspect many science fiction readers agree. After all, SF isn't *just* about the science and technology; if it were, we'd be reading textbooks and technical manuals instead.

I could try to define science fiction by what it isn't. For example, science fiction typically excludes magic and the supernatural as tools or explanations for phenomena. However, many SF novels contain "science" that is, frankly, imaginary, merely handwaved into existence by authors. More than a few science fiction novels feature elements with nothing other than the story's say-so that we are, indeed, presented with an advanced form of science. Some fans might quote Arthur C. Clarke's famous law that "any sufficiently advanced technology is indistinguishable from magic" (Arthur C. Clarke, *Profiles of the Future*. Rev. ed. [New York: Harper & Row, 1973], 21, footnote). Regardless of Clarke's law or a story's assurances, we are faced with the fact that such technology is essentially magical in its presentation and explanation, and the equivalent of magic in its function. Thus, a negative definition of science fiction seems inadequate.

We could try to define science fiction by what it does. Science fiction authors often posit an extrapolation of science and technology and then consider its effect on humanity (or another, fictional species). In detailing the interaction between society and the science fictional element, the author holds up a mirror to aspects of our own societies and cultures. Sometimes the reflection is clear, sometimes it is an absurd, twisted, fun-house distortion, but the best of such fiction reveals insights into contemporary and universal concerns and permits us to see ourselves in a new light.

Except when it doesn't. SF need be neither profound nor revelatory. Many excellent stories are simply fantastic adventure yarns or humorous spoof and satire, meant to entertain and delight. Science fiction need not always demand nor require brow-furrowing, pondering, or deep introspection; it can simply be fun.

Perhaps we should define science fiction by its aspects. It can be visionary and bold. It often focuses on exploration and discovery, regardless of whether the object of such endeavors is a planet, an alien civilization, an extraterrestrial artifact, or a solution to contemporary dilemmas. Science fiction can inspire and elicit a sense of awe and wonder, a sublime joy and a desire to experience the unknown. Many works of science fiction promote peace, progress, and understanding in their pages.

On the other hand, a friend of mine once posited science as "war against nature," and many science fiction stories focus on conquering and mastering our environment. Numerous science fiction stories focus on destruction rather than creation, war rather than peace. Instead of a progressive utopia, we might just as easily find a fascistic dystopia waiting in the pages, and the work may elicit a sense of caution rather than wonder. All of which is good, mind you. Different writers have different purposes in their writing, and sometimes at the end of the day, you want to see stuff blowing up, especially if it's the flagship of an evil alien space emperor.

It seems as if the only requirement of science fiction is that the work includes some form of science or technology, real or imaginary, that builds on or extrapolates from contemporaneous or imagined scientific or technological concepts or knowledge. The science in a work of fiction may be the primary focus; the plot hook; the jumping-off point; the solution to a mystery; the tool we use to explore ourselves, our cultures, and our civilizations; or simply the set dressing. Even if the scientific elements turn out to be pseudoscience or outdated views of science, utterly imaginary technology, the key to averting impending disaster, simply the trappings of science, or even the existence of alternate realities that science suggests, we'll call the work science fiction. To do otherwise would cut us off from some of the most beloved, imaginative, and influential work in the genre—an unacceptable outcome, I'm sure you'll agree.

This inclusive attitude toward science fiction encompasses the adventure stories of C. L. Moore and Leigh Brackett as easily as it does the cyberpunk novels of William Gibson or the transhumanist works of Charles Stross. The creations of Isaac Asimov can share space with those of Mary Shelley, H. G. Wells, E. E. "Doc" Smith, Roger Zelazny, and Masamune Shirow, and none of them seems out of place. Octavia Butler's parables can be told in the same breath as Jack Vance's tales, and Michael Moorcock's *Dancers at the End of Time* can perform with Anne McCaffrey's *Crystal Singer*. The Mars of Edgar Rice Burroughs can orbit next to that of Kim Stanley Robinson, and the cosmic horror of H. P. Lovecraft can rest beside the cosmic awareness of Arthur C. Clarke. The Minds of Iain M. Banks can share thoughts with Alfred Bester's telepaths, and Robert Heinlein's *Starship Troopers* can muster alongside John Scalzi's *Ghost Brigades*.

I could go on (don't worry, I won't), but suffice it to say that cutting out any of these works over a preference of taste or a nuance of wording would be a shame. It's a big, strange fictional universe. I figure we should keep it that way.

A Journey through Time: A Very Brief History of Science Fiction Literature

Science fiction aficionados and scholars like to speak of science fiction in terms of ages or eras, similar to how historians divide the past by technology level or how biologists divide the geological and evolutionary timeline. I will occasionally do the same thing, simply because the terms are used often enough that they've become part of the SF vernacular. I will certainly admit that this short trip from past to present is neither exhaustive nor objective, but I'll try to identify the broad strokes for readers interested in SF.

While some scholars would trace the origins of science fiction back to the second century A.D. (see, for example, *The History of Science Fiction* by Adam Roberts), many trace modern science fiction to the early nineteenth century. Mary Shelley's gothic novel *Frankenstein; or, the Modern Prometheus*, published in 1818, presents a thoughtful consideration of the promise and perils of scientific endeavor, as well as the archetypal mad scientist. Not long after, Edgar Allen Poe launched a balloon journey to the moon in 1835 with "The Unparalleled Adventure of One Hans Pfaall" and brought space travel to the arena of popular fiction.

Jules Verne kept science fiction firmly in the public eye throughout the nineteenth century with his *Voyages Extraordinaires*, tales that delighted and inspired his readers. Verne was perhaps more stringent than other writers, in that he hewed very close to the actual science of his time, though his novels were also packed with action and adventure. Works such as *From the Earth to the Moon* (1865), *Twenty Thousand Leagues under the Sea* (1870), and *Journey to the Center of the Earth* (1864) captured the imaginations of generations of fans and are considered classics today.

Even more fanciful fare could be found in American dime novels with the Edisonades (named after Thomas Edison), stories that featured the exploits of inventors and their wondrous creations. Just as fantastic, though perhaps more thoughtful, H. G. Wells's stories proved to be pioneering science fiction. Wells revived the mad scientist in works like *The Invisible Man* (1897) and *The Island of Doctor Moreau* (1896), as had Robert Louis Stevenson with *The Strange*

Case of Dr. Jekyll and Mr. Hyde (1886), all of which expanded on the themes in Shelley's *Frankenstein* and included examinations of humanity, the nature of good and evil, and the unexpected consequences of scientific discoveries. Wells also took his writing beyond the laboratory, devastating the Earth in *The War of the Worlds* (1898), traveling to the far future in *The Time Machine* (1895), and following Poe and Verne before him in *The First Men in the Moon* (1901), all the while composing reflective social commentary.

Edgar Rice Burroughs burst onto the science fiction stage with his serialized story *Under the Moons of Mars*, later collected and retitled *A Princess of Mars* (1917). Full of alien races, swashbuckling action, and strange technology, Burroughs's series on Barsoom (as the native residents of Mars call their planet) and its dashing hero John Carter garnered him substantial attention before the popularity of the Tarzan stories made Burroughs a household name. These planetary romances would be the inspiration for later action-oriented science fiction like Alex Raymond's *Flash Gordon* comic strip, as well as sword and sorcery pulp fiction stories.

In 1926, author and editor Hugo Gernsback founded *Amazing Stories,* the first magazine devoted exclusively to the burgeoning genre of "scientifiction," a clumsy, unwieldy early term for SF that thankfully fell out of use. Gernsback and *Amazing Stories* changed SF forever. Originally offering reprints of stories by Wells, Verne, and others, the magazine soon introduced new fiction from authors like E. E. "Doc" Smith, known for his <u>Skylark</u> and <u>Lensman</u> series, and Philip Francis Nowlan, creator of Buck Rogers. Later magazines that worked hard to keep science fiction alive and well include John W. Campbell's magazine *Astounding Stories* (1930, which later changed its title to *Astounding Science Fiction* and, still later, *Analog Science Fiction and Fact*); *New Worlds* (1946); *The Magazine of Fantasy and Science Fiction* (1949); *Galaxy* (1950); and *Isaac Asimov's Science Fiction Magazine* (1977, later simply *Asimov's Science Fiction*), among others.

Thanks in large part to these magazines and the authors they showcased, and despite the interruption of World War II, science fiction experienced its Golden Age from the 1930s through the early 1950s. Authors such as Isaac Asimov, E. E. Smith, C. L. Moore, Leigh Brackett, Robert A. Heinlein, and A. E. van Vogt were early North American luminaries. Other writers like Aldous Huxley, Olaf Stapledon, and George Orwell were also crucial to establishing the genre.

Science fiction continued to flourish in the 1950s, aided in no small part by both the cinema and, as larger publishers saw opportunities for profit, the expanding paperback market. During this time, Isaac Asimov grew in stature and importance as an author, and many more writers contributed their voices and works to the genre. Arthur C. Clarke, Ray Bradbury, Fritz Leiber, Theodore Sturgeon, Walter M. Miller Jr., Philip José Farmer, Jack Vance, Andre Norton, and Poul Anderson are only a few of the authors who penned some of their most famous work during this time. Exploration was a common theme, and space operas, with their intergalactic empires and vast panoramas, were plentiful.

It was inevitable that changes in culture became mirrored in conceptions of the future. During the 1960s and 1970s, science fiction writers began incorporating more of the social sciences—fields such as psychology, sociology, and politics—into their work. Authors placed additional emphasis on exploring characters' psyches, a focus on internal realities no less fantastic and wondrous than the fictional external realities. The writers also demonstrated a literary sensibility that was rarely seen in the genre's pulpy roots. This New Wave in science fiction included talents such as Michael Moorcock (who also changed the direction of the British magazine *New Worlds* as its editor), Roger Zelazny, Philip K. Dick, Ursula K. Le Guin, and Samuel Delaney. These authors invented new uses for the earlier tropes of science fiction and challenged contemporary cultural notions of gender, religion, sexuality, political thought, the nature of humanity, and the nature of reality.

SF proceeded from sober to somber as the Cold War and continued abuse of the environment forced people to realize that humanity had the ability to utterly devastate the planet and drive itself into extinction. Whether the end came through nuclear conflict, a fatally damaged ecosystem, or a killer virus, science fiction reminded us of our fragility and warned us against a headlong path to destruction.

The overcast mood found its way into the four-color world of comics to varying degrees. The pulpier, action-oriented SF found a comfortable home in comics, particularly publications such as Britain's *2000 AD*, but themes of humanity's hatred of the other and post-apocalyptic landscapes crept into these tales for younger readers. Certainly the changing mood found its way into France's *Metal Hurlant* (published in the U.S. as *Heavy Metal*), a magazine that reflected the influence of SF's New Wave, and contributors such as Jean Giraud (a.k.a. Moebius) influenced SF comics worldwide. As U.S. comics primarily fixated on superheroes, characters such as the X-Men confronted prejudice while simultaneously opening up cosmic realms of adventure. Japan's *manga* also evolved alongside SF's general mood; *Astro Boy* captured a youthful exuberance, while later Japanese titles, such as *Akira*, were profoundly affected by the dark themes to come.

Despite the resurgence of space opera in film (thank you, *Star Wars!*), during the late 1970s and early 1980s, the bright memories of futures past were fading away rapidly (as beautifully related in William Gibson's story "The Gernsback Continuum") . These flashbacks yielded to new visions of tomorrow that highlighted contemporary concerns, including rampant capitalism and the growing divide between the rich and poor. William Gibson's classic novel *Neuromancer* and the film *Blade Runner* essentially defined the cyberpunk subgenre, with assistance from writers like Pat Cadigan, Bruce Sterling, Walter Jon Williams, Norman Spinrad, and Melissa Scott. These authors wed cutting-edge technology with street-level concerns and global perspectives, all the while developing convincing protagonists concerned with making a buck.

The grand vistas of space opera were bound to return, however, and did so in the form of the New Space Opera movement. Iain M. Banks, Dan Simmons, Peter F. Hamilton, Ken MacLeod, Alastair Reynolds, Stephen Baxter, Paul J. McAuley, and a host of other authors brought back the spectacle and breadth of the older SF. The mood and plots seem more complex in this revival, however. The protagonists aren't necessarily good guys, and the antagonists aren't necessarily bad guys. A moral grayness pervades the New Space Opera, and there's no guarantee of a happy ending.

Time and technology advance apace. Biotechnology and nanotechnology in particular spark minds with possibility and potential. There is a resurgent hopefulness in humanity's ability to shape its future, a confidence that puts a new spin on SF. Concepts such as transhumanism, posthumanism, and the singularity allow for new and grand varieties of science fiction. Transhumanist fiction combines tropes of cyberpunk and New Space Opera with faith in sentient species' ability to overcome age-old obstacles like illness and death and competently face whatever new problems may arise. Charles Stross, Justina Robson, and their contemporaries write of sentients, including humanity's descendents, which adapt, change, grow, and see all the wonders the universe has to offer.

(Not) The Encyclopedia Galactica: What This Book Is For, and How to Use It

As I mentioned at the beginning of this introduction, think of *Read On . . . Science Fiction* as a traveler's guide to the imagination organized in chapters, lists, and individual entries. The different chapters—Story, Character, Setting,

Mood, and Language—cover broad areas of appeal. Each chapter has a variety of list headings that (I hope) are memorable and at least mildly witty. Each list identifies and groups books by a general theme and gives readers entry points to the universes of science fiction that may generate interest and elicit further exploration.

Each entry within a list is structured the same way:

- the author's (or authors') last and first name(s) in bold print

- the title of the book in italics and bold print

- the series that book belongs to, if applicable, underlined

- the publication year of the edition of the book I listed, followed by the book's original publication year, if applicable

- the publisher of the edition I listed

- the ten and thirteen digit International Standard Book Numbers (ISBNs) assigned to the edition I listed

- the page count of the edition I listed

Here's an example:

Bujold, Lois McMaster

The Warrior's Apprentice. <u>Vorkosigan Saga</u>. 2002 (1986). NESFA Press, ISBN: 1886778272, 9781886778276, 309p.

You may also encounter the occasional symbols within an entry. In each list, one entry will have an arrow ⇒ next to it. The arrow indicates a good introductory book within a given list, an excellent place to start exploring. The other symbol, **GN**, indicates that the book is a graphic novel—comics bound into a book format.

When possible, I tried to choose books that are available in recent editions through libraries and bookstores. The annotations accompanying each entry are not exhaustive summaries—I don't want to give away all the surprises, after all. Rather, they serve as quick snapshots of the book—trailer, teaser, and representative appeal all in one—with just enough information to spark curiosity.

The only real downside of presenting a guide to science fiction is that there are simply too many science fiction novels for any author to be able to cover the entire genre. (If your favorite book is missing, *mea culpa*.) Faced with the impossibility of an exhaustive resource, I present you with what I hope is a representative sampling. In writing this work, I tried to include a variety of books ranging from the foundational to the most recent that cover a broad cross-section of subgenres. This breadth of scope increases the likelihood that any given reader will find something of interest in these pages.

So now that you know how the book is organized, what do you do with it? Librarians can use this book as an on-the-spot resource for making specific science fiction recommendations tailored to their patrons' tastes. Patrons often approach librarians and ask them to recommend a good book, a vague request at best since the parameters of what constitutes a good book will vary with each patron. The chapter headings map the appeal factors that many librarians use as guidelines when they perform readers' advisory interviews to clarify what their patrons desire. For example, if a patron is new to SF and wants something light and humorous, the librarian could turn to the Mood chapter and find a list of humorous novels that may interest the patron.

If a patron has already ventured into science fiction, librarians can ask about books the patron previously read and enjoyed. Our friendly neighborhood librarian could then look up those titles and their authors in the index. From there, it's a simple matter of turning to the lists containing those books and authors' names and recommending similar works from those lists. Librarians can also use these lists when creating bookmarks and bibliographies for their patrons, or when devising read-alike lists for their libraries' Web sites.

Of course, individual readers, including patrons who are too shy to approach their librarian, can simply access this book themselves. Some readers may open a page at random and let chance decide their next great read. Old hands at navigating literary space can use the index to look up specific authors and works, or scan the lists in the table of contents until inspiration strikes. In any event, when readers discover their next fantastic read, they have a ready list of future options awaiting them.

Ultimately, this book is yours to do with what you will. I sincerely hope that you will find it useful to you in your exploration of the science fiction genre. If you do, please take a moment to let me know at steven.torres.roman@ gmail.com. I appreciate your comments.

Now get out there and discover something new.

Chapter One

Story

Story in science fiction can seem a fragmented, dissociated concept. For some, the words "science fiction" elicit visions of ray guns, swashbuckling adventures, exotic planets, alien empires, and massive ships that would require an entire planet's resources in metal. For others, science fiction is strictly about the soundness of the science and the author's extrapolative skill in crafting the story around a new technology, and society's reaction to it.

Fortunately, because of this very dissociation, a large number of themes, both universal and topical, fit under the umbrella of science fiction and provide a variety of stories as numerous as the stars and as unique as the writers and readers of these tales. Even better, as the range of authors and dates demonstrates, each new generation of writers redefines these themes for a new generation of readers. In the following lists, inquisitive and industrious seekers of every stripe will find a host of story types arrayed like a wine rack with vintages recent, classic, and rare to delight and satisfy the reader's discerning palate.

Science Fiction 101: Opening Doors to Wonder

Science fiction is a big genre with a long and storied history, and readers may have difficulty accessing the genre for a variety of reasons. Many SF novels, for better or worse, assume an experience and facility with the genre that readers may not possess. Concepts like transhumanism and nanotechnology may cause readers to stumble unsatisfactorily in their tentative first steps into the genre. In addition, some readers may believe that SF, with its aliens and space ships, is too divorced from the real world. Others may have encountered science fiction only through films and television and feel lost as to where to begin reading, intimidated by the multiplicity of books and authors available in stores and libraries. This list will hopefully give librarians and new readers a bit of guidance and relief. Some of the stories contain perpetually relevant themes; others may attract new readers due to their humor, their recognizable settings, or their crossover with other genres. I hope that readers will step right through these beckoning gateways, enter new worlds, and experience a genre filled with imagination, hope, humor, adventure, and wonder as they gain familiarity with the tropes, the vocabulary, and the imaginative visions of science fiction.

Adams, Douglas

⇒ *The Hitchhiker's Guide to the Galaxy.* The Hitchhiker's Guide to the Galaxy. 1995 (1979). Ballantine, ISBN: 0345391802, 9780345391803, 216p.

If you have friends you'd like to introduce to SF, then this is the novel to put into their hands. It's refreshingly and delightfully irreverent look at science fiction covers many of the genre's major tropes. Alien researchers like Ford Prefect live and move among us, study us (in this case, for the eponymous guide), and occasionally get things wrong (Ford thought that the Earth's dominant life forms were automobiles). Other aliens are more than willing to destroy our planet (the new hyperspace bypass has to go *somewhere*, after all) and use us in their experiments (wait until you learn about the real creators of the Earth). We even get a bit of interspecies communication! (Do *not* let Vogons read their poetry to you.) *The Hitchhiker's Guide to the Galaxy* is accessible, hilarious, and the first in a series that will draw readers into further exploring the genre.

Barry, Max

Jennifer Government. 2004 (2003). Vintage, ISBN: 1400030927, 97814 00030927, 321p.

Readers with little interest in spaceships and aliens will enjoy Barry's pointed satire, breezy pace, and his ability to extrapolate the free market to a sly, snide extreme. He envisions a world where the incorporated police require proof of payment before investigating crimes, and corporate culture and brand identification extend to the point where employees take company names as their own. And when major corporations think that they can get away with murder if it means a sales boost, they find themselves in an adversarial relationship with the government—just like in our world! Readers will find a comfortable introduction to SF as slang replaces technobabble, and the empires are corporate rather than galactic, but no less ruthless.

Gibson, William

Pattern Recognition. 2005 (2003). Berkley Books, ISBN: 0425198685, 9780425198681, 367p.

Gibson's novel takes place in a recognizable world and focuses on how we shape our media, and how it shapes us. His protagonist, Cayce Pollard, is a coolhunter: she has an intuitive ability to sniff out the next big thing, discover trends about to explode in popularity, and package them for maximum profit. She impresses her latest client so much that he asks her to track a series of Internet clips that developed a cult following, as the genius behind the cult media would boost any marketing department. Cayce accepts the job and follows a trail into a dark world filled with hackers, cryptographers, and gangsters. Fans of contemporary thrillers will discover a science fiction author who speaks their language and will enjoy this easy introduction to SF with a world just around the corner from our own.

Greenland, Colin

Take Back Plenty. Tabitha Jute/Plenty. 1992 (1990). Avon, ISBN: 0380763958, 9780380763955, 484p.

Film and television fans that enjoy the adventures of Captain Mal Reynolds in *Firefly* and *Serenity* will find this novel a good gateway to science fiction novels. Unlike the high-falootin' planetary princesses and intergalactic globetrotters in so many other novels, Tabitha Jute is a space trucker, the pilot of the artificially intelligent spacecraft *Alice Liddell*. Readers will appreciate this frank, sharp, and realistic working-class heroine as she tries to earn an honest buck. When she finds herself deep in debt she accepts what should be a simple job from acquaintance Marco Metz. The simple transport to the satellite Plenty turns perilous, and Jute soon finds herself in too deep and over her head. Greenland's wild and humorous adventure will ease newer readers into space opera. This well-told tale won the British Science Fiction Award, the Arthur C. Clarke Award, and the Eastercon Award.

L'Engle, Madeleine

A Wrinkle in Time. The Time Quintet. Square Fish, ISBN: 0312367546, 9780312367541, 245p.

L'Engle's classic children's novel serves as an excellent gateway for younger readers to the worlds of science fiction. The author employs the elements of fairy tales and children's literature—young characters that children can identify with, learned fairy godmothers and guardians, travel to other realms, and a choice between right and wrong—even as she bends vocabulary to serve science fictional needs. *A Wrinkle in Time* has the young protagonists, guided by the mysterious Mrs. Whatsit, Mrs. Who, and Mrs. Which, use a tessaract, a wrinkle in time, to travel across the universe, meet alien beings, and confront a dreaded evil that threatens the entire universe.

Robb, J. D. (a.k.a. Nora Roberts)

Naked in Death. In Death. 1995. Berkley, ISBN: 0425148297, 9780425148297, 313p.

Nora Roberts used the pen name of J. D. Robb when she wrote this vision of the far future. Eve Dallas is a New York City detective in 2058. Most guns are in museums or private collections, but somebody killed Sharon DeBlass, licensed companion and prostitute, with a firearm. All evidence points to Roarke, a billionaire who sometimes skirts the law. Dallas isn't convinced, but what if her desire for the handsome suspect is playing havoc with her instincts? Smart, capable female character? Check. Handsome, irresistible, wealthy suspect? Check. Smoldering passion mingled with murder? Double check. Put these together with a jump forward in time, and you get a science fiction series that speaks to mystery and romance readers in their own language. And with nearly forty novels and novellas in this best-selling series, Roberts shows no evidence of slowing any time soon.

Virtual Realities: Artificial Intelligence, Digital Dreams, and Cognitive Constructs

While Gibson's cyberpunk novel *Neuromancer* popularized the possibility of artificial intelligence (A.I.) and the effect of computer technology on society, he was by no means the first nor the last to do so, as Isaac Asimov's robots, Philip K. Dick's novels, HAL 9000, and *The Matrix* demonstrate. The rapid spread of computers and Internet use have certainly benefitted society, but the diffusion of computer technology has also exacerbated humanity's discomfort with the unpleasant potential of its creations. Will artificial intelligences conquer humanity, *Terminator* style? Or will our ability to subcreate in virtual reality create vistas and worlds of unparalleled beauty and a bounty of pragmatic and profitable interactive technology? Only time will tell, but if you start reading now, you might get ahead of the learning curve.

Ballantyne, Tony

Recursion. 2006 (2004). Spectra, ISBN: 0553589288, 9780553589283, 432p.

Herb Kirkham tried to build his own city using self-replicating Von Neumann machines. Unfortunately, they appear to have run rampant and devoured the entire ecosystem, something the Environmental Agency takes a dim view of. The Agency is willing to cut a deal with Herb, if he'll help stop a fleet of spacecraft coming to Earth. Herb's storyline mingles with that of Eva Rye, a suicidal girl suspicious of an omnipresent being she calls the Watcher, and Constantine Storey, a "ghost" to whom computers and surveillance turn a blind eye. When these plots converge, they reveal the secret behind humanity's development, and who's been manipulating us from the shadows.

Brooke, Keith

The Accord. 2009. Solaris, ISBN: 1844165892, 9781844165896, 442p.

Scientist Noah Barakh builds the Accord, a virtual reality that stores people's minds after death and permits them to live on, as a partial solution to Earth's overpopulation and chaos. Noah pursues an affair with Priscilla, wife to powerful politician Jack Burnham. When Jack discovers their relationship, he murders Priscilla; in turn, Noah commits suicide so that he can be with Priscilla in the Accord. Jack, furious over their escape and intent on possessing Priscilla with an obsession that borders on madness, finds his own way to gain power within the Accord so that he can utterly own his wife and destroy Barakh. Brooke offers a full view of how the Accord affects society even as the tense and deadly love triangle drives the plot to conclusion, all without relinquishing the story's grip upon the reader.

De Abaitua, Matthew

The Red Men. 2007. Snowbooks, ISBN: 190500558X, 9781905005581, 377p.

Nelson Millar works for Monad. They specialize in designing virtual workers, A.I.s called the Red Men that take some of the burden off of executives' shoulders. But the Red Men have a rather serious glitch, a flaw that pushes the simulated men to extremes. Monad, however, is already pushing to extend the program. Imagine an entire virtual city patterned off of real people: Redtown! Naturally, Millar becomes increasingly worried about who decides what the future will be. This sharp criticism of corporate culture will appeal to fans of Philip K. Dick and other writers of surreal SF.

Gibson, William

⇒ *Neuromancer*. <u>Sprawl</u>. 1984. Ace, ISBN: 0441569595, 9780441569595, 288p.

Case is a console cowboy, an elite cyberspace hacker whose gift was taken from him after he tried to cheat an employer. When Molly Millions, a cybernetically enhanced mercenary, and her mysterious employer Armitage offer to return Case's gift in exchange for working a dangerous and lucrative job, Case jumps at the chance. Soon, however, Case realizes the need to discover the true mastermind and purpose of this caper if he is to survive. This novel, a brilliant combination of noir, sleek stylish prose, and 1980s zeitgeist, won the Hugo, Nebula, and Philip K. Dick Awards.

McDonald, Ian

River of Gods. 2006 (2004). Pyr, ISBN: 1591024366, 9781591024361, 597p.

The year is 2047, one hundred years after India declared its independence from colonial rule. In that time, the country has fragmented into autonomous regions. Society has been radically altered by technology, including: rogue A.I.s; the creation of a new caste of gender-neutral humans; and a popular soap opera in which the actors are entirely computer generated. McDonald thrusts a host of characters into this setting, including cops, politicians, tycoons, fanatics, and housewives, and their different plot streams flow and coalesce into a narrative whole that explores humanity and reality. While the author immediately immerses fans in the novel's setting, the book does include a handy glossary to help guide readers down the *River of Gods*. This novel was nominated for a Hugo Award and won the British Science Fiction Association Award.

Powers, Richard

Galatea 2.2. 2004 (1995). Picador, ISBN: 0312423136, 9780312423131, 329p.

Powers becomes a character in his own novel in this modern take on the Pygmalion myth, as he returns from overseas to a university as a resident writer. He meets Philip Lentz, a computer scientist, and agrees to an unusual experiment: Lentz has established a computer network, and wants Powers to expose it to literature. As the simulation, named Helen, learns to appreciate beauty, she develops consciousness, but the ugliness of the world threatens her bond with Powers.

Robson, Justina

Silver Screen. 2005 (1999). Pyr, ISBN: 1591023386, 9781591023388, 383p.

Anjuli O'Connell works for OptiNet as the psychologist for the company's A.I., named 901. She discovers the body of her coworker, Roy, who may have uploaded himself into 901 after suing to have the World Court recognize the computer consciousness as a sentient being. Robson considers issues of the division between artificial and natural life and the possibility of machine evolution, and foregrounds the inevitable societal conflict over these issues.

Sawyer, Robert J.

WWW: Wake. <u>WWW</u>. 2009. Ace, ISBN: 0441016790, 9780441016792, 356p.

Caitlin Dector is blind. Her mathematical genius and proficiency with the Internet opens the world to her, but when she has the opportunity to receive an implant that can grant her vision, she eagerly accepts. When she opens her eyes to see for the first time, she instead perceives the complex construct that is the World Wide Web. She also discovers something unprecedented: a new, evolving intelligence within the sea of information. Echoes of William Gibson, Helen Keller, and *Ghost in the Shell* combine into a symphony of science fiction devoted to a new sentience.

Suarez, Daniel

Daemon. 2009 (2006). Dutton, ISBN: 0525951113, 9780525951117, 432p.

Matthew Sobol, computer programmer and game designer, succumbs to cancer. Before his death, he unleashes a program, a Daemon, onto the Web. While investigating the murders of programmers from Sobol's company, Detective Peter Sebeck discovers that Sobol's Daemon has insinuated itself into computer networks worldwide. The program uses the ubiquity of computers to play out Sobol's last, most horrific game. Suarez demonstrates how our society's dependence on computers can be used against us in this novel. Fans of Michael Crichton's books will find much to enjoy here.

Vinge, Vernor

Rainbows End. 2006. Tor, ISBN: 0312856849, 9780312856847, 364p.

A cure for Alzheimer's disease awakens poet Robert Gu to a new world that has no place for him, where people wear computers in their clothes and interact with a virtual world that overlays the actual world using special contact lenses. Gu suffers a bruised ego when he must return to high school and learn how to use the new technology everyone else takes for granted. His ego also leads him to become the pawn of a massive global conspiracy. Vinge manages to deliver a believable future, extrapolating from both current technology and the speed with which technology outstrips humanity. This technological thrill-ride coupled with a very human sense of displacement earned Vinge the Hugo Award.

Walton, David

Terminal Mind. 2008. Meadowhawk, ISBN: 0978732634, 9780978732639, 270p.

A balkanized United States sharply divides the rich and the poor, but the friendship between wealthy Mark McGovern and underprivileged Darin Kinsley flourishes despite class differences. The two young hackers soon find themselves out of their depth when they accidentally release an artificial intelligence and it begins causing incredible damage. Walton considers class conflict and corporate corruption in this suspenseful story.

Celestial Harmonies: The Sounds of Science Fiction

In times past, people equated the mathematical precision of the heavenly bodies' movements with the complex harmony of music. Some science fiction authors clearly follow suit, as they gain inspiration for their futurological imaginings from their own rhythmic and melodious compositions, or the artistic strains of their more musically inclined compatriots. More simply, writers likely get ideas from wherever they can, including the acoustics that stimulate their brains. This particular list emphasizes the importance of musicians and their music to society, whether they express freedom, inspire hope, challenge authority, or expose us to new thoughts. In these ways and others, music and science fiction enjoy common cause, so make sure to play it loud while reading these high notes from the genre!

Asaro, Catherine

Diamond Star. Skolian Empire. 2009. Baen, ISBN: 1416591605, 978141 6591603, 494p.

Rock singer Del is actually Del-Kurj, empathic scion of the Ruby Dynasty's interstellar empire. Rejected by his family, Del finds new life and purpose in his music, but his political ties to family, enemies, and the Earth that adores his music may provide more conflict than he can handle. Asaro lets readers see humanity through Del's alien eyes, even as readers identify with his struggle for the freedom to live his life as he chooses. And what's a rock story without music? Asaro's fans will be thrilled to learn of the author's collaboration with the band Point Valid to produce an album to accompany the novel; it shares the title *Diamond Star*.

Denton, Bradley

Buddy Holly Is Alive and Well on Ganymede. 1992 (1991). Avon, ISBN: 0380718766, 9780380718764, 290p.

Mild-mannered Oliver Vale is, like so many Americans, watching his television when a live broadcast from Jupiter's moon, featuring none other than Buddy Holly, invades the airwaves. But isn't Buddy Holly supposed to be dead? Even stranger, Buddy's asking for Oliver by name. Soon Vale is on the run from a host of unusual pursuers, including a cyborg dog, aliens, a CIA assassin, and religious fanatics. Can Oliver discover what's going on before the FCC finds him? This wild John W. Campbell Memorial Award–winning novel will warm readers' hearts as it keeps them laughing.

Disch, Thomas M.

On Wings of Song. 2003 (1979). Carroll & Graf, ISBN: 0786711221, 9780786711222, 315p.

Daniel Weinreb lives in a deeply divided America. Imprisoned for a trivial offense in the theocratic, oppressive Midwest, he becomes obsessed with the act of "flying": using music and technology to separate consciousness from the body. When flying, Daniel experiences complete freedom and unimpeded travel and can explore and discover anything he desires. Disch's novel of social schism, longing, and transcendence won the John W. Campbell Memorial Award.

Gibson, William

Idoru. Bridge. 2003 (1996). Berkley, ISBN: 0425190455, 9780425190456, 308p.

Rock band front man Rez intends to wed Rei Toei, a complicated arrangement since Toei is an *idoru*, an A.I. personality. This seemingly impossible plan highlights Gibson's sharp exposé of mass media and popular culture and explores when a simulacrum becomes "real."

McCaffrey, Anne

Crystal Singer. Crystal Singer. 1985 (1982). Ballantine, ISBN: 0345327861, 9780345327864, 311p.

Killashandra Ree becomes frustrated when her vocal training fails to pay off in musical roles, but a unique need for her talents leads her to the planet Ballybran. She becomes a crystal singer for the Heptite Guild and uses her voice to locate the elusive and highly valuable Black Crystal, an element essential for communications technology. McCaffrey's stubborn and determined lead character provides an excellent example of how persistence pays off.

Spinrad, Norman

⇒ *Little Heroes*. 1987. Bantam, ISBN: 0553052071, 9780553052077, 486p.

Muzik, Inc. has a brilliant idea—do away with the actual music stars and put money behind artificial personalities that the company owns outright! Unfortunately, sales continue to slip; the digital stars lack something essential. Enter Glorianna O'Toole, the Crazy Old Lady of Rock and Roll, who knew all the greats when they were still alive. She has to teach programming nerds Bobby Rubin and Sally Genaro about the soul of rock and roll, and the biggest lesson is rebellion! Spinrad's tale of urban blight and the power of music remains timely in this era of American Idol, cloned boy bands, and digital rights management.

Get Your *Bildungsroman* On!: Coming of Age in the Future

Put simply (perhaps too simply), a *bildungsroman* is a story in which a young person leaves home and embarks on a journey or adventure that mirrors an internal odyssey of growth, maturation, and discovery. At the conclusion of that journey, the youth returns with a better sense of the world and his or her place in it. In the many worlds of science fiction, these journeys from childhood to maturity are correspondingly weird, wondrous, bizarre, and glorious. At their roots they also remain recognizable and moving as readers identify and empathize with the protagonists' fumbling and floundering, epiphanies and pitfalls, betrayals, compromises, and victories. Readers making their way across the alien landscape of transformation and experience may find hope and courage in the following pages. These stories might also reawaken some spark of youth within adult readers and remind us of the need to continue growing.

Brooke, Keith

Genetopia. 2006. Pyr, ISBN: 1591023335, 9781591023333, 303p.

In a world of biotechnology run rampant, "True" humanity prides itself on its genetic purity and shuns or enslaves mutants. When Flint's sister Amber goes missing, he abandons his home and scours a world full of change and uncertainty to find her.

Bujold, Lois McMaster

The Warrior's Apprentice. Vorkosigan Saga. 2002 (1986). NESFA Press, ISBN: 1886778272, 9781886778276, 309p.

When Young Miles Vorkosigan fails his military physical due to ill health, the young man decides to take a vacation to his mother's homeworld and forget his troubles. Miles unexpectedly encounters one character after another whom he aids or befriends and soon finds himself with an entourage, a spacecraft he can't pay for, and a job running guns to a distant, war-torn planet as the admiral of the Dendarii Free Mercenaries. When Miles learns that his family's enemies have accused the Vorkosigan family of treason, he races home and hopes that his quick wit and fast tongue can salvage his family's honor. This delightful novel is a fast-paced, comedic, fabulous *bildungsroman* and picaresque all in one. Readers will delight to Miles's adventures as his silver tongue gets him out of trouble time and again, only to entrap him in yet another sticky and perilous situation.

Card, Orson Scott

⇒ *Ender's Game*. Ender Wiggin. 1992 (1985). Tor, ISBN: 0312853238, 9780312853235, 226p.

Ender Wiggin is a brilliant child, a prodigy selected by Earth's military as the ideal candidate for an advanced training school in its war against an insectoid race. Chosen for his intelligence, ruthlessness, and empathy, Ender becomes a master strategist and commander. Pushed to the edge of sanity by a grueling series of exams and combat simulations, Ender Wiggin must reconcile himself with his actions as a child bred for war, a hoped-for savior of humanity whose success at war games may spell the end for an entire species. Winner of both the Hugo and Nebula Awards, *Ender's Game* is both a gifted child's coming-of-age story and a meditation on military conflict.

Grant, Richard

Through the Heart. 1992 (1991). Bantam, ISBN: 0553293206, 9780553293206, 376p.

Grant's Philip K. Dick Award–winning novel depicts a young man struggling to find his place in a bizarre world gone sour and bitter. Kem's father trades him to the monstrous *Oasis*, a massive mobile city that roams the wastelands and barters with other settlements. Compared with the drudgery Kem experiences, the residents aboard live lives of luxury. But during Kem's daily servitude, he stumbles upon a variety of the leviathan dwelling's mysteries, like how the *Oasis* seems to have the sole treatment for the fatal illness known as the Crying. Grant's genius lies in making Kem and his fragile existence believable enough for readers to empathize with them; this same empathy enables the readers to utterly inhabit the bizarre landscape and accept its strange denizens with nary an eyeblink.

Herbert, Frank

Children of Dune. <u>Classic Dune</u>. 1987 (1976). Ace, ISBN: 0441104029, 9780441104024, 416p.

Paul Atreides, former Emperor of the known universe, walked into the desert and is believed dead. In his stead, his younger sister Alia rules as regent and raises Paul's children, Leto and Ghanima. As a Reverend Mother, Alia has access to the genetic memories of her ancestors, supposedly ensuring her wisdom, but her inherited abilities drive her mad and leave the royal family open to scheming and insurrection. Leto, determined to continue the work his father began, must find his way through betrayal and danger to lead humanity along its Golden Path and ensure its future.

Hopkinson, Nalo

Midnight Robber. 2000. Warner, ISBN: 0446675601, 9780446675604, 329p.

Young Tan-Tan lives on the utopian planet of Toussaint, settled by Carib peoples. Tan-Tan's favorite story is of the Midnight Robber, and she dreams of being a Robber Queen. When her father commits murder, the two are banished to the planet of New Half-Way Tree, an extradimensional alternate version of Toussaint. Forced to endure the harsh environment and the sexual predations of her father, Tan-Tan takes on the mantle and new identity of the Midnight Robber in order to survive. This novel, written in a dialect that immerses readers in the culture, is a powerful tale that combines science fiction and folklore and earned both Hugo and Nebula Award nominations.

Ness, Patrick

The Knife of Never Letting Go. <u>Chaos Walking</u>. 2008. Candlewick, ISBN: 0763639311, 9780763639310, 479p.

The Noise germ killed all the women and left the men able to hear each other's and animals' thoughts. Todd Hewitt is the only boy in Prentisstown, a community of men, and will soon undergo his rite of passage when he turns thirteen. When Todd comes across a girl named Viola, the rest of his town instantly knows of his discovery and begins to hunt down the pair. Viola's existence hints at a terrible secret and a terrible truth about the men of Prentisstown. But with all the men able to hear Todd's thoughts, how long can the two youths evade capture? Patrick Ness uses Todd's simple voice to relate a complex tale of gendered roles and vulnerability, lies, and hatred.

Stephenson, Neal

The Diamond Age; or, a Young Lady's Illustrated Primer. 2000 (1995). Bantam, ISBN: 0553380966, 9780553380965, 455p.

Nanotechnology is at its peak. Structures made of diamond shine brightly, and tiny machines called mites monitor people's health. But society is highly stratified, divided into cultural groups called phyles and firmly separated by economic class. In a phyle patterned after Victorian society, a Lord commissions the development of an interactive primer that promotes intellectual and personal growth and self-determination. He intends to give the primer to his daughter, but the device falls in the hands of young Nell, a thete—a member of a permanent underclass without phyle, money, hope, or future. Nell's acquisition and use of the primer leads to unexpected results. Stephenson's novel touches on themes of nature versus nurture, the role of technology in society and education, and the cruel inequities of wealth, status, caste, and class, while playfully conjuring Dickensian society as seen through a futuristic funhouse mirror.

Shipshape and Ship-to-Ship: Fleet-ing Glimpses of Naval SF

Space battles between fleets of ships are a standard feature of science fiction, particularly space operas and military SF. Over time, authors have put more care and thought into describing the military life and mind-set and into depicting space combat with accurate scientific and tactical details. Over this same period of time, more than a few military minds have become authors themselves. These writers used their talents and experience to inform their stories and developed quite a fan base among both military and civilian readers. Interested parties will find plenty of action in the following books, as well as insight into the moral obligations and responsibilities of military command.

Campbell, Jack

Dauntless. Lost Fleet. 2006. Ace, ISBN: 0441014186, 9780441014187, 293p.

The long war between the Alliance and the Syndic finds the former on the brink of defeat. When the Alliance fleet is trapped behind enemy lines, they stumble upon their long-revered war hero, Captain John "Black Jack" Geary, floating in suspended animation. Geary's rude awakening renews the hope of Alliance forces and leads to the service members idolizing him. Unfortunately, the Alliance fleet is badly disorganized, inept, and inefficient. Outnumbered and outgunned, Geary must restructure his forces and retrain them in strategy and tactics before the Syndic destroys them all. Campbell provides plenty of battles and action, and his excellent portrayal of a man forced by circumstance to become a hero and legend will keep readers coming back for more.

Cook, Glen

The Dragon Never Sleeps. 2008 (1988). Night Shade, ISBN: 1597800996, 9781597800990, 290p.

Intelligent Guardships protect the Canon of worlds, a series of planets linked by a Web of routes permitting faster-than-light travel. The Guardships, each named after a Roman legion, carry massive crews in suspended animation and the uploaded minds of legendary military advisors. The vessels have proven themselves capable of patrolling and protecting human space, but the mercantile houses that created the Guardships rankle under their law, and one house in particular has hidden allies that could end Guardship rule. Glen Cook, perhaps best known for his military fantasy series The Black Company, takes his military fiction to a different plane with sufficient intrigues, plots, and counterplots to keep readers guessing.

Hunt, Walter

The Dark Wing. Dark Wing. 2002 (2001). Tor, ISBN: 0765340690, 9780765340696, 474p.

The Solar Empire finds itself repeatedly at war with the avian Zor. Despite their defeats, the Zor continue their war out of religious zeal, since they view humans as an affront to their beliefs. Lord Admiral Ivan Marais writes a treatise on the Zor mentality and finds himself suddenly in command of the fleet combating the aliens. But the admiral's solution amounts to genocide, and it's quite possible that Marais is fulfilling the Zor's apocalyptic prophecy. Excellent tactical descriptions combine with disturbing philosophical questions in this opening novel of Hunt's Dark Wing series.

Moon, Elizabeth

Victory Conditions. Vatta's War. 2009 (2008). Ballantine, ISBN: 0345491629, 9780345491626, 403p.

Kylara Vatta rose from Academy expulsion to admiral. In this conclusion to the five-part Vatta's War series, she faces her nemesis, the pirate Gammis Turek. Vatta seeks to end Turek's threat against the galaxy and gain revenge for the murder of her family, but Turek's plans and assets are greater than anyone imagined. A wounded Kylara must rally an alliance and lead a last, desperate confrontation. Moon artfully blends military strategy with strong character growth as Vatta accepts the responsibility—and the cost—of leadership.

Weber, David

⇒ *On Basilisk Station*. <u>Honor Harrington</u>. 2002 (1993). Baen, ISBN: 0743435710, 9780743435710, 448p.

When Commander Honor Harrington of the Royal Manticoran Navy assumes command of the HMS *Fearless*, she soon learns the perils of politics. A spiteful superior officer reassigns Harrington to the busy wormhole junction of Basilisk station near the backwater world of Medusa. Despite having only a single ship with an understaffed crew, Honor creatively fulfills her duties, successfully enforces the customs laws, and regains the trust of a Medusan government used to the excesses and incompetence of the previous naval administrator. Just as she manages to restore order to a problematic command, a native insurgency blossoms on Medusa, and the attentions of the hostile Republic of Haven threaten Honor's crew and the lives of everyone on the planet. Weber set new standards with his very popular <u>Honor Harrington</u> series, incorporating realistic physics of astromilitary engagement, a flawed but committed crew, thrilling ship-to-ship combat, and a noble female lead character into a notable series opener.

Gendered Space: Science Fiction and the Sexes

Sexism is particularly pernicious throughout human history and society, with effects that range from the demeaning to the utterly horrific. Science fiction, however, is nothing if not a literature of possibilities, and many authors have envisioned alternate relationships between men and women, sometimes for the better, sometimes worse, sometimes simply because they can, and perhaps because someone should.

Bear, Elizabeth

Carnival. 2006. Bantam, ISBN: 0553589040, 9780553589047, 392p.

The New Amazonian gynarchy, fearing men's aggression, uses them only for labor and breeding. The oppressive Coalition sends ambassadors Vincent and Michelangelo to New Amazonia, ostensibly to return precious stolen art but in actuality to serve as spies and discover the Amazonians' secret energy technology. The Amazonians find the male diplomats acceptable because they are gay, and thus underestimate their assumedly "gentle" nature. But the New Amazonians' city, built long before by aliens, houses secrets that could alter both Coalition and Amazonian societies. Bear's complex play of social agendas and the politics of gender and sexuality enrich this tale of intrigue.

Brin, David

Glory Season. 1994 (1993). Bantam, ISBN: 0553567675, 9780553567670, 772p.

Stratos houses a matriarchy founded by feminist separatists. Cloning serves as the primary means of reproduction, and cloned women dominate the political and economic hierarchy. They do retain some men, altered for reduced aggression, as a necessity for genetic variation. Maia is one such naturally born variant; discriminated against and banished from society, Maia hopes to be successful enough to someday found her own cloned matrilineal line. When she discovers and befriends an outworld man, his presence causes immense political upheaval. The complexities and intricacies of Brin's imagined society will interest and challenge readers—although the society seems a practical and stable feminist structure, it is by no means perfect, as it enforces and perpetuates unjust treatment of its variant underclass.

Griffith, Nicola

Ammonite. 2002 (1992). Ballantine, ISBN: 0345452380, 9780345452382, 397p.

In her James Tiptree, Jr. and Lambda Award–winning novel, Griffith explores a single-sex society while demonstrating that human behaviors are not necessarily gendered behaviors. The Durallium Company sends anthropologist Marghe Taishan to investigate their investment, a colony on the planet GP, as the Company wants to exploit the planet's resources. A deadly virus killed all the men and many of the women, but altered the remaining females, enabling them to maintain a viable population and culture, and a sustainable and harmonious relationship with the planet, if not always with each other.

Jones, Gwyneth

Life. 2004. Aqueduct, ISBN: 0974655929, 9780974655925, 370p.

Bioengineer Anna Senoz makes a startling discovery: the very concept of gender itself may be irrevocably altered due to ongoing changes in male DNA. This same controversial revelation, however, turns Anna into a target for prejudice and fear. Jones's metaphorical extrapolation highlights the continuing and crushing gender inequities in society.

Le Guin, Ursula K.

⇒ ***The Left Hand of Darkness.*** 2000 (1969). Ace, ISBN: 0441007317, 9780441007318, 304p.

Genly Ai is an ambassador on a mission to convince the inhabitants of the world of Gethen to join a larger confederation of planets. The people of Gethen are gender neutral and have the ability to be either male or female depending on physiological and environmental conditions. Various factions attempt to use Genly as a political pawn, and he soon finds himself imprisoned. When Genly's Gethen contact, Estraven, comes to rescue him, the two embark on a journey and relationship that explores and transcends the concept of gender. A feminist SF classic, *The Left Hand of Darkness* won the Nebula Award in 1969.

Russ, Joanna

The Female Man. 2000 (1975). Beacon, ISBN: 0807062995, 9780807062995, 213p.

> Four women from four alternate Earths meet and challenge one another's concepts of gender roles. Joanna strives for respect and aspires toward equality in then-contemporary 1970s Earth. Jeannine is a librarian from a world that never recovered from the Great Depression; she struggles with her own depression and listlessness in a world with far more restrictive social norms. Janet comes from Whileaway, a world where plague destroyed the male population, and has never experienced sexism. Finally, Jael's world is consumed by a devastating war between the sexes, and she brings the four women together hoping to plant training camps for women across all dimensions. Russ's bold polemic is a foundational work of feminist SF and serves as challenging fare for readers who enjoy heavy amounts of philosophical, political, and social contemplation and confrontation.

Tepper, Sheri S.

The Gate to Women's Country. 1989 (1988). Bantam, ISBN: 0553280643, 9780553280647, 328p.

> In the aftermath of a nuclear war, the matriarchal communities of Women's Country develop a sustainable, if tenuous, society. The Women's Council restricts men to either military garrisons that protect the women's enclaves or positions of servitude—the council forbids teaching soldiers to read, and no men have a voice in their governance. Stavia becomes a woman in this society, and as she grows, she wrestles with rebellion and her community's imperfect aspects. When she becomes a doctor and explores beyond Women's Country, however, she experiences one of the alternatives to her home: the communities of the vicious, polygamist, and misogynist Holylanders. Tepper's homage to the ancient tragedy *The Trojan Women* depicts difficult decisions and complex morality in an imperfect world. Her gendered use of language, which defaults to feminine, poses an interesting contrast to contemporary usage and exposes hegemonic assumptions in modern society.

Tiptree, James, Jr. (a.k.a. Alice Sheldon)

Houston, Houston, Do You Read? 1996 (1976). Doubleday, ISBN: 1568652518, 9781568652518, 150p.

> Three astronauts radio Earth when a solar flare damages their ship, but get only female voices in reply. When a spacecraft comes to their rescue, an all-female crew greets the astronauts. Somehow, the three men have traveled into their future. A plague apparently killed every human male on Earth, and in the meantime women reproduce by cloning. While two of the men have rather selfish designs for a planet of women, the third realizes that the astronauts are, at best, scientific and anthropological curiosities. Alice Sheldon, who wrote under the pseudonyms Raccoona Sheldon and James Tiptree, Jr., was a key feminist SF author whose somewhat darker visions enlightened many in the field.

Not-So-Civil Wars: Worlds Torn Asunder

Civil wars are anything but. When fellow citizens and kin violently fall upon one another, the damage done and painful memories last even longer. A variety of internal conflicts that become conflagrations await your attention. Whether they occur in another galaxy or in America's past and present, you can be sure the strife will get very ugly, very quickly.

Abnett, Dan

Horus Rising. The Horus Heresy. Black Library, ISBN: 184416294X, 9781844162949, 412p.

> At the height of the Imperium, in the days before the emperor was a rotting corpse on his throne, the Great Crusade against heretics and Chaos was in full swing. The emperor makes Horus the head of his legions, but the new Warmaster is plagued by doubt and uncertainty, fertile ground for the seeds of corruption. Abnett's gothic SF set in the *Warhammer 40,000* universe begins an unforgettably epic tale of fallen heroes and betrayal.

Card, Orson Scott

Empire. 2007 (2006). Tor, ISBN: 0765355221, 9780765355225, 355p.

> When the U.S. president and vice president die in a terrorist attack on the White House, a group calling itself the Progressive Restoration takes over the U.S. government using incredibly high-tech mechs and hovercraft. U.S. Army Major Reuben Malich leads the battle to defend against all enemies, foreign and domestic, and to retake our government for the people. But are Malich's forces and the Progressive Restoration simply pawns in a much larger game?

Card, well known for science fiction epics, takes on a contemporary conflict within U.S. borders.

Forstchen, William, and Newt Gingrich

⇒ *Gettysburg: A Novel of the Civil War.* 2005 (2003). Tor, ISBN: 0312987250, 9780312987251, 544p.

The Battle of Gettysburg was a decisive victory in the Civil War. Forstchen and Gingrich have General Robert E. Lee make crucially different and thoroughly plausible strategic and tactical decisions that ensure the Confederate victory over the Union forces.

Moore, Ward

Bring the Jubilee. 2001 (1953). Gollancz, ISBN: 1857987640, 9781857987645, 194p.

The War of Southern Independence saw the Confederate States of America victorious. In the decades since that fateful day, the C.S.A. continued to prosper until it became a major world power, in contrast to the broken North, which slipped into sharp decline. Hodge Backmaker, eager to study history in person, manages a trip back in time to a crucial battle in the Civil War, but his presence causes events to go awry.

Turtledove, Harry

How Few Remain. 1998 (1997). Del Rey/Ballantine, ISBN: 0345406141, 9780345406149, 595p.

Turtledove takes famous personages and gives us an update on their activities since the Confederate States of America won the War of Secession. Lincoln leaves the presidency in shame and becomes a proponent of Marxism. The U.S. enters into a second disastrous war with the Confederacy but is stymied by Southern leadership and its foreign alliances. And a rather frightening alliance is developing between the United States and Germany, leading into some of Turtledove's later series.

The Great Unknown: Cosmic Mysteries

One common view of scientists depicts them as people obsessed with knowledge. Some of these learned individuals want to enable humans to become masters of their world and fates. Others are driven simply to explain the unexplainable, to ask piercing questions and discover brilliant solutions, and to see beyond the next horizon. Despite centuries and millennia of curiosity and experimentation, there are a number of questions that science cannot answer (not yet, anyway), mysteries currently beyond the reach of researchers. Fortunately such limitations do not prevent the speculation of SF writers. Take a look at these thoughtful examinations of cosmic mysteries, then take a moment to gaze at the stars and wonder.

Reynolds, Alastair

Revelation Space. <u>Revelation Space</u>. 2002 (2000). Ace, ISBN: 0441009425, 9780441009428, 585p.

> Big ideas abound in this series opener that explores why there are so few intelligent races in the universe. Dan Sylveste is working on an archaeological dig on the world Resurgam. He's trying to discover what happened to the planet's inhabitants and discovers a clue to a being called the "Sun Stealer." Ilia Volyova, one of three cyborgs on the awesomely powerful ship *Nostalgia for Infinity*, needs Dan's help to save her captain from a virulent nanoplague. Ana Khouri, an assassin, simply needs to kill Dan. When these three plot threads weave together, the solution to an ancient mystery reveals a cosmic threat that endangers worlds.

Sagan, Carl

Contact. 1997 (1985). Pocket, ISBN: 0671004107, 9780671004101, 434p.

> Eleanor Arroway, an astronomer and avowed agnostic working on SETI (the Search for Extra-Terrestrial Intelligence), receives a message from space that consists of prime numbers and demonstrates an alien intelligence behind the broadcast. The transmission contains encoded plans for an unusual vehicle that Arroway and her crew construct and board to meet the mysterious aliens. Arroway's meditation on her encounter suggests an intelligence behind all creation. Sagan's unconventional use of intelligent design points to far greater enigmas than most SF stories hint at.

Sawyer, Robert J.

⇒ ***Calculating God.*** 2000. Tor, ISBN: 0312867131, 9780312867133, 334p.

> Tom Jericho is a paleontologist whose expertise is mass extinction events. He receives a visit from an alien scientist, the spider-like Hollus, who comes to Jericho with no less than evidence of the existence of God. When the two compare notes, they realize that the same extinction events have occurred on other planets, a pattern that suggests an intelligent entity in the background. Dying of cancer, Jericho must reconcile his science and Hollus's evidence with his reasons for disbelief. While science fiction has not been kind to intelligent design, Sawyer has written a novel that addresses the issue with humor and warmth and received a Nebula nomination for his achievement.

Stapledon, Olaf

Star Maker. 2008 (1937). Dover, ISBN: 0486466833, 9780486466835, 192p.

One night, a man sits upon a hill and admires the firmament above. Suddenly, unexpectedly, his mind goes spinning on a journey through the universe. He telepathically links with other beings and sees aliens, civilizations, and planets across the cosmos, before finally encountering the first mover, the Great Creator. Stapledon's thoughtful, philosophical science fiction portrays a being whose values and virtues do not match our own, and readers may find themselves challenged by the novel's higher power.

Willis, Connie

Passage. 2001. Bantam, ISBN: 0553111248, 9780553111248, 594p.

Psychologist Joanna Lander and neurologist Richard Wright investigate the phenomenon of near-death experiences from a scientific viewpoint, but best-selling author Maurice Mandrake, with his insistence on a spiritual explanation that includes angels and the presence of loved ones in the hereafter, frustrates their efforts. When Lander agrees to undergo a chemical procedure simulating a near-death experience, she finds herself aboard a version of the *Titanic* as it sinks. Willis's thriller takes us to the brink of death and beyond and offers a glimpse of what may come after. Her passage into the unknown earned both Hugo and Nebula nominations.

Wilson, Robert Charles

Spin. Spin. 2005. Tor, ISBN: 0765309386, 9780765309389, 364p.

Without warning, a strange membrane encloses the Earth and blocks out the stars. The membrane does strange things to time: for every year that passes on our planet, the universe ages over a hundred million years. As the moment swiftly approaches when our sun will go nova and destroy the planet, we see how four people choose to face the end. Will they succumb to despair, or strive for greater understanding? Will they discover what, or who, created the membrane? And will the human race survive? This novel of cosmic mystery and human relationships earned a Hugo Award.

Gilligan's Universe: Lost and Stranded

Space is an inhospitable and dangerous place. Any number of accidents, errors, and unforeseen circumstances can occur that will test the mettle of explorers and travelers. In the following novels, some characters will panic, some will rally, and some will simply accept the inevitability of their hopeless situation.

Anderson, Poul

Tau Zero. 2006 (1970). Gollancz, ISBN: 0575077328, 9780575077324, 189p.

The fifty passengers of the *Leonora Christine* set out to colonize a planet light years away. They travel at relativistic speeds, so as time races by in the universe outside the ship, relatively little passes within the craft. When the ship suffers damage to its decelerator, the crew members must face the loss of everything they know, as they are trapped within a ship speeding toward the end of the universe.

Clarke, Arthur C.

A Fall of Moondust. 2002 (1961). Gollancz, ISBN: 0575073179, 9780575073173, 224p.

Technology advances to the point where a lunar colony is feasible. Tourists can even ride in special vessels that sail the lunar dust seas. However, when a quake traps the cruise ship *Selene* beneath the moon's surface, the colonists must stage a daring rescue.

Mitchell, Syne

⇒ *End in Fire*. 2005. New American Library, ISBN: 0451460332, 9780451460332, 337p.

Astronaut Claire Logan finds herself stranded in space when a limited nuclear conflict breaks out on Earth. She manages to make contact with the Chinese space station but fears that the war below may be mirrored in orbit.

Russ, Joanna

We Who Are about To . . . 2005 (1977). Wesleyan University Press, ISBN: 0819567590, 9780819567598, 118p.

When their ship goes off course, a group of tourists become stranded on a hostile world. Most of the survivors unreasoningly insist on colonizing the planet, and begin a desperate, futile struggle to live despite their lack of skills and resources. One lone dissenter refuses to be forcibly bred to populate the planet and crafts a lethal response to her fellow passengers' demands. Russ writes a forceful tale of life, death, and the importance of individual will versus the needs of the group.

Vinge, Vernor

A Deepness in the Sky. Qeng Ho. 2000 (1999). Tor, ISBN: 0812536355, 9780812536355, 774p.

Two factions, the Qeng Ho traders and the Emergent slavers, receive signals from an arachnoid race and respond hoping to exploit this new opportunity. When the two factions clash, they become stranded in space and form an uneasy truce as they wait until the arachnoids develop an economy and technology sufficient for their needs. Readers of Hard SF will enjoy the arachnoids' struggles to overcome obstacles and advance their scientific knowledge, struggles that mirror our own world's history.

Greed Is Good: Extrapolating Capitalism

Proponents of capitalism and corporate culture argue that competition and the free market create wealth, foster progress, and eliminate waste. Detractors of said viewpoint are quick to point out that, without proper oversight, laws, and regulation, greed inevitably leads to ethical compromise and to the haves trampling over the rights and humanity of the have-nots. The following works explore the heights and depths of corporate ambition and the consequences thereof.

Barrett, Neal, Jr.

Prince of Christler-Coke. 2004. Golden Gryphon, ISBN: 1930846282, 9781930846282, 244p.

In the far future, capitalism has morphed into neofeudalism, and old corporations lend their names to noble lineages. Asel Iacola, Prince of Christler-Coke, falls victim to a hostile takeover from the lord of Disney-Dow in Califoggy. Banished to Oklahomer, Iacola experiences the disparity between wealthy and poor firsthand as he escapes captivity and journeys the length and breadth of this bizarre U.S. Readers looking for sharp wit and strange humor will enjoy this dark picaresque.

Buckner, M. M.

War Surf. 2005. Ace, ISBN: 0441013201, 9780441013201, 375p.

What's a bored, wealthy, virtually immortal corporate executive to do when overwhelmed by ennui? Clearly, he outfits himself with the latest in upgrades and high-tech weaponry. He then joins a team of like-minded individuals and war surfs, a pastime in which players rudely interrupt wars and fight against both sides for points. Nasir Deepra's team is one of the highest rated, most popular groups of surfers around, but a catastrophic loss forces them to go up against the toughest challenge to rebuild their rep: the orbital factory Heaven. Deepra's company owns Heaven, and he dreads both what they'll encounter and what secrets their surf might bring to light. Worse, when Deepra's equipment malfunctions, he finds himself facing the realities of class conflict and the new economy he helped found.

Ellis, Warren, et al.

Ocean. 2009 (2005). DC Comics/Wildstorm, ISBN: 1401223540, 9781401223540, 168p. GN

U.N. Weapons Inspector Nathan Kane reports to a research station orbiting Jupiter's moon Europa. When he arrives, he learns that the scientists aboard discovered coffins beneath Europa's ocean that contain a slumbering race of hostile aliens. They also have evidence of a device capable of generating wormholes and destroying planets. A nearby satellite belonging to the DOORS Corporation is also interested in the find and refuses to cede its rights to the new technology. Ellis delivers a fast-paced thriller coupling science fiction with corporate intrigue and greed in this stellar (lunar?) graphic novel.

Irvine, Alexander

Buyout. 2009. Del Rey-Ballantine, ISBN: 0345494334, 9780345494337, 319p.

In the year 2040, prison overpopulation is a serious problem, and the cost of housing so many inmates has become staggering. Martin Kindred facilitates a solution: specifically, a buyout. Prisoners with life sentences and no hope of release may sign their lives over for execution. In exchange, the prisoners' beneficiaries receive millions of dollars. This system, although controversial, is cheaper than maintaining the convicts in prison with the requisite housing, food, medical care, and facilities costs. Kindred markets the plan as empowering prisoners, enabling them to make their final choice with dignity. Irvine deftly explores the politics underlying the justice and prison systems in this surprisingly dark, humorous novel about the worth of human life.

Kollin, Dani, and Eytan Kollin

The Unincorporated Man. 2009. Tor, ISBN: 0765318997, 9780765318997, 478p.

Justin Cord is a forward-thinking twenty-first century businessman, so when he develops a terminal illness, he funds a secret cryogenic chamber for himself. In the twenty-fourth century, people discover Justin's chamber, thaw him out, and give him a fantastic new, healthy body. Understandably, Cord is also an instant celebrity. But the world three hundred years later is a very strange place. At first it seems a veritable utopia, but there's one small exception: after an economic disaster, society's financial solution was to force citizens to incorporate themselves. People own shares in one another, so getting jobs or an education requires them to trade stock in themselves, and the government owns a percentage of everyone. Most people spend their considerably extended lives trying to get a majority share in themselves, and terrible things can happen to those who fail. Cord, however, finds the situation untenable and refuses to sign an incorporation agreement. In doing so, he threatens the system and those with a vested interest in the status quo. The Kollins' brilliant socioeconomic thought experiment is engaging and frighteningly plausible, even as it redefines private property.

Marusek, David

Counting Heads. 2007 (2005). Tor, ISBN: 0765317540, 9780765317544, 336p.

Over a hundred years from now, humanity feels overwhelmed by getting everything it ever wanted. Everyone has their own artificial intelligences, although capacities may vary according to your bank account. Robots and clones perform all the undesired labor, although unemployment is a problem. Nanotechnology allows for the custom creation of any desired possession and rejuvenates bodies to the point of immortality—if you can afford it. Unfortunately, neither the Earth nor the economy can support the population. Eleanor Starke plans to transfer humanity to space to give people more room and allow the Earth to rejuvenate itself. Unfortunately, corporate assassins strike before she can carry out her plan. The cryogenically preserved head of Starke's daughter survives, however, and its vital memories and inside information are valuable prizes for several factions out to claim the cranium. Marusek dazzles readers with a gonzo world plagued by its own achievements and provides a wildly entertaining ride through tomorrow's madness.

Morgan, Richard K.

⇒ *Market Forces.* 2005. Del Rey/Ballantine, ISBN: 0345457749, 9780345457745, 441p.

The unfettered capitalism of 2049 takes war profiteering to a new level. Chris Faulkner, a hotshot member of Shorn Associates, works in Conflict Investment. This new market features massive corporations financing Third World governments, rebels, and tottering regimes to prolong and manage conflicts for maximum profit. Unfortunately for Chris, success brings its own perils in the form of cutthroat competition and betrayal. Even worse, Chris may be developing a conscience. Warning: readers may experience a growing sense of unease at corporate power and an unreasonable fear of stock quotes.

Pohl, Frederik, and C. M. Kornbluth

The Space Merchants. 1985 (1953). St. Martin's, ISBN: 0312749511, 9780312749514, 169p.

Mitchell Courtenay works for the Fowler Schocken advertising and marketing firm. In a world where corporations rule rather than governments, the gulf between haves and have-nots is insurmountable, overpopulation strains the environment to the breaking point, and even the most basic resources are scarce. Courtenay works to convince people to colonize the nearly uninhabitable planet Venus. Soon, Mitch finds himself the victim of conspiracy and identity theft. Imprisoned in conditions he didn't even know existed, Mitch sees the horrors of rampant consumerism and rabid capitalism firsthand and becomes an advocate for conscientious conservationism. Pohl and Kornbluth scribe a prophetic tale, far ahead of its time, and address issues that are timeless and timely with economy and humor.

Spinrad, Norman

Bug Jack Barron. 2004 (1969). Overlook, ISBN: 1585675857, 9781585675852, 254p.

Entertainment star and talk show host Jack Barron goes toe-to-toe with corporate heavyweight Benedict Howards. Howards runs a foundation that promises immortality thanks to perfected cryogenic science and is trying to ease legislation through Congress that could give him a monopoly on the technology. Although Howards and Barron spar in the public arena, Barron is game for a bit of bribery until he discovers the horrifying secret of Howards's procedure. Spinrad takes on corruption, politics, big business, and the media in this unforgettable novel.

Invasion!: Space Invaders and Hostile Takeovers

First contact with an alien species is a staple of science fiction stories. As the film *E.T.* demonstrates, sometimes extraterrestrials that visit our planet simply want to waddle around, drink our beer, and eat our delicious candy. On the other hand, they may try to contact us in confusing ways and encourage us to build mountains out of our mashed potatoes, as in *Close Encounters of the Third Kind*. But these are perhaps best-case scenarios. What happens when things go horribly, terribly wrong? What if humanity acts in an untoward manner, and the aliens take offense? What if they do to us what humanity has done to itself for millennia; to wit, what if they see something we have, such as our lovely blue planet with all its resources, want it, take it, and enslave or kill all of us to get it? What if they simply decide that humans are delicious? The result may be all-out war. Unfortunately, there's no guarantee that humanity will win . . .

Christopher, John

The Tripods

The White Mountains. 2003 (1967). Simon Pulse, ISBN: 0689856725, 9780689856723, 195p.

The City of Gold and Lead. 2003 (1967). Simon Pulse, ISBN: 0689856660, 9780689856662, 209p.

The Pool of Fire. 2003 (1968). Simon Pulse, ISBN: 0689856695, 9780689856693, 176p.

Alien Masters rule the Earth from their tripods, three-legged massive war machines. But their more insidious means of ensuring obedience comes from the "caps," mind-control technology the invaders affix to children at the age of fourteen. Young Will and his friends, frightened by the effects caps have on others, decide to escape to the White Mountains, a refuge for free humanity. Over the course of the trilogy, Will joins the resistance, infiltrates the Masters' cities, and strikes at the heart of their power. Breakneck suspense and escapes make Christopher's novels compelling reading for younger readers and adults alike.

Ellis, Warren, et al.

Switchblade Honey. 2003. AiT/Planet Lar, ISBN: 1932051139, 9781932051131, 88p. GN

When humans first encountered the alien Chasta, we treated them like animals. Imagine our surprise when they demonstrated greater technological advancement and capacity for war than humanity. Earth is steadily losing the war, and decides to recruit a black-ops team of guerrillas to fight suicide missions behind enemy lines. Captain John Ryder and his crew are criminals in the eyes of the authorities, although their primary offenses were rebelling against illegal orders and refusing to abandon their ethics. With their advanced starship, the *Switchblade Honey*, the team takes the war to the Chasta. When they discover the Chasta's doomsday weapon, will the misanthropic squad warn the Earth, or abandon the planet that imprisoned and condemned them? Ellis provides a very humorous and cynical take on *Star Trek* and similar shows while addressing ethical dilemmas and assembling a memorable cast of characters.

Emshwiller, Carol

The Mount. 2002. Small Beer, ISBN: 1931520038, 9781931520034, 232p.

In the not-so-distant future, the alien Hoots take over our planet and breed humans as mounts for their use. Charley, a mount of high pedigree, is proud of his accomplishments and devotes himself to his Little Master. Charley's father, however, is dedicated to freeing humans from Hoot domination. This internal conflict forces Charley to choose between the only life he has ever known, that of a pampered slave, and the very frightening alternative of freedom. A thoughtful meditation on slavery and humanity, *The Mount* earned a Nebula nomination.

Gerrold, David

A Matter for Men. <u>War against the Chtorr</u>. 1989 (1983). Bantam, ISBN: 0553277820, 9780553277821, 435p.

The Chtorr, a carnivorous race of huge, wormlike creatures, set their sites on Earth. Their insidious invasion plan consists of planting alien creatures into Earth's ecosystems. These life forms crowd out the native organisms, slowly infest our planet, and turn our world against us. Reviewers favorably compared this novel to Heinlein's classic *Starship Troopers*, and the 1989 edition of the novel replaces material deleted by a previous publisher.

King, Stephen

The Tommyknockers. 1998 (1997). Penguin, ISBN: 0451156609, 9780451156600, 747p.

Bobbi Anderson, a writer and resident of the small town Haven, Maine, stumbles across the remains of an extraterrestrial craft. The ship begins slowly transforming the townsfolk into aliens, granting them a mad mechanical genius while simultaneously eliciting psychotic behavior. Only Bobbi's friend, Jim Gardener, seems immune to the ship's influence, but with the entire town and alien technology arrayed against him, his chances at defeating the invasion seem slim. King brings his trademark flair for horror to science fiction and thrills readers with the creepy violation of Haven's citizens by gory violence and possession.

Knight, E. E.

Way of the Wolf. <u>Vampire Earth</u>. 2003. Roc, ISBN: 0451459393, 9780451459398, 391p.

The Kurian Invasion took Earth completely by surprise. In their opening salvo, the Kurians bribed humans to sell out their race, caused natural disasters to devastate our planet, and then released the horrific Ravies plague, the infected becoming akin to ravening zombies. The Kurians' genetically engineered soldiers, known as Grogs, adapted to battle on land, in the air, and in the sea. But worst of all are the Reapers, who drain captives of their blood and transfer their victims' life essence to their Kurian masters. Guerrilla fighters and freeholds sustain hope that someday Earth will be free. The Lifeweavers, kin to the Kurians but opposed to their enslavement of Earth, enhance soldiers who prove worthy to varying degrees. These warriors, called Wolves, Cats, and Bears, gain the gifts of greater speed, strength, and endurance, and heightened senses. David Valentine is one such guerrilla, a Wolf who grows from rescued orphan to lieutenant. Readers will discover his tale to be equal parts pulp adventure, military fiction, and *bildungsroman* as he makes his way through a world transformed by war, terror, and hope.

Meyer, Stephenie

The Host. 2008. Little, Brown, and Co., ISBN: 0316068047, 9780316068048, 619p.

    The parasitic Souls assumed control of humanity with the best intentions, and indeed created a peaceful, nearly utopian, society on Earth. But a takeover is still a takeover, hostile or not, and "wild" humanity intends to take Earth back from the aliens. When the Soul named Wanderer enters the mind of Melanie Stryder, she fights back and refuses to relinquish control. Melanie's strong desire to find the man she loves forces a truce with Wanderer, and the two escape to find the rebels, giving Wanderer the opportunity to see beyond humanity's destructive nature. Stephenie Meyer's first science fiction work maintains the same blend of action and romance that fueled her popular Twilight series—fans of the vampire novels will likely find this book just as entertaining.

Ringo, John

A Hymn before Battle. Legacy of the Aldenata/Posleen War. 2006 (2000). Baen, ISBN: 1416533214, 9781416533214, 467p.

    The Galactic Federation contacts Earth's governments and warns them of imminent invasion by the alien Posleen. The pacifist Federation, led by the mysterious race called the Darhel, need soldiers to fight the war for them. In exchange, the Darhel offer rejuvenation therapy that can restore youth to willing veterans and advanced technology to use in the coming battle. Earth mobilizes its military, scientists, strategists, and even its science fiction writers in an effort to defeat the ravening Posleen horde. Intrigues among Earth's command, however, provide hints of sinister hidden agendas and suggest that our Darhel allies have additional plans for humanity. Ringo's praise and criticism of Earth's military response to alien invasion adds a layer of thoughtful credibility to the exciting battles, and his roving viewpoint offers perspectives from a variety of angles and adds fullness to the narrative.

Wells, H. G.

⇒ *The War of the Worlds.* 2005 (1898). Penguin, ISBN: 0141441038, 9780141441030, 199p.

    Mysterious cylinders crash-land on Earth following a series of explosions on the surface of Mars. Martians emerge from the cylinders and use their overpowering technology, including heat rays, chemical weapons, and enormous mobile tripods, to invade and conquer. A mysterious Martian red weed overwhelms the ecology as quickly and effectively as the Martians overwhelm Earth's opposition. Horror mounts as Martians begin feeding off of human blood in grisly exsanguinations. In the face of such devastating power, it appears humanity's end is at hand. H. G. Wells's novel of extraterrestrial conquest, despair, and terror provides the primary template for alien invasion stories. *The War of the Worlds* has numerous adaptations in comics and films, and panicked the United States in the form of Orson Welles's 1938 radio drama. Want to know where the idea for movies such as *Independence Day*, *Mars Attacks*, and *Signs* originated? Then read this novel.

Wyndham, John

The Day of the Triffids. 2003 (1951). Modern Library, ISBN: 0812967127, 9780812967128, 228p.

The triffids, ambulatory carnivorous plants with poisonous stings, are Soviet creations that other nations soon exploit for their oil. When a bizarre celestial event blinds most of humanity, the triffids take advantage of the situation to break free and feast on humanity. Although some aspects of the story may seem dated, particularly the characters' Cold War paranoia, Wyndham handily demonstrates how, even in the middle of worldwide catastrophe, humanity can be its own worst enemy in this tense, classic novel.

Hold the Line!: In the Trenches with Military SF

Conflicts can erupt over any number of causes, from limited resources to opposing ideologies to terrible misunderstandings. Sometimes, peaceful interventions win the day, but when diplomacy fails, worlds go to war. While spacecraft may duel from long distances and never actually see their opposition, the soldiers and ground pounders charge through the mud and blood to go hand-to-hand and lasrifle-to-battle armor with their enemies as they hold the line, take the hill, and win the war. Some of these characters fight for money, others because they must, still others for glory or a cause. Beyond the descriptions of battles, weapons, tactics, and strategies, however, many readers become hooked on a book or series because of the camaraderie between characters and the authors' convincing portrayals of the grave costs of war.

Abnett, Dan

The Founding. Gaunt's Ghosts. 2007. Black Library, ISBN: 1844163695, 9781844163694, 767p.

Commissar Ibram Gaunt serves the emperor by commanding humanity's soldiers in never-ending warfare against aliens, heretics, and the forces of Chaos. When Gaunt founds a new warrior chapter on the planet Tanith, a violent incursion strikes the world, forcing Gaunt to abandon most of the population to Chaos. The Tanith First and Only initially despises Gaunt, hating him for leaving their world to the enemy. In time, however, their charismatic and noble leader forges the team into an elite scouting and fighting unit renowned for their stealth—Gaunt's Ghosts—committed to avenging their home by defeating enemy forces in theatres of battle across the universe. This series of novels, set in the world of Games Workshop's miniatures wargame *Warhammer 40,000*, is extremely popular with fans of military science fiction. This omnibus contains the novels *First and Only* (1999), *Ghostmaker* (2000), and *Necropolis* (2000).

Buettner, Robert

Orphanage. <u>Jason Wander</u>. 2008 (2004). Orbit, ISBN: 0316019127, 9780316019125, 302p.

After alien Slugs use Ganymede as their forward base in a war against Earth, young Jason Wander gets to choose between prison and military service. Humanity manages to cobble together a spaceworthy vehicle and sends a contingent of soldiers into the void to take the fight to enemy territory as Earth's only hope. Buettner writes an homage to classic military SF novels and uses his own military experience to good effect to capture the essence of soldiers' bravery and fellowship.

Dickson, Gordon R.

Dorsai Spirit. <u>Childe Cycle</u>. 2002. Orb, ISBN: 0312877617, 9780312877613, 432p.

This omnibus contains the books *Dorsai* (1959) and *The Spirit of Dorsai* (1979). *Dorsai* relates that, when humanity went to the stars, it splintered into a myriad of customs and cultures. The Dorsai come from a proud military tradition and earn money for their world by hiring themselves out as mercenaries. Donal Graeme's tactical gifts border on the superhuman, and he uses them to lead his forces to victory time and again while defeating enemies across the known worlds. Dickson's novel *Dorsai* set an early standard for military science fiction, but although the book is a classic, it also dates itself in its depiction and treatment of women, which Dickson only somewhat compensates for in *The Spirit of Dorsai*. The second novel shows the mettle of the Dorsai women through the character of Amanda Morgan, who leads the resistance against bold invaders of her native planet.

Drake, David

The Complete Hammer's Slammers. <u>Hammer's Slammers</u>.
Vol. 1. 2006. Night Shade Books, ISBN: 189238969X, 9781892389695, 395p.
Vol. 2. 2006. Night Shade Books, ISBN: 1892389738, 9781892389732, 505p.
Vol. 3. 2007. Night Shade Books, ISBN: 1892389800, 9781892389800, 514p.

As humans move outward to the stars, the expansionist policies of politician armchair generals necessitate warfare. Colonel Alois Hammer and his eponymous mercenary tank regiment are on the front lines of this conflict, and their exploits are gritty fare from the viewpoint of common soldiers in a war-torn universe. These classic military science fiction stories have a variety of features to satisfy readers: ethical dilemmas and contemplation of the horrors of war for conscientious consideration; enough military hardware and tactics to satisfy the intellect; and plenty of adventure to entertain the action junkies.

Finley-Day, Gerry, et al.

Rogue Trooper, Vol. 1: The Future of War. Rogue Trooper. 2005. Rebellion, ISBN: 1904265286, 9781904265283, 157p. **GN**

Nu-Earth bears the depredations and damage of the terrible war between the Norts and the Southers. The Southers create Genetic Infantry, altered troops that can withstand the hostile environment warped by biological, chemical, and radioactive warfare. When the Norts slaughter Rogue's entire group, he retrieves three teammates' biochips and implants their personalities into his equipment. Together they scour Nu-Earth, searching for the Traitor General who betrayed their unit to the Norts. Finley-Day combines wild military SF and over-the-top action with a revenge story. He also strikes an unusual balance between Rogue's incredible competence and heroism and a criticism and condemnation of war.

Haldeman, Joe

The Forever War. Forever War. 2009 (1974). St. Martin's Griffin, ISBN: 0312536631, 9780312536633, 264p.

William Mandella is one of the soldiers chosen under the Elite Conscription Act, legislation that ensures humanity's best, brightest, and most highly trained professionals serve in the military. Mandella spends weeks and months on ships that go faster than light, while decades, even centuries, pass for others. Each time Mandella returns, it's to a world, culture, and people that he barely recognizes, and soon the military becomes the only stability he knows. Haldeman, who served in the Vietnam War, won both the Hugo and Nebula Awards for *The Forever War.* His experiences enable him to communicate effectively a soldier's sense of confusion, frustration, and displacement, as well as the seeming insanity and absurdity of war.

Heinlein, Robert A.

Starship Troopers. 2006 (1959). Ace, ISBN: 0441014100, 9780441014101, 279p.

Juan Rico lives in a society where completion of military service is a requirement for full citizenship. Rico enlists soon after graduation and is placed in the Mobile Infantry division whose troopers wear powerful hi-tech battlesuits in combat against the insectoid "Bugs" of the planet Klendathu. Heinlein spends a good portion of the novel describing the philosophy behind Rico's society and examines the themes of personal and social responsibility, sacrifice, and military life. One of the first novels I'd ever read that hinted at an ethnically diverse human presence in space, this philosophically controversial novel won the Hugo Award.

Leiber, Fritz

The Big Time. 2001 (1961). Orb, ISBN: 0312890788, 9780312890780, 128p.

Two factions, the Snakes and the Spiders, fight an eternal war for control of history. Soldiers from every era battle one another without ever seeing the beings that guide the war, and none understand the reason for the conflict or their place in it as combatants. In a small place called The Big Time, the warriors rest, recuperate, philosophize, and enjoy what entertainments and services the establishment offers before going off to fight once more. Leiber penned a Hugo Award–winning character piece, told in the first person, that explores an almost timeless cluelessness and curiosity about the place of small people in large, and apparently never-ending, conflicts.

Scalzi, John

⇒ *Old Man's War.* Old Man's War. 2007 (2005). Tor, ISBN: 0765348276, 9780765348272, 318p.

The Colonial Defense Force only accepts elderly recruits. They can give you your youth back, but they need men and women with a lifetime's experience in their ongoing conflicts with other intelligent races over inhabitable planets. This breezy novel takes a matter-of-fact approach to the basis of conflict with other intelligent species—competition over limited resources—and Scalzi brings humor, adventure, and a touch of romance to future war.

Shepard, Lucius

Life during Wartime. 2006 (1987). Orion, ISBN: 0575077344, 9780575077348, 418p.

U.S. soldier David Mingolla fights in war-torn Guatemala as the Cold War progresses. America's Psicorps recruits him, and Mingolla soon develops into one of the most powerful psychics ever seen, even as his personality warps due to the training and drugs coupled with the chaos of war. Shepard delves into the psychic damage of war and holds out hope for redemption and, perhaps, freedom.

Zelenetz, Alan, et al.

Alien Legion Omnibus, **Vol. 1.** <u>Alien Legion</u>. 2009. Dark Horse, ISBN: 1595823948, 9781595823946, 352p. GN

The Alien Legion accepts all sentients, no questions asked, from the noblest of beings to the dregs of the universe. Heroes, hellions, warriors, and scum—all may enlist. But the Alien Legion also gets the worst and most dangerous assignments the Galarchy has to offer. Once your term is up, you can start a whole new life, the slate wiped clean—if you survive. This long-running classic SF comic book series featuring a "French Foreign Legion in space" is now back in print; hopefully, new stories will soon follow.

Mind Games: Psychology in Science Fiction

Space was never the final frontier. The mind houses intelligence, emotions, and the sense of self; its vast potential, its hidden depths, its capabilities and malleability fascinate scientists, writers, and readers alike. But power over the mind represents absolute domination, and this cornucopia of possibility draws those who wish to control such a wealth of resources. The books on this list host a variety of explorations and exploitations by both scrupulous healers and unethical experimenters, so focus your mind's eye on the enjoyment, edification, and enigmas offered in this section.

Faust, Minister

From the Notebooks of Dr. Brain. 2007. Del Rey, ISBN: 0345466373, 9780345466372, 390p.

The superheroes of FOOJ (the Fantastic Order of Justice) have done their job too well. With a decided lack of any more supervillains to fight, they've turned their hostility toward one another. Dr. Eva Brain-Silverman, psychologist to the superhuman community, becomes their therapist and delves deeply into their dysfunctionality. But an investigation into the death of Hawk King leads to startling and unsettling revelations about the so-called heroes' psyches. Faust's fantastic send-up of comics, talk show hosts, and pop psychology also offers a sophisticated, satirical, and unsettling look at racial issues in society.

Keyes, Daniel

⇒ *Flowers for Algernon.* 2005 (1966). Mariner, ISBN: 0156030306, 9780156030304, 311p.

Charlie Gordon, IQ 68, is the ideal candidate for an experimental surgery that increases intelligence. As Gordon's intellect soars, he discovers troubling emotional barriers between himself and others: his acquaintances become resentful around a paragon who used to be the butt of their jokes, and he can't seem to come to terms with feelings of intimacy and love. But when the first recipient of the surgery, a laboratory mouse named Algernon, begins to deteriorate, Gordon must come to terms with losing all he's gained. Keyes's ennobling and heartbreaking story is on the bookshelves of most schools and public libraries and will capture the imaginations and tug at the heartstrings of both teen and adult readers.

Le Guin, Ursula K.

The Lathe of Heaven. 2008 (1971). Scribner, ISBN: 1416556966, 9781416556961, 184p.

George Orr abuses drugs to prevent himself from dreaming, because whatever George dreams becomes reality. When Orr's psychotherapist, Dr. Haber, realizes the existence and effectiveness of George's ability, he has George tamper with reality to remake a world plagued by overpopulation, war, famine, and pollution into something better. Unfortunately, playing god has its price, and Orr's well-intentioned dreams create unexpected consequences. Haber's growing hunger for power leaves Orr desperate to escape his therapist's influence. Le Guin's thoughtful meditation demonstrates that even if one person gained the power of a god, humanity would still lack easy solutions to the world's problems.

Robson, Justina

Mappa Mundi. 2006. Pyr, ISBN: 1591024919, 9781591024910, 523p.

Genius Dr. Natalie Armstrong develops a program that can map brains and reprogram living minds. She intends to use the technology to heal patients suffering from psychological disorders, but the potential to rewrite personalities interests the U.S. government, which desires the secrets of mind control. Robson deals thoughtfully and effectively with conceptual technology that could change the world forever. She touches on possible abuses, but thoughtful readers will also consider the fact that once the genie is out of the bottle and the technology proves viable, its use for good and ill is practically guaranteed.

Slater, William

House of Stairs. 1991 (1974). Puffin, ISBN: 0140345809, 9780140345803, 166p.

Five orphans find themselves trapped in a bizarre structure containing a single landing with a fountain, an unusual food-dispensing machine, and stairs that lead nowhere. While the machine dispenses food freely at first, the children soon learn that only certain bizarre behaviors earn a reward of sustenance. Despairing of rescue, the children know helplessness, deprivation, and panicked fear as they try to determine what they must do to be fed. When the machine begins to reward them for vicious, aggressive, and sadistic behavior, the children must decide whether they will submit to the machine or resist and retain their humanity. Slater's excellent book, written for a young adult audience, explores the horrors of psychology without morality, research without ethics, and conditioning for conformity.

Zelazny, Roger

The Dream Master. 2001 (1966). Ibooks, ISBN: 0743413016, 9780743413015, 256p.

Charles Render is a therapist who treats people with a device that lets him manipulate their dreams. When he takes on an apprentice therapist and guides her in the use of the machine, their contest of wills spells disaster for them both. "He Who Shapes," the original novella that formed the basis of this book, won the Nebula Award.

Moving up the Food Chain: Becoming, Evolving, Transforming, and Transcending

Science posits the theory of evolution, allowing for species to change gradually over extensive periods of time. SF authors and fans, however, don't have the luxury of millions of years to wait and see what humanity may become, which results in speculation of a broad array of exciting, unusual, and terrifying possibilities. Authors' visions of evolution often come in radical leaps forward, whether through genetic tampering, alien interference, or, more recently, nanotechnological bootstrapping. These leaps allow writers to explore baseline humanity's reactions to the beings that will replace them, and this glimpse of the mortality of *Homo sapiens* leads to reactions of fear, denial, and conflict, also touching upon themes of race relations and genocide as humanity struggles with becoming more than it is. But there is also the potential for new understanding and acceptance. After all, the children are our future.

Baxter, Stephen

Coalescent. <u>Destiny's Children</u>. 2004 (2003). Ballantine/Del Rey, ISBN: 0345457862, 9780345457868, 527p.

In the aftermath of his father's death, George Poole learns that he has a sister, Rosa, whom he didn't know existed. Rosa belongs to a religious community in Rome called the Puissant Order of Holy Mary Queen of

Virgins. Regina, George's ancestor, cunningly created the Order to preserve a bloodline through the tumultuous instability of a Rome wracked by violence and bloody upheaval, but over centuries the subterranean community evolves into a another species. Fans of *The Da Vinci Code* and similar novels in which an ancient secret has grave consequences will enjoy Baxter's efforts.

Bear, Greg

Darwin's Radio. Darwin. 2000. Ballantine, ISBN: 0345435249, 9780345435248, 538p.

Worldwide panic ensues over a strange virus dubbed "Herod's flu" that deforms and kills fetuses. The government is trying to cover up the true reasons for the phenomenon, but evidence from several sources leads a discredited anthropologist and a molecular biologist to the terrible conclusion that the fetuses, and parents, are actually evolving into a new species. Bear's portrayal of an evolutionary leap and society's reaction to it netted him a Nebula Award.

Butler, Octavia

Lilith's Brood (formerly Xenogenesis). 2000. Warner Books, ISBN: 0446676101, 9780446676106, 746p.

Lilith Iyapo awakens to discover Earth devastated by nuclear war. The alien Oankali, a race with three sexes, recruits humanity against its will. The third sex, the ooloi, allows the melding of Oankali males and females but also enables the Oankali to meld with other races. The aliens' price for saving humanity and repopulating Earth is the blending of human and Oankali into something new. Some humans, including Lilith herself, resist the merging of species, and others revile the aliens and hybrids that result, but humanity must come to grips with its own forced evolution and the new beings among them if it is to survive. Formerly known as the Xenogenesis trilogy, this omnibus was originally published as three separate novels: *Dawn* (1987), *Adulthood Rites* (1988), and *Imago* (1989).

Clarke, Arthur C.

⇒ *Childhood's End.* 2001 (1953). Del Rey, ISBN: 0345444051, 9780345444059, 240p.

Just as humanity is primed to explore the universe, mysterious alien spaceships arrive bearing the enigmatic Overlords. Initially hiding their appearance, the extraterrestrials usher in a golden age of peace and prosperity for humanity, at the cost of restricting scientific endeavors and preventing people from living among the stars. Some rebel against the Overlords, decrying the resultant stagnation and loss of ambition, but their objections become moot as children begin to develop powerful psionic abilities. The

Overlords reveal their purpose: to shepherd humanity and prepare it for an evolutionary leap to join with a powerful being known as the Overmind. Like caterpillars that devour the plant they live on before metamorphosing into butterflies, the children lay waste to Earth prior to experiencing a Rapture unexpected by humanity. Clarke combines a frightening evolutionary transformation with a decidedly non-Western apocalypse as humanity leaps forward into destiny but abandons its individuality in this unusual and disturbing book.

Kress, Nancy

Beggars in Spain. Sleepless. 2004 (1991). Eos, ISBN: 0060733489, 9780060733483, 400p.

Originally a novella, *Beggars in Spain* garnered Kress both the Hugo and Nebula Awards before she expanded the work into a full novel. In a world that values productivity, some people begin genetically engineering their children for sleeplessness, which grants them increased efficiency, ability, and opportunity for achievement. The children also gain heightened intelligence and, inadvertently, agelessness, creating an intellectual and technological elite. But what happens to society when the Sleepless utterly outstrip the Sleepers, normal humanity, and the Sleepers feel weighed down by their inferiority? And what happens when the children of the Sleepless outstrip their parents?

Morrison, Grant, et al.

New X-Men, **Vol. 2**. X-Men. 2008. Marvel, ISBN: 078513252X, 9780785132523, 360p. GN

Guardians of a humanity that fears and hates them, the X-Men get a fantastic twenty-first-century makeover by comics legend Grant Morrison. Professor Xavier's graduates repeatedly save the world in their guise as superheroes, but as these famous outsiders try to earn humanity's trust, unrest foments and threatens to destroy the team. The world seems determined to maintain its hatred of mutants, and Professor Xavier's next generation of students distances itself from his noble ideals.

Robson, Justina

Natural History. 2005. Bantam, ISBN: 0553587412, 9780553587418, 325p.

The Unevolved, unmodified humanity, cling to hierarchical dominance and create beings of blended biology and high technology called the Forged. The Forged have bodies created for specific purposes, and the Unevolved use them to perform a variety of work, much of it difficult and dangerous to standard humans. When a Forged named Isol discovers a mineral that enables her to travel anywhere instantaneously, she also discovers a deserted world that she claims as a potential home and refuge for dissatisfied Forged. Earth sends archaeologist Zephyr Duquesne to ensure that the world is truly dead and abandoned. But in the midst of potential schism, the unusual mineral exhibits a disturbing effect on those it alters. Robson builds a brilliant and engrossing new universe while simultaneously posing difficult questions about creators and their creations, oppression, and responses to transcendence.

Rucker, Rudy

Postsingular. <u>Hylozoic Era</u>. 2009 (2007). Tor, ISBN: 0765318725, 9780765318725, 320p.

Computer corporation billionaire Luty uses nanotechnology to transform Earth into a better, virtual world. But nanotechnologist Lundquist and his son, Chu, alter the program to make humans hyperintelligent and connect all minds. This alteration has its problems, as the artificial intelligence Big Pig makes its own plans and the interdimensional Hibraners try to confine humanity to its pocket of reality. Rucker's mad extrapolation and warm humor make for a wonderful, whimsical experience.

Ryman, Geoff

Air; or, Have Not Have. 2004. St. Martin's Griffin, ISBN: 0312261217, 9780312261214, 390p.

The tiny village of Kizuldah, Karzistan, becomes the focal point of the information revolution when the new technology called Air is tested on the local populace. Air allows people to access and send information globally by thought. When Third World tradition meets First World technology, villager Chung Mae must prepare her people for the changes that are yet to come and lead them into the future. Ryman explores the effects of radical technological change upon humanity, and earned a Nebula nomination doing so.

Stapledon, Olaf

Last and First Men. 2008 (1930). Dover, ISBN: 0486466825, 9780486466828, 246p.

Stapledon's classic SF novel relates the history of the human race from the twentieth century across two billion years forward in time. Humanity evolves and develops, civilizations rise and fall, but actual growth is slower than mere change. Stapledon's philosophical meanderings range from the plausible to the utterly bizarre; he also portrays early examples of science fictional tropes such as genetic engineering and telepathic gestalts.

Get a Clue: Mystery, Crime, and SF Noir

The science fiction and mystery genres have quite a bit in common. Classic science fiction stories often feature an urgent problem that characters solve creatively using knowledge, logic, and reasoning from observed phenomena to arrive at a solution. In the same manner, detectives must use their intelligence and talents, as well as the clues and tools available, to solve crimes. When the two genres overlap one another, readers get a dual thrill from world-building and whodunit, often with a dash of Chandlerian noir in the characterizations to satisfy their more cynical sides. Pick up one of the following titles and test yourself against these science fictional sleuths.

Asimov, Isaac

The Caves of Steel. Robot. 1991 (1954). Bantam, ISBN: 0553293400, 9780553293401, 270p.

New York City detective Elijah Baley lives on an overpopulated Earth covered with massive cities housed in domes, caves of steel. He has to solve the murder of a wealthy Spacer, a man who was trying to relax Earth's prohibitions on despised robot labor. Worse, Baley's boss has assigned him a new partner, R. Daneel Olivaw, and the R stands for "robot." Asimov demonstrates the compatibility of SF and the mystery genre, while examining the potential humanity of a being created by humans in this classic science fiction novel.

Cadigan, Pat

Tea from an Empty Cup. Artificial Reality Division. 1999 (1998). Tor, ISBN: 0812541979, 9780812541977, 254p.

Artificial reality (AR) allows game players to experience anything and everything they can't in real life. Yuki Harame searches AR for signs of the man she loves, putting her in danger's path. Meanwhile, a series of gamers' deaths that mirror their avatars' demises in AR requires detective Doré Konstantin to patrol the virtual post-apocalyptic streets of Noo Yawk Sitty and find a serial killer. But how do you find a murderer in a world where everything is a lie?

Effinger, George Alec

When Gravity Fails. Marid Audran/Budayeen. 2005 (1986). Orb, ISBN: 0765313588, 9780765313584, 284p.

Multicultural SF fans will delight in Effinger's novels; they're set in a twenty-second century when body and mind are easily malleable, with an

Islamic world in political and economic ascendance over the West. This high point of Middle-Eastern civilization still has its low places, however, and a serial killer with downloadable psychopathic personalities stalks the Budayeen underworld. Crimelord Friedlander Bey initially suspects streetwise Marid Audran of the crimes and later coerces him to hunt down the murderer. With American and Asian settings dominating the rest of the subgenre, this Arabic cyberpunk noir novel shines like a cigarette tip in a dark alley.

Grimwood, John Courtenay

Pashazade. <u>Arabesk</u>. 2005 (2001). Bantam, ISBN: 0553587439, 9780553587439, 354p.

Ashraf al-Mansur steps out of an American prison and into a dynastic North African family—out of the frying pan and into the fire. Lady Nafisa, noblewoman of the cosmopolitan city El Iskandryia, informs Raf of his unknown heritage, as well as new obligations and privileges, including an arranged marriage. Nafisa's murder leaves Raf the only suspect and desperate to clear his name. But as Raf investigates the murder, he uncovers secrets about his own past. Grimwood continues this series in *Effendi* and *Felaheen*.

Harrison, M. John

Nova Swing. <u>Kefahuchi Tract</u>. 2009 (2006). Bantam, ISBN: 0553590863, 9780553590869, 315p.

After the events in *Light*, Harrison returns to the mysterious Kefahuchi Tract, an area of space dropping bits of itself planetside. One of the zones affected is the Saudade Event Site, where living algorithms and warped physics damage local reality. Vic Seratonin is a "travel agent"—he guides tourists looking for artifacts and thrills in and out of the zone for a modest fee. His latest client, Elizabeth Kielar, needs Vic's help to access the site. Lens Aschemann, intrigued by the site's bizarre effects on reality, is a police detective investigating the traffic in and out of the event site. The convergence of these characters' goals affects all those who observe and interact with them in this warped Schrödinger's noir.

McDevitt, Jack

Seeker. <u>Alex Benedict</u>. 2005. Ace, ISBN: 0441013295, 9780441013296, 368p.

Thousands of years ago, the passengers of one of the first faster-than-light ships, *Seeker*, set out to escape tyranny and find a new world. The story of *Seeker* has passed into legend, but when relic hunters Alex Benedict and Chase Kolpath come across a cup from that fabled ship, they begin their search for it and the lost colony founded by *Seeker*'s passengers. This novel of mystery and future archaeology netted its author a Nebula Award.

Meaney, John

To Hold Infinity. 2006 (1998). Pyr, ISBN: 1591024897, 9781591024897, 499p.

Yoshiko Sunadomari seeks her estranged son, Tetsuo, on the world of Fulgar, and discovers that he is a wanted criminal. Tetsuo has run afoul of the Luculenti, wealthy and powerful enhanced humans that run Fulgar's society. He flees capture into an unterraformed no-man's land while Yoshiko uses her scientific and martial skills to clear his name and pursue a murderer who preys on Fulgar's elite. Meaney provides plenty of thrills even as he portrays the inequities between technologically enhanced haves and unmodified have-nots.

Morgan, Richard K.

⇒ *Altered Carbon*. <u>Takeshi Kovacs</u>. 2003. Ballantine, ISBN: 0345457684, 9780345457684, 375p.

In a future where human consciousness can be encoded digitally, Takeshi Kovacs is taken out of storage and "sleeved" into a rented clone body so that he can solve the murder of a powerful businessman. Richard Morgan revives the cyberpunk subgenre and blends it with a stylish noir sensibility with plenty of twists to keep the reader guessing. Along the way, Morgan manages to raise some interesting questions about the uses and abuses of technology that render people virtually immortal.

Parker, Danielle L.

The Infinite Instant. 2008. Lachesis, ISBN: 1897370539, 9781897370537, 275p.

Minuet James offers rather exclusive services to her clientele. She's an athletic, beautiful, and brilliant detective, as well as a powerful registered psychic. But James is going through a rather difficult time: her business suffers due to outside pressure, an unknown persecutor holds a secret over her head, and someone's framed her for murder. She's forced to work with her mob boyfriend and an adversarial cop to solve her problem, and there's also the small matter of a rogue A.I. she created.

Somers, Jeff

The Electric Church. <u>Avery Cates</u>. 2007. Orbit, ISBN: 0316021725, 9780316021722, 373p.

Dennis Squalor preaches salvation from the pulpit of the electric church and promises eternal life in a cyborg body. His growing power worries the System Security Force, so the authorities hire assassin Avery Cates to kill Squalor. Fans of dystopian urban settings, cyberpunk, capers, and crime noir will readily identify with Cates and his team of criminals and devour this novel whole. Later installments of the series include *The Digital Plague*, *The Eternal Prison*, and *The Terminal State*.

Stross, Charles

Halting State. 2007. Ace, ISBN: 0441014984, 9780441014989, 351p.

An Edinburgh detective, a London insurance agent, and a programmer are all drawn into a bank robbery. The trouble is, the crime took place in virtual reality through the interface of a popular online role-playing game! As the team investigates, they discover that the magnitude of the break-in and its implications could have devastating consequences. A brilliant technothriller set in a future just around the corner, the novel is also an interesting experiment in writing, as Stross uses the second-person voice throughout.

The New Neighbors: First Contact

What do you do when you contact a new alien race? Above and beyond the challenges of communication and the necessary skill of navigating the untested waters of cultural contact, extreme caution, open minds, thoughtful action, and an attitude of acceptance all help the success of first contact situations. Unfortunately, even these precautions are no guarantee of an amicable or successful alliance, as some of the following novels demonstrate.

Flynn, Michael

Eifelheim. 2007 (2006). Tor, ISBN: 0765319104, 9780765319101, 320p.

At the time of the Black Plague, the alien Krenken crash near a small German town and form a fast friendship with the local pastor. In the present, a historian and a physicist become embroiled in the mystery surrounding the abandoned fourteenth-century town and discover strange manuscripts that could provide the answers to their research. Flynn's blend of historical and science fiction is notable both for its accuracy in depicting a late medieval village and for its first contact narrative, in which beings of different species and different mind-sets meet and communicate. This novel was nominated for a Hugo Award.

MacLeod, Ken

Learning the World. 2006 (2005). Tor, ISBN: 0765351773, 9780765351777, 384p.

The crew members of the huge starship *But The Sky, My Lady! The Sky!* arrive at their destination prepared to colonize the planet. Imagine their surprise when they discover the new world is already inhabited by a race of batlike beings. Even more, imagine the surprise the world's inhabitants experience when they discover that the object hurtling toward them through space is actually artificial. MacLeod weaves a first contact story in which the races involved both have elements of the other while also seeming utterly human, and he received a Hugo nomination for his efforts.

Niven, Larry, and Jerry Pournelle

The Mote in God's Eye. 1991 (1974). Pocket, ISBN: 0671741926, 9780671741921, 560p.

The destruction of the former human empire gave rise to a militant new one. When humans discover an alien solar sail craft, complete with dead pilot, they determine that it came from the star known as the Mote. Commander Lord Roderick Blaine, captain of the INSS *MacArthur*, uses the Alderson jump drives to travel the distance instantaneously and discovers an alien species that is drastically subdivided according to function. The aliens appear peaceful but conceal a terrible secret about their species that leads them to consider conquering human worlds. Niven and Pournelle write a groundbreaking work, fully flesh out their alien species, and consider how differences in biology and physiology might produce accompanying differences in psychology and society. Unfortunately, no species seems immune to conflict, and the authors also consider the necessity of war.

Resnick, Mike

A Miracle of Rare Design. 1996 (1994). Tom Doherty Associates, ISBN: 0812524241, 9780812524246, 256p.

Xavier William Lennox works as a first-contact specialist and spy, securing treaties and new business opportunities for his employers. For him to succeed, Lennox experiences a variety of alterations to his body to blend in with the alien species, but with successive surgeries and changes, he risks losing his humanity.

Russell, Mary Doria

⇒ *The Sparrow.* 1997 (1996). Ballantine, ISBN: 0449912558, 9780449912553, 408p.

In 2019, the Arecibo observatory in Puerto Rico picks up an interstellar broadcast of exquisite music. Jesuit priest Emilio Sandoz leads an expedition to the planet Rakhat, convinced that God has ordained him to make the journey to bring His word to a new planet. Forty years later, a U.N. ship sends a mutilated Sandoz back to Earth, where he relates his story concerning the deaths of every other member of the expedition and the devastating consequences that resulted from misunderstandings and mistakes. Russell's first contact story asks hard questions of religious faith and ponders the true reasons and motives behind even the noblest actions.

Tepper, Sheri S.

Grass. 1993 (1989). Bantam Spectra, ISBN: 055376246X, 9780553762464, 449p.

Humanity, although spread among the stars, suffers from a terrible plague on all its worlds save one: the planet Grass, named for its key feature that coats and covers it like a rolling ocean. Rigo and Marjorie Westriding travel to the planet hoping to find a key and cure for the plague, but Grass' ruling families, the bons, refuse to cooperate with the scientists. The nouveau noble class spends its leisure time participating in hunts, using the intelligent native Hippae as mounts and the equally sentient foxen as their prey. The secrets Marjorie discovers about the connection between Grass' life-forms and the plague ravaging humanity challenges her faith, her marriage, and her ingenuity. Tepper's novel is a wonderful mélange of feminist thought, examination of colonialism, and challenge to the assumed privileges of nobility, all wrapped in an involving first contact story.

Traviss, Karen

City of Pearl. <u>Wess'Har</u>. 2004. HarperCollins/Eos, ISBN: 0060541695, 9780060541699, 392p.

Shan Frankland leads a crew of scientists and marines to the planet of Cavanagh's Star. Frankland needs to discover the fate of a Christian colony that settled decades ago, and the scientists want a new planet to explore and exploit for corporate interests. They arrive to find the colonists safe and a delicate balance among the native aquatic bezeri, the expansionist isenj, and the powerful, environmentally conscious, and protective wess'har. When the isenj threatened to drive the bezeri to extinction, the wess'har intervened and devastated the isenj. When humans don't adhere to the wess'har strictures, they risk the same fate in this first contact story cum morality play.

Wilson, Robert Charles

Blind Lake. 2002. Tor, ISBN: 0765302624, 9780765302625, 399p.

At Blind Lake, Minnesota, Marguerite Hauser studies aliens on another planet with the use of a unique telescope. Restricted to observation, unable to communicate in any way with the creatures she watches, she persists in researching the possibility of understanding a completely alien civilization. When a reporter sneaks into the facility and the base is locked down, Marguerite begins to suspect that one of the aliens is aware of her and is trying to send her a message. This SF thriller and xenopological novel was nominated for the Hugo Award.

Dangerous Game: On the Hunt and on the Run

Hunters have a variety of motivations, from necessity to cruelty. They may long to test their mettle against nature, to stalk the most dangerous game, or to protect others from danger. The intended prey must be cunning enough to evade detection and capture. Whether you focus on the sport of the chase and the thrill of the kill, or the drive to survive another day, will depend on whether you identify with the hunters or hunted in these novels.

Martin, George R. R., Gardner Dozois, and Daniel Abraham

Hunter's Run. 2009 (2008). Eos, ISBN: 0061373303, 9780061373305, 287p.

Three authors jointly pen this tale of desperation and examination of identity. In a universe already colonized by more advanced races, Ramon Espejo, like many other humans, uses employment by aliens as a means to leave Earth. When Espejo stumbles across a hidden base, the aliens capture him and use him to hunt down a second intruder whom Espejo knows all too well.

Moon, Elizabeth

Hunting Party. Serrano Legacy/Familias Regnant Universe. 1993. Baen, ISBN: 0671721763, 9780671721763, 364p.

Rather than face an unjust court-martial, Heris Serrano leaves the military and signs on as captain of an interstellar luxury yacht, the *Sweet Delight*. She quickly befriends the owner, the wealthy Lady Cecelia, as they fly to an annual foxhunt. Serrano's alarm at the presence of smugglers aboard ship soon fades in the face of a very different kind of hunt than expected, one that uses humans as prey. As always, Moon keeps the action moving while simultaneously writing characters that mature and grow, keeping the reader engrossed in their fates.

Nolan, William F., and George Clayton Johnson

Logan's Run. Logan. 2000 (1967). Bantam, ISBN: 0553025171, 9780553025171, 148p.

Logan 3 lives in an enclosed society of youth that wards against overpopulation by enforcing a mandatory age of death. Upon reaching twenty-one years old, on a person's Lastday, citizens report for euthanasia. Logan is a Sandman, an agent who tracks down runners who hope to survive their Lastday and escape to Sanctuary, a refuge where they might live the rest of their natural life spans. But Logan's attempt to track down and eliminate Sanctuary becomes a flight for survival when he reaches his own Lastday.

Nolan and Johnson pen a classic SF tale of youthful authoritarianism and survival.

Patterson, James, and Michael Ledwidge

The Dangerous Days of Daniel X. <u>Daniel X</u>. Vision, ISBN: 0446509132, 9780446509138, 269p.

    Daniel X has the power to create anything he can imagine. As a child, he saw his parents killed before his eyes and inherited the role and responsibility of Earth's alien hunter. Daniel depends on trial and error and is unsure of himself and his abilities because he lacks a mentor or guide. Nonetheless, he pledges himself to protect our planet and someday hunt down his parents' murderer. Patterson's second series for teen readers, after <u>Maximum Ride</u>, recalls young comic book heroes and their perils and problems in striving to attain an ideal while learning more about themselves.

Sarban, a.k.a. John William Wall

The Sound of His Horn. 1960 (1952). Ballantine, ISBN: n/a, 125p.

    Captured World War Two Ally soldier Alan awakens a century later to a future where Nazi Germany conquered the world. Alan's captors have a vicious and dangerous sport they enjoy: they alter humans into hunting animals and release captives like Alan into the wilderness to serve as prey. Sadly, this book is long out of print, but interested readers can obtain a free copy at Munseys (www.munseys.com).

Wagner, John, et al.

Strontium Dog: Search/Destroy Agency Files 01. <u>Strontium Dog</u>. 2006. Rebellion, ISBN: 1905437153, 9781905437153, 336p. **GN**

    In the aftermath of the last world war, Strontium-90 fallout mutated a portion of the population. The norms' abundant discrimination and hatred leaves mutants with few rights and fewer options: they can live in poverty, turn to lives of crime, or become Search/Destroy agents, bounty hunters also called Strontium Dogs. Johnny Alpha and his norm partner, Wulf, travel across space and time to apprehend the worst criminals the universe has to offer. John Wagner, as well as later creators like Alan Grant and Carlos Ezquerra, depict a series full of action and strange adventure, while also addressing issues of racism and inequality in terms that younger readers can comprehend.

Westerfeld, Scott

⇒ *Peeps*. 2005. <u>Peeps</u>. Razorbill, ISBN: 1595140832, 9781595140838, 288p.

    Cal came all the way to New York City, lost his virginity, and became a disease carrier. Fortunately for Cal, being parasite positive—i.e., peep—means that he has all the advantages of being a biological vampire with none of the drawbacks. Rather than being an insane cannibal, Cal simply craves a lot of protein. The Night Watch hires him to hunt other peeps, including his ex-girlfriends, but soon he'll have something worse to worry about. Westerfeld handles this somewhat cautionary young adult tale with flair and skill. Fans of *Buffy the Vampire Slayer* and similar fare will find a new favorite to add to their list.

Yadate, Hajime, and Yutaka Nanten

Cowboy Bebop, **Book 1.** Cowboy Bebop. 2002. TokyoPop, ISBN: 1931514917, 9781931514910, 184p. **GN**

Martial artist Spike Spiegel once belonged to the criminal underworld. Jet Black was a cop. Both of them nearly died due to romantic entanglements. They work with Faye Valentine, a femme fatale, con artist, and compulsive gambler, and Radical Edward, a computer genius. This team of bounty hunters crews the *Bebop* and tries to make ends meet by bagging crooks and cons. Fans of Joss Whedon's *Firefly* will want to give this series a try, both in *manga* and *anime* formats. *Cowboy Bebop*, with its magnificent visual style that combines jazz, Westerns, noir, and SF elements, perfected the concept of a madcap crew doing whatever's necessary to pay the bills, put food on the table, and keep flying.

Peeping Time: Glimpses of the Future

What would you do if you could pierce the veil of time and see into the future? Would you concern yourself with selfish gain, perhaps take a peek at some winning lottery numbers? Would you try to change the path you took in life, try to change your future? Or would you go much further and try to direct the fate of all humanity? Even more terrifying, what if you couldn't change the future? What if all our lives are predetermined, and you discovered that we are all simply puppets who cannot see the strings? The following books concern those individuals who peer through time. Whether or not they try to change their futures, what they see indelibly changes them.

Asimov, Isaac

Foundation. Foundation. 1991 (1951). Spectra, ISBN: 0553293354, 9780553293357, 320p.

Hari Seldon pioneered the science of psychohistory, the mathematical study of large-scale societal trends that allows him to predict the future course of civilization. When he discovers that the Galactic Empire is slowly sliding into a decline, he plans a sequence of events that will shorten the coming dark ages to a mere millennium. Seldon sets up the Foundation of the Encyclopedia Galactica, the sanctuary for and core of all humanity's knowledge to be safeguarded through the difficult centuries ahead. The Foundation will also be the base for a new and better Empire. Asimov is one of the founding fathers of science fiction, and with good reason: he pioneered much of what is currently taken for granted in the genre. This book consists of tales that first appeared in the magazine *Astounding*; they still read very well and are essential for serious study of the genre's roots.

Bear, Greg

Eon. Eon. 2002 (1985). Gollancz, ISBN: 0575073160, 9780575073166, 512p.

A large, potato-shaped asteroid appears in Earth's orbit. Investigating scientists discover that the asteroid is the work of an intelligent species. It contains historical information about an imminent nuclear war, indicating that the artifact comes from Earth's future. Of even greater interest are seven hollowed-out chambers, one of which seems to go on forever but actually links to humanity's far-off descendents. Bear's novel possesses a Cold War sensibility, with grave tensions between America and the Soviet Union, and warns against the consequences of hostility that is both suicidal and genocidal.

Dick, Philip K.

The World Jones Made. 1993 (1956). Vintage, ISBN: 0679742190, 9780679742197, 199p.

After ideological insanity causes an apocalyptic nuclear war that devastates the Earth, the new world authority FedGov decrees relativism as the new orthodoxy and criminalizes the promotion of belief as fact. FedGov agent Doug Cussick is simply doing his job when he arrests Floyd Jones, a fortune-teller who works in a mutant carnival, but Jones soon shocks and dismays the entire world when he proves that his precognition is genuine. Jones can see one year into the future and justifies FedGov's fears when he rises to power with his charisma and talent, becoming a demagogue and despot. But Jones doesn't just see the future; he's trapped by it, and plays out the role he knows he must. Philip K. Dick crafted a thoughtful pondering of free will, predestination, and politics in this early novel.

Gibson, William

All Tomorrow's Parties. Bridge. 2003 (1999). Berkley, ISBN: 0425190447, 9780425190449, 339p.

Colin Laney once moved among the corridors of power; now he lives in a cardboard box in San Francisco. Laney has the ability to see nodes of information in events and media patterns that predict the future course of events. He's just found the almighty node of all nodes, something that could change the world forever, and determines to ease society through this transition. As the node approaches, Laney's efforts become intertwined with a security guard, an artificial intelligence, a killer invisible to Laney's ability, a bicycle messenger, and a power-hungry billionaire, all playing their part to change the direction of tomorrow.

Sawyer, Robert J.

⇒ *Flashforward.* 2000 (1999). Tor, ISBN: 0812580346, 9780812580341, 319p.

Two CERN physicists striving for a Nobel prize enact an experiment that sends the minds of humanity two decades into the future, where all people experience a brief period of their lives-to-be. Meanwhile, everybody's out-of-body experiences cause a variety of incidents and catastrophes. Upon returning, each individual must come to terms with what they saw. Some insist on free will and work to ensure or change their fate, while others' acceptance borders on fatalism. Sawyer engages in another brilliant thought experiment sure to capture readers' imaginations.

Vonnegut, Kurt, Jr.

The Sirens of Titan. 2006 (1959). Orion, ISBN: 0575079029, 9780575079021, 272p.

While traveling between Earth and Mars, Winston Niles Rumfoord encounters a chronosynclastic infundibulum. This bizarre phenomenon converts him into a being of pure energy that can only take physical form once every fifty-nine days; it also grants him complete knowledge of the past and future, all of which converges toward one rather anticlimactic and absurd purpose. Rumfoord forms the Church of God the Utterly Indifferent and manipulates entire planets with war and faith. He also has the sorry duty of informing Malachi Constant, the Earth's richest and luckiest man, of his unavoidable fate. This satirical novel takes a darkly comic jab at religion and considers humanity's rather limited perspective of an absurd, deterministic universe.

Hail to the Chief!: The Perils of Politics

Politics is full of backstabbing, scheming, sabotaging, cheating, lying, vilifying, villainizing, patronizing, pandering, grandstanding, and bribery. And that's just during campaign season. Actually achieving high office guarantees a host of enemies, hangers-on, and sycophantic parasites that hope to exploit their connections until the politician has nothing left to give. For better or worse, just as many news outlets show current affairs of state in a negative light, many science fiction authors depict tomorrow's politics with a similar cynical/pessimistic/realistic (choose which adjective you prefer) attitude. One thing is for sure: with so many people hungry for power, it's a full-time job to ensure that you're not on the menu.

Dick, Philip K.

Now Wait for Last Year. 1993 (1966). Vintage, ISBN: 0679742204, 9780679742203, 230p.

The Earth is on the wrong side of an interstellar war, having sided with Lilistar against their enemies, the Reegs. Gino "The Mole" Molinari is Earth's supreme leader, and desperate to get out from under the control of the 'Starmen. Surgeon Eric Sweetscent is puzzled by Molinari's ability to rule and appear well and healthy in public, given that the ruler suffers from severe ailments, and even appears to have died several times! The terrifyingly addictive drug JJ-180, a chemical that enables its users to visit alternate timelines, may hold the answer to the mystery of Molinari's success in office, and the key to slipping the noose of the 'Starmen.

Heinlein, Robert A.

Double Star. 1986 (1956). Ballantine, ISBN: 0354330137, 9780345330130, 243p.

Lorenzo Smythe is a remarkably talented and insufferably arrogant actor who happens to be down on his luck and out of work. He takes a job to stand in for a kidnapped politician who supports Martian rights, a position Smythe despises, and unexpectedly becomes locked into the role. Heinlein's character piece, which won the Hugo Award, touches on the theme of identity, as Smythe moves from imitation to emulation, overcoming his own prejudices in the process.

Stephenson, Neal, and J. Frederick George

Interface. 2005 (1994). Bantam, ISBN: 0553383434, 9780553383430, 618p.

A stroke leaves Governor William A. Cozzano with brain damage, but a shadowy corporate conspiracy offers to fund a cutting-edge operation for the governor. With a new biochip, Cozzano receives polling information directly into his brain. The information gives him an advantage over his competition, but the hardware also leaves the new presidential candidate vulnerable to outside control. Stephenson's fast-paced political thriller will keep readers speeding through the text to discover what happens next!

Sterling, Bruce

Distraction. 1999 (1998). Bantam, ISBN: 0553576399, 9780553576399, 532p.

The year 2044 finds the no-longer-United States of America a schismatic mess. Sixteen political parties vie for power and deadlock the government, which may soon be at war with the Netherlands. Climate change is devastating the environment, information warfare is rampant, and the military is resorting to bake sales for funding. In these troubled times, Oscar Valparaiso moves like a shark through turbulent waters. You could call him a born political fixer, if he had actually been born. He was actually grown in vitro and genetically altered as part of a Columbian baby racket. Valparaiso sees incredible opportunity in the Collaboratory, a corrupt scientific hothouse for brilliant minds, but good-ol'-boy Louisiana governor "Green Huey" wants the facility for illegal scientific experimentation. The resulting duel of disinformation, savvy, and spin, fueled by Sterling's sharp political satire, will keep readers turning pages and chuckling wickedly.

Vaughan, Brian K., et al.

⇒ *Ex Machina,* Vol. 1: *The First Hundred Days.* Ex Machina. 2005. Wildstorm, ISBN: 1401206123, 9781401206123, 136p. **GN**

When Mitchell Hundred discovered a strange device near the Brooklyn Bridge, it gave him the ability to communicate with machines. He became the world's first (and only) superhero, the Great Machine, with mixed success. But what does a superhero do with all that good public relations capital? Hundred wanted to make a real difference, so he ran to become mayor of New York—and won! Ex Machina chronicles the career of Mitchell Hundred from beginning to end, his triumphs and failures, and the moments of wonder in between. Political junkies and avid viewers of shows like *The West Wing* will thoroughly enjoy this meaty and thoughtful graphic novel series.

Red Alert!: Distress, Despair, and Disaster

The following novels feature a variety of scenarios in which humanity faces impending disaster and the resultant chaos and breakdown of society. The cataclysms may be entirely natural or due to humanity's shortsightedness and are often ecological and astronomical in origin. In some of the works, humanity perseveres and demonstrates compassion and nobility. Sadly, our species more often appears brutal, savage, and even suicidal in the face of these cataclysms. Certainly, whenever humans contend with dire straits, they must ultimately confront themselves as well.

Barnes, John

Mother of Storms. 1995 (1994). Tor, ISBN: 0812533453, 9780812533453, 560p.

A military operation causes a nuclear explosion that releases voluminous amounts of methane from the ocean floor. The sudden heat and temperature increase results in a multiplication of hurricanes of unbelievable intensity, leading to catastrophic suffering. Politicians and scientists scramble to solve the crisis even as fearful humanity, fully immersed in virtual reporting, watches the events in real time.

Baxter, Stephen

Flood. 2009 (2008). Roc, ISBN: 0451462718, 9780451462718, 496p.

In 2016, scientists realize that climate change cannot be solely responsible for rising sea levels. Seismic disturbances have released a vast reservoir of water from beneath the ocean floor. Earth is drowning; governments cannot cope, stopgap emergency measures prove ineffective, and the populace gradually realizes that the sea levels will continue to rise beyond all expectations. The wealthy flee to a massive ship dubbed the *Ark Three*, and officials escape into space, but over the decades the remainder of humanity must adapt to a new environment to survive.

Brunner, John

The Sheep Look Up. 2003 (1972). BenBella, ISBN: 1932100016, 9781932100013, 388p.

Despondent scientist Austin Train is in seclusion. He warned the world of the increasingly severe and devastating effects of pollution, but with little effect. Most of the public ignores Train, even as the increasingly toxic environment bolsters his arguments. Worsening conditions force people to use gas masks and water purifiers, and demand for these items proves lucrative for callous and greedy corporations. The few who did listen to the ecologist's prophetic warnings take their activism to extremes, while the majority, rather than demanding change, become increasingly detached and indifferent to one another even as their planet dies and society crumbles around them.

Leiber, Fritz

The Wanderer. 1999 (1964). E-Reads, ISBN: 1585860492, 9781585860494, 308p.

Without warning, an inhabited planet appears in Earth's orbit. Its presence tears the moon to fragments and unleashes catastrophes across our world, including earthquakes, tidal waves, and massive floods. The novel examines the resulting terror and struggle for survival from multiple viewpoints and depicts a universe uncaring and unresponsive to humanity's plight. Leiber won the Hugo Award for this early precursor to the disaster genre.

Niven, Larry, and Jerry Pournelle

Lucifer's Hammer. 1983 (1977). Del Rey, ISBN: 0449208133, 9780449208137, 640p.

Tim Hamner, an amateur astronomer, discovers a comet heading toward Earth. Fearful and dismayed, a panicked populace begins stockpiling and preparing for the coming apocalypse. When the comet, dubbed Lucifer's Hammer, strikes the planet, it causes earthquakes, converts waters to massive amounts of killing steam, creates horrifying tidal waves, and sends tons of dust and debris into the atmosphere that block out the sun and begin a new ice age. In the aftermath, humanity struggles to survive as barbarism reigns. Cannibals and other marauding bands roam the wastelands, and anti-technology activists who desire humanity to live in harmony with nature oppose those who desire a return to civilization. Niven and Pournelle build their narrative slowly, heightening tension and terror. Even after the disaster, when cooperation is key to survival, the authors portray a humanity divided against itself.

Robinson, Kim Stanley

Forty Signs of Rain. Capital Science. 2005 (2004). Bantam, ISBN: 0553585800, 9780553585803, 393p.

Scientists contending with climate change find their efforts hampered by capitalism and corporate greed. High-powered science requires extensive funding, but corporations, eager for profit, put legal strangleholds on scientists' ability to communicate. As the researchers begin to understand the extent of environmental damage caused by humans, they must also contend with ponderous political bureaucracy. Robinson earnestly pleads the case for environmental awareness and action while portraying the very real frustrations and obstacles scientists face.

Schätzing, Frank

The Swarm. 2006. Regan, ISBN: 0060813261, 9780060813260, 881p.

Whales attack ships! Crustaceans poison cities! Monstrous storms devastate populated coasts! As these freak accidents multiply, they begin to form a terrifying pattern. A dedicated group of scientists discovers that the frequency and intensity of the disasters are neither random nor natural. The Yrr, intelligent creatures that manipulate ocean life, are responsible for these essentially terrorist actions, perhaps as a defense against humanity's abuse of the sea. Worse, the military's only means of destroying the Yrr may irreparably damage marine ecology unless the scientists can find a better solution. Schätzing's novel, a huge best seller in his native Germany, communicates an environmental message with global scope.

Shute, Nevil

⇒ *On the Beach*. 1990 (1957). Ballantine, ISBN: 0345311485, 9780345311481, 278p.

World War Three devastated the entire Northern Hemisphere. While the far Southern Hemisphere is still capable of supporting life, the nuclear fallout is slowly moving to cover the entire Earth, poisoning all life. When survivors detect an erratic radio signal from the United States, an expedition sets out by submarine to determine if it's possible to survive the oncoming fallout. However, as the situation becomes bleaker, the few people remaining must come to terms with how they will face their last days.

Sterling, Bruce

Heavy Weather. 1996 (1994). Bantam, ISBN: 055357292X, 9780553572926, 310p.

Jerry Mulcahey leads the Storm Troupers, a group of storm chasers who study heavy weather and analyze the data. Unchecked greenhouse gas production has radically altered weather patterns, and Mulcahey expects the mother of all storms: an F-6 scale twister, far beyond the intensity of anything yet recorded. Sterling combines an exciting and dangerous profession with thrilling action and suspense.

Turner, George

Drowning Towers (**a.k.a.** *The Sea and Summer*). 1996 (1987). Avon, ISBN: 038078601X, 9780380786015, 387p.

Melbourne, Australia, suffers with an economy as damaged as its environment. Government corruption results in joblessness and bleak poverty, with "swills," the poorest citizens, warehoused in high-rise buildings that soon become watery tombs as the sea level rises. Turner won the Arthur C. Clarke Award for his depiction of society slowly spiraling to oblivion and people's desperate attempts at survival.

Religious Rites and Wrongs: Religion and Faith in Science Fiction

Some people regard faith and science as antithetical to one another. Certainly, many science fiction tales regard religious institutions as oppressive and believers as inimical to scientific knowledge and progress. To be fair, there are historical antecedents of said repression, which might explain some prejudice within the genre. Nevertheless, authors' consideration of religion as a sociological phenomenon allows for a host of possible visions of worlds and futures altered by the power of faith.

Abnett, Dan, et al.

Durham Red: The Scarlet Cantos. Durham Red. 2006. Rebellion, ISBN: 1904265863, 9781904265863, 96p. **GN**

Originally a bounty hunter, the mutant vampire Durham Red takes a long sleep in suspended animation. She rests for far longer than she intended, as she discovers over one thousand years later when an academic discovers her sarcophagus. In her absence, humanity continues its policy of persecution against mutants. The oppressed mutants, hoping for a savior, form the Tenebrae cult around the memory of the blessed Saint Scarlet, and Durham Red is faced with unwanted worship and some disturbing expectations.

Atwood, Margaret

The Handmaid's Tale. 1998 (1986). Anchor, ISBN: 038549081X, 9780385490818, 311p.

The Republic of Gilead is an oppressive theocracy that subjugates women and strips them of any rights. As an ongoing civil war has sterilized much of the population, women who prove fertile are trained as "handmaids"—concubines forced to endure rape in the effort to breed children for Gilead. Offred, a handmaid captured when she tries to escape the United States, has her daughter and her name taken from her, wears clothing that readily identifies her status, and is placed with a Gilead commander's family. The disjointed story Offred relates portrays a numb despair at the Republic's horrors, until the faint hope of the Mayday resistance movement leads her to risk everything for her freedom. This dystopian feminist tale of patriarchal religious oppression won the Arthur C. Clarke Award.

Blish, James

A Case of Conscience. 2000 (1958). Del Rey, ISBN: 0345438353, 9780345438355, 242p.

In this Hugo Award–winning novel, a team of four scientists travels to the planet Lithia to make contact with its reptilian inhabitants and determine whether Earth should institute full and open contact with the aliens. Lithian society, lacking war and crime, appears utopian to the visiting humans. Father Ramon Ruiz Sanchez, Jesuit priest and biologist, also discovers that the Lithians have no concept of God, nor any religion. While some team members argue for viewing Lithians as equals, others hope to exploit the planet. But Ruiz-Sanchez considers the Lithians a challenge to religion. Blish considers the role of religious belief and the domino effect that careless first contact sets in motion, leading to intervention, exploitation, and destruction, in this classic encounter between two species.

Hamilton, Peter F.

The Dreaming Void. <u>Void Trilogy</u>. 2009 (2007). Del Rey/Ballantine, ISBN: 034549654X, 9780345496546, 601p.

Although humanity has developed immortality, they still seek enlightenment. The Living Dream movement forms a Pilgrimage to the Void, an artifact at the galactic center that slowly consumes its surroundings to fuel the universe within. A number of other factions and species believe that such a sudden influx would cause the Void to expand radically and are determined to halt the Pilgrimage before it reaches its goal. Characters, plotlines, and intrigue abound in this sprawling space opera.

Levy, Roger

Icarus. 2007 (2006). Gollancz, ISBN: 0575079819, 9780575079816, 423p.

On the world of Haven, the subterranean dwellers make a discovery that calls their entire received truths into question. On another planet, Haze, the city of AngWat sits in its lush jungles; its lords demand tribute and keep the origins of their cruel and vicious traditions from their people. And on Earth, a megalomaniacal preacher uses his influence to devastating effect. In all these tales, authorities control and manipulate the populace until belief substitutes for truth and truth is forgotten.

MacLeod, Ken

The Night Sessions. 2008. Orbit, ISBN: 1841496510, 9781841496511, 324p.

Detective Inspector Adam Ferguson investigates a fatal explosion that caused the death of a clergyman. He discovers evidence of a bomb, a possible terrorist action. In the years since the Faith/Oil Wars and the Great Rejection, religious believers have become a disenfranchised minority. Ferguson himself is a former member of the squads that forcibly and violently ousted believers from public life. But a frightening conversion has taken place, and a set of broadcast sermons, known as the Night Sessions, lead to a new and terrifying radical movement. MacLeod's ability to depict the religious mind-set as alien makes for a convincing extrapolation and a frightening vision of religious extremes.

Miller, Walter M., Jr.

⇒ *A Canticle for Leibowitz*. 2006 (1959). Eos, ISBN: 0060892994, 9780060892999, 352p.

In the wake of a nuclear war that consumed our world, the Catholic Church's Order of Leibowitz seeks out and preserves the technology of the past in preparation for the day when humanity climbs out of barbarism.

Spanning three ages, the novel strikes a perfect balance between the cyclical nature of history, particularly our species' habit of repeating disastrous mistakes due to fear and stupidity, and a belief in our ability to survive and strive for a better tomorrow.

Weber, David

Off Armageddon Reef. <u>Safehold</u>. 2008 (2007). Tor, ISBN: 0765353970, 9780765353979, 788p.

Weber deals with ideology and coerced obedience in this new series of novels. As the Gbaba Empire steadily wipes out humanity, a small colony finds sanctuary on the distant planet Safehold. To prevent the Gbaba from detecting them, a faction of humans insists humanity restricts itself to a low level of technology. To this end, the faction alters historical records and the colonists' minds and establishes a religion that prevents technology from advancing beyond the medieval level. Centuries later, the Church of God Awaiting maintains a stagnating stranglehold over the colonists' development. But at Armageddon Reef, the only survivor of the last war uses an android body and the last cache of high technology to ignite a technological renaissance and awaken humanity from its new dark age.

Willett, Edward

Marseguro. 2008. DAW, ISBN: 0756404649, 9780756404642, 392p.

Geneticist Victor Hansen fled Earth with the new water-dwelling race of Selkies. Earth's religious theocracy, the Body Purified, rules from a position of ideological and genetic purity and sends a force to eradicate the heretical refugees led by Victor's descendent, Richard. Willett highlights the conflict between religious fanaticism and freedom but doesn't skimp on the action and battles many fans enjoy.

Things Left Behind: Xenoarchaeology, Relics, Monoliths, and Artifacts

Our planet is dotted with ancient and mysterious monoliths, from the pyramids to the statues of Easter Island to Stonehenge. These sites have an overwhelming impact on travelers: they command attention and awe viewers with their majesty and suggestions of ancient wisdom and knowledge. I often wonder if these sites inspired authors to create fictional alien ancients and lost artifacts of unguessable technological prowess. Scholars, scientists, treasure hunters, and the terminally curious seem driven to discover and destined to encounter these products of other civilizations and the breakthroughs and revelations they may contain. Unlike those searchers, you, dear reader, need look no further; a veritable trove of wonder awaits you in these books.

Banks, Iain M.

The Algebraist. 2006 (2004). Night Shade Books, ISBN: 1597800449, 9781597800440, 544p.

Young Taak, a xenopologist working for the Mercatoria, studies the Dwellers, a race of beings that inhabit a gas giant. When a rival civilization cuts off the system's wormhole, the Mercatoria orders Taak to discover the Dwellers' secret portals before an invading force and its sadistic leader arrive to take the knowledge for themselves. This novel of mystery and magnificent scope earned a Hugo nomination.

Clarke, Arthur C.

Rendezvous with Rama. Rama. 1990 (1972). Spectra, ISBN: 0553287893, 9780553287899, 243p.

Scientists monitoring space for potential threats to Earth discover an immense alien craft passing through the solar system. The crew of the *Endeavor*, piloted by Commander Norton, intercepts the ship designated as *Rama* and discovers an entire world within. With only a matter of weeks before the craft leaves our solar system, the crew must explore the artifact's wonders and learn as much as they can about its mysterious creators before it journeys beyond our sun. Clarke won the Hugo, Nebula, and John W. Campbell Awards for this classic novel of scientific exploration and discovery. Readers who enjoy characters that use their minds rather than violence to overcome difficulties will revel in exploring the enigmatic vessel. Clarke went on to pen three sequels to *Rendezvous with Rama* with the help of author Gentry Lee: *Rama II*, *The Garden of Rama*, and *Rama Revealed*.

Crichton, Michael

⇒ *Sphere.* 1988 (1987). Ballantine, ISBN: 0345353145, 9780345353146, 371p.

The United States gathers a group of scientists to explore a strange craft discovered on the floor of the Pacific Ocean. Evidence suggests that the submerged ship is at least three hundred years old, and the researchers learn that it comes from the future. Within the ship, they find a mysterious sphere. When a scientist enters the artifact, an entity calling itself Jerry visits the crew. Although Jerry initially seems friendly, his appearance corresponds with bizarre and deadly attacks on the team, even as a terrible storm cuts the crew off from the Navy ships waiting above. As the number of scientists dwindles, psychologist Norman Johnson must unravel the mystery behind Jerry and the sphere before death claims them all. *Sphere* is an intriguing thriller that considers the wonder of exploration, the power of the mind, and the danger of accessing technology that the human race may not be mature enough to use.

Flynn, Michael

The January Dancer. 2008. Tor, ISBN: 0765318172, 9780765318176, 350p.

On the planet Jehovah, a nexus of interstellar travel, a bard, and a scarred man meet in a tavern to converse about an ancient relic. Although this introduction sounds like the beginning of many a *Dungeons & Dragons* adventure, it serves here as the opening scene of a delightful space opera. The January Dancer is an artifact that allegedly gives its possessor the power to control others. Amos January finds the alien object, only to barter it for repairs to his damaged ship. As the artifact trades hands, readers follow it through narrow escapes, pirate attacks, and political intrigue. Flynn's use of future patois and Celticisms may require readers to go at a slower pace, but this same unique language adds to the flavor and richness of the author's universe. Flynn's sharp wit and magnificent turns of phrase—"what can come from nameless places but something unspeakable?"—provide rare gems on every page.

Haldeman, Joe

Camouflage. 2004. Ace, ISBN: 0441011616, 9780441011612, 296p.

When the Navy discovers an impervious artifact, they assign scientist Russell Sutton to provide answers about the enigmatic object. Meanwhile, two immortal aliens who have lived among humanity throughout our history feel the object's summons. One, the changeling, lives by altering its shape, adapting, and learning; the other, the chameleon, has become very good at killing. This novel includes some of the oldest elements and themes of classic SF, including aliens, artifacts, and the discovery of what it means to be human, and earned a Nebula Award.

Hamilton, Peter F.

Fallen Dragon. 2002 (2001). Warner, ISBN: 0446527084, 9780446527088, 630p.

Lawrence Newton dreams of being a pilot as humanity expands across the galaxy. He runs away and works as a soldier for the interstellar corporation Zantiu-Braun and tries to earn enough to make his dream a reality. Lawrence's job, however, is distasteful: he pillages established colonies to acquire "assets" for the corporation. The colony world of Thallspring has no intention of offering up its wealth to Zantiu-Braun and uses a cache of alien technology to fight back against the soldiers. If Lawrence can find the cache, he can smuggle it to Earth. But the technology is linked to an ancient legend, and when Lawrence learns the source of the advanced science, his life takes a drastic turn. Hamilton consistently manages to write epic modern space operas with a sharp focus on the very human concerns and growth of the individuals involved.

Harrison, John M.

The Centauri Device. 2009 (1975). Gollancz, ISBN: 0575082577, 9780575082571, 208p.

When the fabled Centauri Device, supposedly a weapon of incredible power, proves to actually exist, the Israeli and Arab world powers each strive to possess it, but neither can use it. The Device will only manifest its abilities in Centauran hands, and many believe the species is extinct. Pity poor John Truck, starship captain on the seedier side of space, who is also apparently half-Centauran and suddenly wanted by opposing forces eager to use him. Harrison's pessimistic novel reads as a cynical and perhaps necessary counterpoint and antidote to the plethora of politically and sociologically more naïve space operas available.

Niven, Larry

Ringworld. Ringworld. 1985 (1970). Ballantine, ISBN: 0345333926, 9780345333926, 342p.

As Louis Wu celebrates his two hundredth birthday, his intense boredom inspires a desire to explore beyond the boundaries of known space. A visit from Nessus, a member of the two-headed alien species of Puppeteers, cures Wu's ennui with images of an alien structure ripe for adventure and exploration. Wu and Nessus journey with fellow explorers Teela Brown and feline alien Kzin, Speaker-to-Animals. They find a massive ring made of an unknown, incredibly durable substance orbiting a sun. As the ring spins, generating gravity, powerful walls of incredible height maintain an atmosphere for the ecosystems found along the ring's segments. When a defense system forces Wu to crash-land on the ring, the crew must explore its wondrous and strange geography even as they search for a means to escape their discovery. Niven combines humor, pulp action, wondrous technology, and exotic locales to good effect, and won the Hugo and Nebula Awards for this novel.

Pohl, Frederik

Gateway. Heechee. 2004 (1976). Del Rey, ISBN: 0345475836, 9780345475831, 278p.

Robinette Broadhead was stuck living a monotonous existence on an ecologically devastated Earth when his luck turned and he won a small lottery. He used the money to purchase a one-way ticket to Gateway, a space station built into a hollowed-out asteroid by a mysterious race known as the Heechee. Gateway has a number of unusual ships that move faster than light, and explorers can sign on as crew in the hope of discovering new riches and resources to exploit. Unfortunately, nobody really knows how to use the Heechee ships, and new routes are determined randomly. Volunteers may end up hitting the mother lode or find themselves emerging in the middle of a sun. Broadhead strikes it rich, but feels tormented by a troubled conscience. He seeks help from Sigfrid, an artificial intelligence and psychologist, and their ongoing dialogue frames the story and eventually reveals the mystery behind Broadhead's secret shame. Pohl won both the Nebula and John W. Campbell Awards for this classic work that explores humanity's courage and cowardice when facing the unknown.

Wilson, Robert Charles

The Chronoliths. 2002 (2001). Tor, ISBN: 0812545249, 9780812545241, 315p.

Monolithic indestructible monuments to a future conqueror, Kuin, begin appearing all over the Earth, commemorating victories still twenty years in the future. The destruction wrought by the chronoliths' materializations and panic over humanity's seemingly inevitable future lead to confusion and fear, with society drawing lines of allegiance or opposition to Kuin. As the phenomenon continues and the date of Kuin's ascendancy approaches, programmer Scott Ward and physicist Sue Chopra search for an answer before time runs out. This thrilling novel of terror and manipulation was nominated for the Hugo Award.

Time after Time: Moving in Four Dimensions

Science fiction stories can range any*when* as well as anywhere. The ability to travel to any point in time, anywhere in history, would certainly intoxicate the erstwhile voyager. At the very least, you could turn your hindsight into foresight. You could give your younger self tips, warn yourself away from bad blind dates, and get advice from the older (and hopefully wiser) you. More imaginative and adventurous travelers could meet their favorite historical figures, get the real story behind the foundations of religious movements, and perhaps change history altogether! Of course, time travel also has its share of perils, including physical hazards such as dinosaurs and angry witch hunters. Also, the future's denizens might not take kindly to intrusions from the past, and could frown upon anybody tampering with their entire existence, thank you very much. You'd also have to consider the headaches of quantum mechanics, alternate futures, and potentially falling in love with your ancestors and erasing yourself from the time–space continuum. In any event, should you ever find yourself in possession of a time machine, do a bit of reading from this list first and learn from others' mistakes.

Baker, Kage

⇒ ***In the Garden of Iden.*** The Company. 2006 (1997). Tor, ISBN: 0765314576, 9780765314574, 329p.

The Company, an organization with agents spread throughout the timestream, rescues young Mendoza from the Spanish Inquisition, and turns her into an immortal cyborg in exchange for her service. The Company travels in time to preserve treasured and rare lost items, and Mendoza's first assignment is to rescue certain extinct herbs from the garden of Sir Walter Iden. But Mendoza didn't expect to fall in love with doomed Nicholas Harpole, a Protestant in Queen Mary's England. The Company forbids its agents to change recorded history, and Mendoza, torn between love and duty, must choose between them. Baker writes a wonderful blend of romance, historical period piece, and science fiction. Recommend this book to friends who are reluctant to give SF a try.

Baxter, Stephen

The Time Ships. 1995. HarperPrism, ISBN: 0061056480, 9780061056482, 520p.

Baxter revisits H. G. Wells's classic, *The Time Machine*. The original traveler returns to the future intent on rescuing his beloved Weena, only to find that his actions have altered that future. Accompanied by a scientifically advanced Morlock named Nebogipfel, the traveler attempts to foil his original experiments, only to be interrupted by a future government with time travel technology. The traveler ranges far into the future and back to the beginning of time on multiple adventures to a vast array of alternate futures. Baxter uses many of these trips to cleverly reference a number of Wells's other works while simultaneously tackling mind-bending paradoxes and quantum physics. Although many frown on sequels as a rule, and particularly sequels not penned by the original author, this warm and charming novel will delight fans of both Wells and Baxter.

Biggle, Lloyd, Jr.

The Chronocide Mission. 2002. Wildside, ISBN: 1587155494, 9781587155499, 337p.

Student Vladislav Kuznetsov finds himself suddenly three hundred years from home in a war-torn, socially stratified, matriarchal future. He discovers that a special lens acts as both devastating weapon and time travel device and sends two men back in time to kill the lens' creator and hopefully rewrite the world's fate. Biggle's last novel proves a charming, suspenseful, and hopeful tale.

Crichton, Michael

Timeline. 2009 (1999). Ballantine, ISBN: 0345517814, 9780345517814, 496p.

Edward Johnston and his associates are archaeologists and historians exploring a medieval dig. Johnston meets with the funding company, ITC, and soon after his students discover modern artifacts among the ruins. Robert Doniger, head of ITC, has developed a functional time machine and persuades the historians to go back to the fourteenth century to retrieve the lost Johnston. Crichton's novel of quantum physics and time travel will delight readers of science fiction and historical fiction.

De Camp, L. Sprague

Lest Darkness Fall. 1996 (1941). Baen, ISBN: 0671877364, 9780671877361, 336p.

Martin Padway is a twentieth-century scholar of Roman history. A lightning strike suddenly transports him to the sixth century as the Roman Empire totters. Martin is quick to adapt, however, and soon finds a new job cooking up and providing alcohol to the natives. As violent forces slowly encroach upon the city, Martin must turn his anachronistic "innovations" to military and political matters. After all, if Rome falls and the Dark Ages begin, what will become of *him*? Continuing in the tradition of Mark Twain, De Camp entertainingly writes about a man out of his time. Fans of Harry Turtledove, S. M. Stirling, and Eric Flint would do well to find a copy of this charming, humorous, and ingenious novel.

Finney, Jack

Time and Again. 1995 (1970). Scribner, ISBN: 0684801175, 9780684801179, 399p.

In 1970, the U.S. government approaches Simon "Si" Morley with a unique proposition. They believe that Si has the special type of mind necessary for their program, a method of hypnosis to psychically send subjects back in time. Si's girlfriend, Kate, has an unusual keepsake, a postcard dating from 1882 in New York that references the destruction of the world. Si travels through time to investigate the artifact and falls in love with a young woman, Julia, in the process. As the unexpected consequences of Si's investigation threaten the couple's safety, Si wonders if his actions might change history, and if he will have to risk doing so. Next to H. G. Wells's classic, Finney's novel is considered a quintessential time travel story.

Flint, Eric

1632. <u>Assiti Shards</u>. 2001 (2000). Baen, ISBN: 0671319728, 9780671319724, 597p.

The entire town of Grantville, West Virginia, disappears from the twenty-first century and reappears in Thuringia, Germany, in the seventeenth century. The townsfolk attempt to cope with the mysterious journey and deal with basic survival, their difficulty communicating with the natives, and the small matter of the Thirty Years War. Over time, they find acceptance despite their strange ways, and consolidate themselves into a power to be reckoned with. Flint's novel of military conflict, clashing politics, and time travel has generated both an avid fan base and a large number of sequels, many of which are collaborations with other authors who want to play in the *1632* universe.

Haldeman, Joe

The Accidental Time Machine. 2007. Ace, ISBN: 0441014992, 9780441014996, 288p.

Matt Fuller is an MIT student who creates a calibrator that, to his surprise, is also a time machine. There are only two hitches: first, it only goes into the future; and second, every time he activates it, it travels exponentially further in time. While Matt enjoys exploring the future, he's not sure he'll ever be able to go home again. A fast read with plenty of adventure and glimpses into interesting worlds, this novel was nominated for the Nebula Award.

Moorcock, Michael

The Dancers at the End of Time. 2003. Gollancz, ISBN: 0575074760, 9780575074767, 664p.

Jherek Carnelian belongs to a future beyond our wildest dreams, where humans regularly reshape reality with nary a thought to using technology beyond our comprehension. They live life beyond the conventions of morality, where virtue is unknown, boredom is the only enemy, and innocent decadence is indulged in the face of final entropy. When Jherek decides to declare his love for the proper and distinctly Victorian Mrs. Amelia Underwood, an inadvertent time traveler, he considers it a brilliant aesthetic choice, an artistic statement like no other. As Jherek follows Mrs. Underwood across the seas of time, he and his love mature, but his pursuit may cost him his life. Moorcock's homage to the *fin de siècle* movement will delight readers interested in late-nineteenth-century literature and comedies of manners. This omnibus edition contains the works *An Alien Heat* (1972), *The Hollow Lands* (1974), and *The End of All Songs* (1976).

Stirling, S. M.

Island in the Sea of Time. <u>Island in the Sea of Time</u>. 1998. Roc, ISBN: 0451456750, 9780451456755, 608p.

The island of Nantucket, Massachusetts, and its inhabitants, as well as the U.S. Coast Guard ship *Eagle*, are swept back three thousand years to the Bronze Age. The Nantucketers must stave off panic and starvation, learn how to survive while cut off from the modern world, and make alliances with the Native Americans in their area. The transplanted Americans have the knowledge and ability to create technology far more advanced than other peoples possess, which gives them an edge, but a rogue member of the community desires to use that advantage to build himself an empire. Stirling's popular series continues with *Against the Tide of Years* and *On the Oceans of Eternity*.

Swanwick, Michael

Bones of the Earth. 2002. Eos/HarperCollins, ISBN: 0380978369, 9780380978366, 335p.

Paleontologist Richard Leyster receives an offer he can't refuse when the enigmatic Griffin walks into his office with an ice chest containing a freshly severed dinosaur head. The mysterious beings called the Unchanging offer Leyster time travel technology to study his subjects in their natural environment but warn against changing recorded history. However, between Creationists desperate to halt his research and a colleague interested in pushing the envelope, Leyster must focus on his and his future's survival. This work of time travel received Hugo and Nebula Award nominations.

Turtledove, Harry

The Guns of the South. 1997 (1992). Ballantine, ISBN: 0345413660, 9780345413666, 517p.

South African white supremacists travel back in time to the American Civil War and offer modern weapons to Robert E. Lee. With this aid from the future, Lee manages to defeat the Northern armies and secures a Confederate nation in the South. When Lee considers the abolition of slavery, however, the travelers' plans appear to backfire, and they begin to plot against the new president of the Confederacy.

Twain, Mark (a.k.a. Samuel Clemens)

A Connecticut Yankee in King Arthur's Court. 2008 (1889). Oxford University Press, ISBN: 0199540586, 9780199540587, 400p.

Hank Morgan, a nineteenth-century laborer, suffers a blow to the head and awakens in the sixth century. He encounters King Arthur, uses his advanced know-how to bluff his way to a position of importance, and manages to discredit the charlatans that surround Arthur, including self-important Church officials and Merlin himself. Hank begins the Industrial Revolution a number of centuries early and imparts modern ideas and ideals to a group of apprentices. Twain's satirical literary classic is particularly apt for inclusion in this book thanks to its protagonist's use of science to overcome superstition.

Vonnegut, Kurt

Slaughterhouse-Five; or, The Children's Crusade, a Duty Dance with Death. 1999 (1969). Dell, ISBN: 0385333846, 9780385333849, 275p.

Billy Pilgrim becomes unstuck in time, and observes the entirety of his life from beginning to end, including his time as a POW in World War II and the bombing of Dresden. Billy also travels in space when aliens abduct him and transport him to the planet Tralfamadore, where Billy learns that while we may have no control over the course of our lives, we can choose what to focus on. Pensive readers will spend time thoughtfully meditating on this absurd, fatalistic story.

Wells, H. G.

The Time Machine. 2005 (1895). Penguin, ISBN: 0141439971, 9780141439976, 104p.

A Victorian scientist and inventor discovers a means of traveling in the fourth dimension. He builds his time machine and journeys to the year A.D. 802,701. He finds a paradise populated by the Eloi, beautiful and peaceful, though primitive and dull, descendents of humanity. The illusion of paradise vanishes, however, with the appearance of the Morlocks, a second strain of cannibalistic human descendents that prey on the Eloi. When the vicious creatures steal the traveler's machine, he must brave their dark subterranean caverns to retrieve it and return home. In this early time travel story, Wells establishes the scientist as adventurer and explorer, a trope that carries through the Golden Age of SF and well into the modern era. This classic is required reading for science fiction fans.

Willis, Connie

Doomsday Book. 1993 (1992). Bantam, ISBN: 0553562738, 9780553562736, 578p.

Kivrin, a history student in the mid-twenty-first century, travels back in time to study England during the fourteenth century. An accident deposits her during the outbreak of the Black Plague, while in her own time an unknown epidemic panics the populace. Fans of historical fiction, particularly of the medieval period, will enjoy this Hugo and Nebula Award–winning novel, as Willis takes great pains to depict the past accurately while shaping her story.

Infectious Imaginations: Contagion and Disease

These novels are proof positive of something frighteningly wrong with the headwiring of science fiction authors. The books on this list, clearly the creations of fever dreams and night sweats, should serve as sufficient evidence to have a few of them put away. Stories of hyperintelligent viral mass consciousnesses and deadly microbes seem eerily more plausible now, given today's fears of fatal epidemics and the potential for biological warfare. Enjoy the books that follow, but remember to wash your hands before and after.

Bear, Greg

Blood Music. 2008 (1995). E-reads, ISBN: 0759241740, 9780759241749, 296p.

Brilliant scientist Vergil Ulam creates new creatures from cells, intelligent biocomputers called noocytes. When his employers fire him, Ulam injects himself with his creation rather than have the project completely destroyed. (Important note: it is never a good idea in science fiction or real life to inject yourself with your own untested technology, no matter how confident you are.) The highly infectious noocytes evolve incredibly fast and soon overwhelm America and panic the world as their numbers begin to cause alterations to reality itself. Bear takes biotechnology and physics to the edge and reexamines reality with a massive new collective consciousness.

Crichton, Michael

⇒ *The Andromeda Strain.* 2008 (1969). Harper, ISBN: 006170315X, 9780061703157, 384p.

The Wildfire lab deals with the possibility of biological threats in the form of extraterrestrial bacteria making their way to Earth, but the scientists never actually believed it would happen. When a satellite crashes in Piedmont, Arizona, a new microbe kills everyone in the town except an old man and a crying baby. As the scientists work to discover what the two survivors have in common, a containment breach increases the tension by triggering the lab's final contingency: a nuclear weapon designed to destroy the lab before any threat can escape. Michael Crichton was a household name by the time of his death in 2008, but this book helped establish his career as a novelist with its solid science and suspense.

Ghosh, Amitav

The Calcutta Chromosome. 2001 (1995). Perennial, ISBN: 0380813947, 9780380813940, 311p.

Antar discovers an anomalous record in company data, the ID of a missing worker named Murugan who, obsessed with Ronald Ross's late-nineteenth-century work on malaria, went to Calcutta to learn more about Ross's research. The novel's various strands span one hundred years, moving between Ross, Murugan, and Antar, as the latter traces the paths of the first two men and stumbles across a mystic society with the key to immortality . . . of a sort. Ghosh artfully blends medical mystery, suspense, and secret history with a postcolonial air to his narrative, a combination that earned the Arthur C. Clarke Award.

Sigler, Scott

Infected. 2008. Three Rivers, ISBN: 030740630X, 9780307406309, 384p.

CIA agent Drew Phillips and Centers for Disease Control scientist Margaret Montoya are on the trail of an infection that transforms its victims into homicidal killers. They need a live host to study, but Montoya has already determined that the parasite isn't a product of nature. Meanwhile, former football player Perry Dawsey discovers unusual triangular marks on his body, and soon begins a vicious war against the disease within him. Sigler's series of podcast downloads are an Internet sensation with their taut, suspenseful plots. Be warned, though, that his descriptions can be powerfully graphic.

Suzuki, Koji

Ring. 2004 (1991). Vertical, ISBN: 1932234411, 9781932234411, 282p.

Asakawa is a reporter investigating the inexplicable simultaneous deaths of several teenagers. His snooping leads him to a mysterious videotape with surreal imagery, and a final warning: people who view the tape are doomed to die in one week's time. There is, apparently, a way to avert the fatal curse, but somehow that portion of the footage was taped over! Further research reveals that the psychic virus transmitted through the video has its origins in a sordid murder, but can Asakawa discover the cure before time runs out?

Chapter Two

Character

Although SF authors must ensure that their characters are not so alien as to be completely incomprehensible, the breadth of the genre allows for a host of memorable personalities with more than a few peculiarities. Authors may showcase a host of imaginative divergences in cultures, languages, mores, mannerisms, even biologies, all of which can highlight a book's themes. But characters need not be alien to be effective. There are a whole host of archetypes that, with a bit of tweaking, can comfortably ease readers into a story and act as tour guides to brave new worlds. It is unlikely that any technological breakthrough will create a shortage of familiar roles like hustlers, rogues, diplomats, soldiers, cops, and heroes. These character types also allow for unusual and unique crossovers between genres and can attract new readers to SF.

Whether you're fascinated by the unusual and strange or drawn to the common and familiar, this chapter's lists contain a varied catalog of intriguing character types for you to become acquainted with and join on their journeys. As you select choices from this roster, I'm confident that these protagonists will meet your exacting standards. In fact, as you sort through all the extrapolations and oddities, perhaps you'll find more than a little in common with them as well.

Negotiating Hostile Territory: Ambassadors, Diplomats, and Mediators

Excellent intermediaries possess a wide variety of talents, including empathy, linguistic skill, and finely cultivated perception. But conflict negotiation is a tricky business, and diplomats must also deal with gossip, intrigue, and espionage, not to mention the occasional assassination attempt. Still, mediation, cooperation, and compromise are usually preferable to war and devastation, so experienced diplomats find themselves in high demand. The accomplished ambassadors described in this section all display intelligence, wit, and wisdom in the performance of their duties and serve to maintain the peace in a hostile universe.

Bujold, Lois McMaster

Diplomatic Immunity. <u>Vorkosigan Saga</u>. 2002. Baen, ISBN: 0743435338, 9780743435338, 311p.

The diminutive hero Miles Vorkosigan and his wife Ekaterin are eagerly anticipating the arrival of their child when the Barrayar Emperor asks Miles to disentangle a legal dispute, an imperial military incident that requires a diplomatic solution. Naturally, the minor trouble turns major, when in the course of Vorkosigan's investigation he deals with murder, genetic politics, and the small possibility of an interstellar war that he must avert. This installment in the long-running <u>Vorkosigan Saga</u> earned a Nebula nomination.

Cherryh, C. J.

Conspirator. <u>Foreigner</u>. 2009. Daw, ISBN: 075640570X, 9780756405700, 370p.

This installment in Cherryh's <u>Foreigner</u> series continues an excellent and successful trend of demonstrating the careful negotiation and understanding between two cultures that are alien to one another. Long ago, humans colonized a planet inhabited by the native Atevi, and a war between the species led to a diplomatic arrangement in which one capable and worthy human would act as mediator between the two factions. Bren Cameron is the current mediator, and he has a warm relationship with Cajeiri, the son of a powerful Atevi leader. Cajeiri's life among humans ensures an even greater understanding between the cultures, although some of his people believe that he has become too human. While Bren negotiates plans to prevent human technology from thoroughly disrupting Atevi culture, a violent incident gives Cajeiri the opportunity to demonstrate his maturity and capability in the face of danger.

Hairston, Andrea

Mindscape. 2006. Aqueduct, ISBN: 1933500034, 9781933500034, 445p.

When the Barrier dropped, it enveloped the Earth and divided it into warring zones that could only occasionally access one another. Assassins murder the ambassador whose treaty could have ended the warfare, but her protégé, Ellini, intends to fulfill her mentor's goal. Ellini is one of the few who can navigate the Barrier, but she begins to see strange visions each time she does so, visions that point to terrible secrets in her Zone's past. Hairston creatively examines extreme culture clash, and readers will appreciate the honest efforts of her characters to surmount the barriers—physical, emotional, and philosophical—that confront them.

Moon, Elizabeth

⇒ *Remnant Population*. 2003 (1996). Ballantine, ISBN: 034546219X, 9780345462190, 325p.

Elizabeth Moon's Hugo-nominated novel is a powerful portrayal of strength in adversity and the value of wisdom. When the massive company Sims Bancorp decides its colony is no longer profitable, it uproots its colonists and leaves for greener pastures. Elderly Ofelia Falfurrias, a liability to her employers, decides to remain behind and discovers strength and wisdom in her solitude. When she encounters the native population, she feels compelled to act as their mediator with a returning humanity.

Simak, Clifford D.

Way Station (a.k.a. *Here Gather the Stars*). 2004 (1963). Old Earth, ISBN: 1882968271, 9781882968275, 225p.

Simak's philosophical and hopeful tale, fraught with alienation and overflowing with empathy, earned him a Hugo Award. Civil War veteran Enoch Wallace runs Earth's sole interstellar way station for aliens. Unfortunately, his youthful energy and appearance attract the attention of the U.S. government, as Enoch is well over a century old. A government agent unwittingly angers Wallace's alien overseers, even as political tensions promise a seemingly inevitable nuclear annihilation. Wallace must defuse the intergalactic incident and convince the rest of the universe that humanity is ready for a grander destiny than extinction.

Tepper, Sheri S.

The Fresco. 2002. Eos, ISBN: 038081658X, 9780380816583, 472p.

Tepper addresses the difficulty and necessity of change in the face of unpleasant truths. Representatives of a multi-species Confederation require a mediator between themselves and the human race and choose Benita Alvarez-Shipton because they believe that she represents common humanity.

The Confederation demands that our species change its ways in order to join the alien alliance. Their sacred fresco, coated with layers of grime due to a taboo preventing anyone from cleaning the piece, depicts the entirety of their religious and societal traditions and directs their actions. When Benita accidentally reveals images that contradict the visitors' received wisdom, the aliens must reexamine themselves, even as they force humanity to do the same.

Willett, Edward

Lost in Translation. 2006 (2005). Daw, ISBN: 0756403405, 9780756403409, 304p.

The conflict between humanity and the batlike S'sinn is on the brink of full-scale interstellar war. Translators Kathryn and Jarrikk have both lost loved ones to violence perpetrated by the other's species, but the pair must overcome their differences to save both races from the catastrophic consequences of their planets' hostilities. Both adults and younger readers can enjoy this tale of cooperation, finding common ground, and respecting the other's right to live, particularly relevant topics at this or any time in history.

It's Not Easy Being Teen: Young Protagonists

Many consider teen rebellion a normal part of the growth process, but the teens in the following books experience growing pains unlike anything we can imagine outside of a science fiction novel. First date jitters, breakups, and acne on prom night are nothing compared to coping with unique powers, overthrowing dystopian societies, and deciding the fate of the world. Compared with the characters in this list, kids these days have it easy.

Baxter, Stephen

The H-Bomb Girl. 2008 (2007). Faber, ISBN: 0571232809, 9780571232802, 288p.

Young Laura Mann lives in Liverpool in 1962, a moment of great potential and crisis. The Beatles are ready to revolutionize music, while the Cuban Missile Crisis escalates out of control. Laura finds herself the focus of various time travelers drawn to this precise moment of history, each trying to ensure their alternate future, and all of them determined to acquire the last gift Laura's father gave to her: an unusual key. Baxter's believable young protagonist, a fourteen-year-old girl making momentous decisions during a difficult time, will resonate with younger readers and inspire adults.

Collins, Suzanne

The Hunger Games. Hunger Games. 2008. Scholastic, ISBN: 0439023483, 9780439023481, 374p.

In what's left of the United States, the government of Pranem demands that each of its twelve districts offer up two of its children every year. These children fight in annual gladiatorial games for the entertainment of the masses. Teenage Katniss goes to the Hunger Games in place of her sister. Accompanying her is Peeta, a boy smitten with her. Their bloody battles and struggles to survive become the latest in reality television, but the rules state that only one child may claim victory. Collins writes convincingly about coming-of-age in a brutal time.

Ford, John M.

Growing Up Weightless. 1994 (1993). Bantam, ISBN: 0553373064, 9780553373066, 261p.

Matt Ronay is an adolescent living in his father's shadow on independent Luna, discovering who he is and who he desires to become. His father is a well-respected, beloved, and important Lunar politician, overwhelmed by precarious economic relations with Earth. As the book progresses, Ford shows the common emotions that link two characters who seem worlds apart.

Gould, Steven

Jumper. Jumper. 2008 (1992). Tor, ISBN: 0765357690, 9780765357694, 345p.

David manages to escape from his abusive father in an unconventional fashion when he discovers his ability to teleport. Over time, David learns how to control his power and explores the lucrative profession of bank robbery. He also learns how to trust and love again, first in a relationship with his girlfriend, Millie, then later by finding his mother. Unfortunately, David also attracts the attention of the government agents who want to study David so that they can understand his unique gift, and they're willing to threaten the people David loves to secure his cooperation. Gould examines the use and misuse of power in David's confrontation with his oppressors, which serves as an appropriate climax to his portrayal of a teenager stumbling toward adulthood and responsibility.

Jodorowsky, Alexandro, et al.

The Technopriests, **Book 1:** *Initiation*. The Technopriests. Translated by Justin Kelly. 2004. Humanoids/DC Comics, ISBN: 1401203590, 9781401203597, 155p. `GN`

The aged head of the Technopriests, Albino, considers his long life and the events that led to his ascendency. His mother, Panepha, was raped by space pirates, and her obsession with revenge was matched only by her disdain for her mutant children, who served as constant reminders of her violation. Albino dreams of becoming the greatest game creator in the galaxy and eventually gets a chance to train for the Technoguild, but nothing could have prepared him for the relentless and brutal instruction he receives. Jodorowsky, an internationally known writer and director, combines his talents with the magnificent art of Zoran Janjetov to create a visionary and beautiful work of art that fans of books like *Ender's Game* will certainly enjoy. Jodorowsky doesn't pull any punches, though, so be prepared for some characters and scenes that are violent and vicious.

Lowry, Lois

The Giver. Giver Trilogy. 2006. Delacorte, ISBN: 0385732554, 9780385732550, 190p.

Jonas's community seems idyllic, free of negative emotions. The society also strictly controls all aspects of its citizens' lives. It determines marriages by testing for compatible partners, assigns children to worthy couples, and older adults experience "release" from the community to ensure a fixed, controlled population. When children reach the age of twelve, the community assigns and trains them in their vocations and roles. Jonas becomes the new Receiver of Memory, the receptacle for all recollections of life before the utopia existed. But Jonas realizes that the community has sacrificed much for its stability and escapes from his society into a new, brighter, harsher world. Lowry's weighty book of compliance and rebellion, with its challenge to uniformity and call to experience the fullness of life, won the Newbery Medal for excellence in American children's literature and is appropriate for both teens and adults.

Takami, Koushun

Battle Royale. 2003 (1999). Viz, ISBN: 156931778X, 9781569317785, 617p.

Every year, Japan's totalitarian government selects a junior high school class for The Program. The government representatives transport the young people to a secluded island, fit them with explosive collars, and equip them with survival packs containing food, water, a map of the island, and a randomly assigned weapon. The students are released onto the island at intervals and ordered to hunt and kill one another. The rules also state that if a single day goes by without any deaths, all of the collars will detonate. As the students divide into enemies, allies, companions, hunters, and prey, all know that the contest only allows for one survivor. This hyperviolent novel with its hypberbolic program serves to criticize scholastic competition even as it thrills and horrifies and will appeal to mature fans of *Lord of the Flies*.

Westerfeld, Scott

⇒ *Uglies*. Uglies. 2005. Simon Pulse, ISBN: 0689865384, 9780689865381, 425p.

Adolescent uglies gaze upon the teenage pretties with envy. Compulsory cosmetic surgery at age sixteen transforms the youths, granting them ideal beauty and lives of leisure. Special Circumstances denies the procedure to young troublemaker Tally, using it as leverage to force her to infiltrate the rebel base called Smoke and reveal its location. When Tally learns a sinister secret about the side effect of becoming pretty, she joins the rebels in their struggle. Westerfeld identifies the milestones that mark transitions from childhood innocence to maturity and effectively translates them into a story about choices and freedom.

Designer Genes: Clones and the Genegineered

Whenever nature presents humanity with a mystery or a challenge, before you can say "Frankenstein," our species will take up that challenge and discover the science behind the mystery. Whether it's a single researcher working out of a lone laboratory or a host of scientists passing down knowledge for millennia, the work continues until somebody solves the puzzle. This drive to learn, to know, is clearly visible in our quest to comprehend the nature of life itself. I wonder if Mary Shelley could have guessed how the living imitators of her eponymous scientist would map the building blocks of biology and even create life. (Hello, Dolly!) We can hope that actual research will bear different fruit than poor Victor's experiments, but scientific breakthroughs tend to outpace our ability to cope with the ethical conundrums presented by progress. The authors in this list examine a number of consequences of cloning and customizing genes; like Shelley, they also consider the thoughts and feelings of the creations themselves. After perusing these books, you may ask yourself if *Frankenstein* should be required reading.

Brin, David

Kiln People. 2003 (2002). Tor, ISBN: 0765342618, 9780765342614, 567p.

In Brin's vision of the future, people can make dittos, clay clones, of themselves. Dittos have the personality and memories of the original, last twenty-four hours, can perform a host of tasks, and transmit their information and experiences to the original when their time runs out. Albert Morris, a detective investigating counterfeit clones, comes across a conspiracy that threatens both his dittos and his body and could change his world forever. This

SF detective novel, with all its implications of the nature of humanity and life, received a Hugo nomination.

Cherryh, C. J.

Cyteen. Alliance-Union Universe. 1995 (1988). Warner, ISBN: 0446671274, 9780446671279, 680p.

Ariane Emory is one of the leading minds of the Union, a vast network of worlds that seceded from Earth's ruling government. When Emory is murdered, her secret project begins: a plan to create as exact a replica of herself as possible. Union scientists create Emory's clone, called Ari, raise and educate her in a controlled environment to mirror the original Emory's childhood, and manipulate her into becoming a future Union leader. When Ari discovers her origins, she must also deal with all the unresolved conflicts the first Emory left behind.

Crichton, Michael

Jurassic Park. Jurassic Park. 1991 (1990). Ballantine, ISBN: 0345370775, 9780345370778, 399p.

Brilliant scientists and geneticists successfully clone dinosaurs using DNA from blood-sucking prehistoric insects trapped in amber. When faced with such a brilliant breakthrough, they do the obvious thing: they turn the discovery into a theme park! As the dinosaur populations break free from their creators' control, the remaining humans on the island find themselves in a competition for survival of the fittest and seek to escape the island and their desperate Darwinian dilemma. You've probably seen the movie, so read the book!

Farmer, Nancy

⇒ *The House of the Scorpion.* 2004 (2002). Simon Pulse, ISBN: 0689852231, 9780689852237, 400p.

Young Matt is a clone of El Patrón, one of the most powerful drug lords that rule nation states in future Mexico. Alternately loved and despised by members of the household, Matt learns the purpose behind his creation and attempts to escape his supposed benefactor. This novel is appropriate for young adults and older readers. The characters, especially young Matt, are credible and believable, and Farmer's critiques range from the ethical uses of science to politics.

Kress, Nancy

Nothing Human. 2003. Golden Gryphon, ISBN: 1930846185, 9781930846180, 300p.

Lillie is one of several teenagers who fall into mysterious comas. When they awaken, the children announce that the Pribir are coming. The alien

Pribir, masters of genetic alteration and biotechnology, intend to save humanity from itself and ensure the survival of our species. Lillie's actions chart a middle path between the two species, even as she redefines humanity. Readers will respond powerfully to Kress's young protagonists as they strive to define themselves.

McHugh, Maureen F.

Nekropolis. 2002 (2001). Eos, ISBN: 0380791234, 9780380791231, 257p.

Hariba grows up in the Nekropolis, an area teeming with Morocco's poorest citizens. To escape this ghetto, she agrees to be "jessed," a process that alters the recipient to ensure loyal servitude. In the house of her master, she encounters Akhmim. Akhmim is a harni, a genetically engineered concubine and slave considered less than human. Hariba eventually falls in love with Akhmim, and her obsession drives her to run away with him. McHugh juggles several fascinating concepts surrounding slavery and biotechnology, including the alteration imposed by jessing and the potential creation of a slave race. The relationship between Hariba and Akhmim also exemplifies the struggle to understand the other, as Hariba comes to terms with Akhmim's altered nature.

Morgan, Richard K.

Thirteen (a.k.a. *Black Man*). 2008 (2007). Del Rey, ISBN: 0345480899, 9780345480897, 544p.

Morgan explores the nature of humanity and the ethics of genetic manipulation in this articulate and violent novel. A populace too indolent to perform its own work creates genetic variants to do the jobs for them. Humans particularly fear members of the thirteenth model, a genetic variant created for its aggression and military applications. Carl Marsalis is a thirteen hit man who hunts his own kind. When a violent thirteen escapes from Mars and goes on a killing spree on Earth, Marsalis's investigation reveals a labyrinthine conspiracy with a vicious agenda. Morgan's stylish noir thriller pays homage to Aldous Huxley's *Brave New World* and the film *Blade Runner* and revitalizes classic SF themes for another generation.

Patterson, James

The Angel Experiment. Maximum Ride. 2007 (2005). Little, Brown, ISBN: 0316067954, 9780316067959, 422p.

Maximum "Max" Ride is the leader of the Flock, a genetically enhanced group of winged children. They escape from the School, the laboratory that created and experimented on them, with the aid of the scientist Jeb. When the School's hunters, the lupine Erasers, recapture the Flock, Max learns the shocking reason behind their creation. Fans of *X-men* and similar titles of mutants on the run will enjoy this series for young adult readers.

Scalzi, John

The Ghost Brigades. Old Man's War. 2007 (2006). Tor, ISBN: 0765354063, 9780765354068, 384p.

When Charles Boutin betrays the Colonial Defense Forces to hostile alien species, the CDF downloads his mind into a new cloned body, hoping to interrogate the copy for information about the original. When the download proves unsuccessful, the clone is sent to the CDF's unique special forces unit, the Ghost Brigades, so named because the unit consists of cloned superhuman troops made from the genetic material of dead conscripts. Jared Dirac is a *tabula rasa*, a childlike mind born into an adult body, and like his fellow soldiers he depends on his implanted BrainPal computer for information and guidance. In time, Boutin's intelligence begins to come to the fore, causing the CDF to question Dirac's loyalty and forcing Dirac to decide if his identity consists of what he was "born" with or what he chooses to be. This excellent sequel to Scalzi's *Old Man's War*, with its issues of identity and loyalty, can be read as a standalone novel.

Sterling, Bruce

The Caryatids. 2009. Del Rey/Ballantine, ISBN: 0345460626, 9780345460622, 295p.

Caryatids are statues of women that act as structural supports in lieu of columns. In the same way, Vera, Radmila, and Sonja, the clones of Balkan war criminal Yelisaveta Mihajlovic, were created to support the world. In this future Earth, the environment is horrifically damaged. Vera belongs to Acquis, a group that uses radical cutting-edge technology to repair and reclaim the environment. Radmila, however, is connected by marriage to the Dispensation, a capitalist enterprise that believes the only way to save the Earth is to make the efforts marketable and profitable. The third clone, Sonja, risks her life to work in what remains of China, using the Gobi Desert as a testing ground for technology. Unfortunately, Caryatids are not Atlases, and the burden of saving the world threatens to overwhelm the cloned women. In both novel and nonfiction, Sterling has long acted as a prophet of the future. He puts his knowledge and extrapolative skills on display in this book and paints a believable picture of environmental and social upheaval in a future not too far from now.

Wilhelm, Kate

Where Late the Sweet Birds Sang. 2006 (1976). Orb, ISBN: 0575079142, 9780575079144, 250p.

Humanity's warfare and carelessness caused extreme changes in the climate and environment, and a corresponding infertility in humanity. A large family secludes itself and continues propagation by cloning, but the clones form their own culture and reject sexual reproduction. The clones' dependence on one another, and the lowered fitness of successive generations, leads to loss of individuality, creativity, and diversity. Wilhelm's cautionary tale of an alternate culture and the costs of change won a Hugo Award.

I Robot, You Jane: Robots and Androids

Sentient robots and androids are further fictional examinations of humanity's desire to create life in its own image. While science and industry create these mechanical constructs to make labor easier and more efficient, their very existence suggests certain uncomfortable questions. If we do create self-aware androids, what uses will we put them to? Would people repeat the crimes of the past and institute a new era of slavery? If even unthinking robots can replace humans on assembly lines, how much more vulnerable will we be to more advanced models that can think for themselves? If we try to prevent a robot revolution by programming laws and obedience into their artificial minds, essentially denying them free will, isn't that simply another form of slavery? A host of possible worlds stemming from the existence of robots awaits you. Interestingly enough, many of these works have something to say about being human.

Abnett, Dan

Titanicus. 2008. Black Library, ISBN: 1844165868, 9781844165865, 399p.

In the Empire of Man, soldiers sacrifice themselves daily in battle to protect humanity against mysterious alien and occult forces. In one branch of service, the crew members are directly linked with gigantic robots called Titans, massive war machines capable of unbelievable devastation. As the forces of Chaos threaten the planet Orestes, Titan Legio Invicta leads the defense, but the god-machine's incredible power could lead to the world's destruction instead of its salvation. Dan Abnett affirms his reputation for hard-hitting military science fiction once again and relates an epic conflict in a universe constantly at war.

Asaro, Catherine

Sunrise Alley. <u>Sunrise Alley</u>. 2006 (2004). Baen, ISBN: 1416520791, 9781416520795, 448p.

Biotech expert Samantha Bryton finds a man washed ashore. He claims to be Turner Pascal, who's supposed to be dead, but Bryton discovers he's an evolved artificial intelligence (EI), an android with Pascal's uploaded mind. When criminal scientist Charon comes looking for his handiwork, the two escape to Sunrise Alley, a safe haven for EI refugees. Unfortunately, the Alley's inhabitants have agendas their creators didn't plan for. Asaro explores the gray areas of love and humanity while continuing her tradition of fine SF seasoned with romance.

Asimov, Isaac

⇒ *I, Robot*. 2008 (1950). Bantam, ISBN: 055338256X, 9780553382563, 224p.

As a reporter interviews Dr. Susan Calvin, he and the reader learn about the history of U.S. Robots and Mechanical Men, and Calvin's career with the corporation as its robot psychologist. Although the Three Laws of Robotics serve as safety measures upon the robots' positronic brains, Calvin relates what happens when the machines' programming goes awry and the safeguards have unintentional consequences. Asimov's book of linked short stories is a foundational text in science fiction; it made history by redefining how SF authors and scientists conceived of robots and artificial intelligence forever afterward. Additionally, Asimov's human characters inspire by using intelligence and logic rather than violence to overcome obstacles, and this insistence on thoughtful, nonviolent solutions combined with a genuine sense of wonder makes the work ideally accessible to younger readers.

Ballantyne, Tony

Twisted Metal. 2009. Tor, ISBN: 0230738605, 9780230738607, 370p.

The Planet Penrose hosts an intelligent robot population that thinks and feels—and some feel too strongly. The fanatics of Artemis City demand conformity and obedience and kill or convert any robot that stands in their way. The zealots have Turing City, a bastion of free thought and individualism, in their sights. As the fates of Artemisian soldier Kavan and the Turing citizen Karel intertwine, they lead to the lost Book of Robots and the secret history of this strange, mechanical world. Ballantyne will make you believe that robots can indeed feel as well as think; his characters are more than mere mechanical constructs, and readers will recall their suffering, struggles, ideologies, and idealism long after they finish the novel.

Dick, Philip K.

Do Androids Dream of Electric Sheep? 1996 (1968). Ballantine/Del Rey, ISBN: 0345404475, 9780345404473, 244p.

The last World War poisoned the Earth and rendered a large number of species extinct. The remaining people treat animals like status symbols, the rarer the better, and those who can't afford real animals keep artificial electric ones to prop up the appearance of affluence. Most humans are desperate to leave the planet, however, and the government encourages emigration to off-world colonies by offering free android servants. Six Nexus-6 models flee slavery and slip away to Earth, where androids are illegal. Rick Deckard hunts rogue androids for a living; he distinguishes between humans and the simulacra using an empathy test, and "retires" the androids he discovers. Deckard comes to doubt his own humanity, however, as his job erodes his compassion. Dick's classic novel of empathy versus entropy, with its challenges to conceptions and assumptions about humanity, is the basis for the film *Blade Runner*.

Lee, Tanith

Metallic Love. Silver. 2005. Bantam, ISBN: 0553584715, 9780553584714, 301p.

Tanith Lee recaptures the romantic heart of *The Silver Metal Lover* while simultaneously delving deeper into the responses of intelligent beings to their status as disposable slaves. Twelve years after the events of the previous novel, young Loren finds Jane's journal and reads of her romance with the android Silver. Although Loren is far more worldly and cynical than Jane, when the META Corporation releases a new series of robots, Loren becomes involved with Verlis, who possesses the original Silver's memories. Even as Verlis passionately teaches Loren to trust and love, Silver's memories drive Verlis to ensure a different fate for himself and his fellow robots.

Martinez, A. Lee

The Automatic Detective. 2009 (2008). Tor, ISBN: 0765357941, 9780765357946, 317p.

You know how mad scientists are always creating powerful robots that serve as killing machines in plots of world domination? Mack Megaton used to be one of those. A robot, that is, not a mad scientist. He overcomes his programming, goes to therapy, and drives a taxi in Empire City, a metropolis filled with mutants, androids, and other bizarre inhabitants. Mack goes from cabbie to gumshoe when aliens kidnap his neighbor's child. Aided by the brilliant Lucia Napier, Mack brings all of his considerable weight to bear in finding the culprits and holding them accountable. Martinez's humorous science fiction noir story deftly blends the tropes of mystery and SF, turns them on their heads, and keeps readers chuckling throughout.

Sawyer, Robert J.

Mindscan. 2006 (2005). Tor, ISBN: 0765349752, 9780765349750, 384p.

Jake Sullivan, desperate to escape an inherited disease, agrees to the mindscan process: his mind is copied into a new, healthy, practically immortal artificial body, and his biological self lives in retirement on the moon after ceding all legal rights to the new android Jake. Delighted with his new lease on life, the new Jake meets Karen, a woman who also agreed to mindscan. When the biological Karen dies, however, her son demands his inheritance and sues, calling into question the android Karen's legal status as a person. Worse, even when biological Jake receives a cure for his condition, the law requires him to remain on the moon, a circumstance that drives him to drastic measures to reclaim his former autonomy and status. Sawyer thoughtfully examines the philosophical and practical consequences of a technology that many other SF writers take for granted, and he won the John W. Campbell Memorial Award for this novel.

Sladek, John

The Complete Roderick. Roderick. 2004. Overlook, ISBN: 1585675873, 9781585675873, 611p.

Sladek uses satire and dark wit to expose the seedier side of humanity's psyche and society in this omnibus collecting the works *Roderick* (1980) and *Roderick at Random* (1983). Roderick is a robot trying to make his way in the world despite people's attempts to take advantage of or destroy him. Unfortunately, he can't seem to logically comprehend or reconcile the behavior of incompetent, deplorable, and prejudiced humanity. A running gag throughout involves people assuming that Roderick is human despite his rather strange appearance; perhaps they mistake Roderick's nature because, of all the characters in the book, he is the most humane.

Stross, Charles

Saturn's Children. 2008. Ace, ISBN: 0441015948, 9780441015948, 323p.

What do robots and androids do when their entire purpose for existence disappears? With all the humans extinct, their mechanical servants end up mimicking their former masters and taking over their roles, practical and societal, even to the point of keeping class systems in place. Courtesan and pleasure robot Freya finds her existential crisis interrupted by her desperate need to escape a wealthy aristo. Freya takes a job as a courier with the Jeeves Corporation but soon discovers that far too many factions and cartels have an unhealthy interest in her package. Stross creates a marvelous, truly posthuman world filled with parody, erotic interludes, gun battles, and a lingering philosophical note about the legacy of slavery.

Venditti, Robert, et al.

The Surrogates. Surrogates. 2006. Top Shelf, ISBN: 1891830872, 9781891830877, 158p. GN

In 2054, most everyone uses android surrogates to conduct their business and indulge in a variety of experiences from the safety of their homes. A vigilante intent on forcing people to actually live their lives begins randomly electrocuting people's surrogates. After an altercation with the vigilante, Detective Harvey Greer must find the culprit while risking his own flesh and in the process rediscovers his experience of the world. Writer Robert Venditti and artist Brett Weldele examine society's dependence on technology in this gripping mystery.

The Flesh Is Weak: Cyborgs

It's certain that if scientists had the capability and technology to rebuild humans—to make them better, stronger, and faster—cyborgs would be a regular feature in our world. Who wouldn't want to be superhuman? We might need a new class in which modified athletes would compete. Governments would leap at the opportunity to have super soldiers (assuming that proper controls were in place, of course). But what do cyborgs do when their parts begin to break down? And how could they retire from government service if the majority of their bodies consisted of proprietary technology? Still, the promise of shiny new parts and the possibility of an extended warranty are tempting. At the very least, cybernetics would take body modification to new levels.

Bear, Elizabeth

⇒ *Hammered*. Jenny Casey. 2005 (2004). Bantam Spectra, ISBN: 0553587501, 9780553587500, 324p.

Jenny Casey, former Canadian special forces soldier, is pushing fifty, with old combat injuries and obsolete cybernetic augmentations that may kill her. Her old commanding officer offers a new lease on life and updated bionics, provided she agrees to a deadly mission, and soon Jenny's up to her cybernetic eyeball in corporate intrigue and betrayal. Post-cyberpunk style and schemes combine with emotional depth to satisfy a variety of fans, and also served to win the 2006 Locus Award for Best First Novel.

Kishiro, Yukito

Battle Angel Alita, Vol. 1. <u>Battle Angel Alita</u>. Translated by Fred Burke. 2003 (1994). Viz, ISBN: 1569319456, 9781569319451, 219p. **GN**

Battle Angel Alita: Last Order, Vol. 1. <u>Battle Angel Alita</u>. Translated by Lillian Olsen. 2003. Viz, ISBN: 1569318247, 9781569318247, 200p. **GN**

In the Scrapyard, the denizens live using the castoffs and junk dropped from the sky city of Tiphares. Daisuke Ido lives as a physician and cybernetic engineer by day and a bounty hunter by night. When he finds the remnants of a female cyborg, he rebuilds her and names her Alita. She has no memories of her past but discovers that she somehow knows the deadly cyborg martial art Panzer Kunst. Soon Alita proves herself an effective bounty hunter in her own right, but Ido is concerned that her mysterious past may catch up with her and sometimes feels overwhelmed by his responsibility as a substitute father. Despite some small changes in translation (the original series title is *Gunnm*, and Alita's name in the Japanese *manga* is Gally), this hyperviolent and high-octane blend of cyberpunk and *Mad Max* style post-apocalyptic adventure fiction has thrilled fans worldwide. The second series, *Last Order*, serves as both a continuation of the first series as well as an alternate universe tale, as the storyline depends on a change to the first series' original ending.

Piercy, Marge

He, She, and It (a.k.a. *Body of Glass*). 1993 (1991). Fawcett Crest, ISBN: 0449220605, 9780449220603, 432p.

Multinational corporations run society. Affluent humanity lives safely sequestered from a damaged world, while most of the population lives impoverished in a devastated environment. The sole exception is the free towns, enclaves that have valuable resources to trade with the corporations but maintain their autonomy. Shira returns to one such free town, the small Jewish community of Tikva, after losing a custody battle over her son. Tikva enjoys the protection of Yod, an illegal cyborg, and Shira comes to love him. Yod's destruction forces Shira to choose between accepting her loss and defying Yod's final wishes. Piercy's novel mirrors the legend of the golem of Prague, adding an additional layer to her unusual love story.

Pohl, Frederik

Man Plus. 2000 (1976). Millennium, ISBN: 1857989465, 9781857989465, 215p.

Deteriorating conditions on Earth, societal breakdown, and increasing tensions among the nuclear powers lead scientists to determine that humanity can only survive if it abandons its home world for another planet. Roger Torraway becomes the first cyborg, Man Plus, designed to explore and live in

Mars' harsh environment. Pohl takes great pains to describe the torment Torraway endures over the course of his gradual transformation. As his body is slowly disassembled, stripped away, and replaced with augmentations, Roger becomes separated from his humanity and emotionally isolated from others. Pohl's insight into the human psyche is evident in Torraway's alienation, and readers will be fascinated by the author's exploration of the ties between biology and psychology.

Shirow, Masamune

Ghost in the Shell. Ghost in the Shell. Translation by Frederik L. Schoot and Toren Smith. 2004 (1989). Dark Horse, ISBN: 1593072287, 9781593072285, 350p. GN

Major Kusanagi leads the elite cybernetic special forces of Section 9 in the fight against security threats, cybercriminals, and terrorists. In addition to gripping crime fiction, mystery, and action, Shirow delves deeply into science fiction's age-old theme on the nature of humanity. Does a cyborg still qualify as human if 99 percent of her body is artificial? How can we determine the nature of reality when the virtual world seems just as real as the one outside the net? How can people speak in terms of "I" in an age when it's possible to reprogram minds; if humans are the sum total of their experiences, what happens when technology allows people to upload, overwrite, and delete memories? Shirow even postulates the possibility of new life and sentience evolving from the Internet's "sea" of information. Fair warning: Dark Horse's more recent edition of Shirow's *manga* is uncensored and includes some explicit sexuality.

From a Certain Point of View: Alien Perspectives and Radically Different Frames of Reference

Eureka moments are tiny flashes of enlightenment and learning where the mind undergoes a sudden paradigm shift that allows for new comprehension and understanding. While perhaps not so sudden, the following books require readers and characters to undergo a similar change in thought processes. Some of these works require radical reconceptions, while others simply hold a mirror to human behavior so that we might see ourselves from the perspective of the other.

Butler, Octavia

Kindred. 2003 (1988). Beacon, ISBN: 0807083690, 9780807083697, 287p.

Octavia Butler's meticulously researched and gripping novel explores the physical, psychological, societal, and institutional aspects of slavery in antebellum America, addresses the question of why anyone would endure or submit to slavery, and considers the necessities of survival against the hope of freedom. Dana finds herself repeatedly and inexplicably transported to an era before the Civil War to save the life of a vicious slave owner, Rufus, who is also her ancestor. During her time in the past, she must endure the life of a slave, full of exhaustion, danger, and abuse, all the while knowing that her own survival depends on Rufus's well-being. This psychologically powerful novel will appeal to fans of Toni Morrison and Gloria Naylor.

Cherryh, C. J.

The Chanur Saga. Chanur/Compact Space. 2000. Daw, ISBN: 0886779308, 9780886779306, 704p.

Cherryh's Compact Space series secured her reputation as a writer of alien perspectives. A faction of the vicious species called the kif captures members of a previously unknown race: humans. Young Tully, a human escapee, finds himself aboard a vessel of Hani, lion-like humanoids. When the Hani pilot, Pyanfar Chanur, finds the young stowaway, she refuses to hand him over to the kif, an action that endangers herself and her crew. Although some find it difficult to read, Cherryh's writing style throughout the series puts fans in the mind of an alien species, with many of the cultural and linguistic differences that entails. This volume is an omnibus edition containing the novels *The Pride of Chanur* (1981), *Chanur's Venture* (1984), and *The Kif Strike Back* (1985).

Chiang, Ted

Stories of Your Life and Others. 2003 (2002). Orb/Tom Doherty, ISBN: 0765304198, 9780765304193, 333p.

Ted Chiang writes primarily in short fiction, with the occasional novella thrown in for good measure. He creates magnificent and mind-bending stories that require readers to upend their assumptions and consider situations from new angles. Tales of particular note in this collection include: "Story of Your Life," in which a researcher's attempt to understand an alien language utterly alters her thought processes and perceptions; "Division by Zero," where a breakthrough in mathematics has unforeseen effects upon physics and the emotional health of its discoverer; and "Tower of Babylon," in which a miner's persistence results in a new attitude toward God and Creation.

Heinlein, Robert A.

⇒ *Stranger in a Strange Land*. 1987 (1961). Berkley, ISBN: 0441790348, 9780441790340, 438p.

When the ship *Champion* journeyed to Mars, it returned with the only survivor of an earlier, doomed expedition: Valentine Michael Smith, the son of two Earth astronauts and the only human to be raised by Martians. While Michael's unique education grants him powerful psychic abilities, his innocence and naïveté put him at the mercy of powerful political and corporate interests. Aided by his nurse, Gillian Boardman, and sheltered by the powerful and wealthy Jubal Harshaw, Michael comes to understand humanity and introduces the planet to the language, wisdom, and powers of the Martians through a mystery religion called the Church of All Worlds. When a rival religious group, the Fosterites, feel threatened by Michael's revelations, they try to silence him through propaganda and violence, but Michael's final teaching has yet to be revealed. This controversial Hugo Award–winning novel was drastically edited and denounced for undermining sexual mores, organized religion, and authority, but was simultaneously praised as a Bible for the counterculture. It also added the word "grok" to the world's vocabulary.

Kelly, James Patrick

Burn. 2005. Tachyon, ISBN: 1892391279, 9781892391278, 178p.

New colonists on the planet Walden willingly give up technology to create a simpler utopian society. The original settlers, the pukpuk, resist the newcomers' extensive terraforming and reforestation by burning down the new woodlands. While recovering from his injuries, fireman Prosper "Spur" Gregory Leung uses the hospital's otherwise forbidden technology to contact others sharing his name and gains the attention of High Gregory, King of Kenning. The king is so intrigued that he decides to visit Leung. Even as Spur tries to hide the consequences of his contact, High Gregory challenges Spur's accepted view of Walden's society. Kelly confronts the consequences of acting from even the noblest motives, and fans of thoughtful SF will want to give this book a chance.

Moon, Elizabeth

The Speed of Dark. 2003. Ballantine, ISBN: 0345447557, 9780345447555, 340p.

Lou Arrendale is a man with autism. He's able to blend in with so-called normal society and earns a living using his unusually sharp pattern recognition skills. When a new surgical procedure offers the hope of a cure for autism, Lou must decide whether to bow to pressures from his employer and his own desires for a relationship or continue being the person he is. Moon's deft, thoughtful, and touching examination of autism and Lou's struggle whether to alter, and perhaps lose, his sense of self earned a Nebula Award.

Silverberg, Robert

Downward to the Earth. 2004 (1977). Gollancz, ISBN: 0575075236, 9780575075238, 213p.

Edmund Gundersen once administrated the colony world of Belzagor. Because of the elephantine appearance of the native species, the authorities refused to recognize their sentience for far too long. Now Gundersen returns to the planet seeking redemption and atonement for his actions toward the aliens. He intends to take part in their rebirthing ceremony, and the experience will change him utterly. Silverberg places his protagonist in an alien environment that leads to a mystical understanding of the other in this story that echoes Joseph Conrad's *Heart of Darkness.*

I Am the Law!: Guardians of Order and Justice

In lieu of a perfect world (see the list titled "We Shall Think for You: Dystopian Dilemmas" in Chapter Three for more on that topic), civilization necessitates laws to govern human interaction and requires individuals who will dedicate themselves to enforcing law, order, and (one hopes) some measure of justice. The following books feature men and women who earn little pay and less thanks for their efforts at keeping the peace. Some of them operate by the book, and some have no choice other than to write the book as they go, given the bizarre nature of the crimes and dangers the future holds, but they all hold unswervingly to their codes. Respect the badge and read on.

Abnett, Dan

Eisenhorn. Eisenhorn Trilogy. 2004. Black Library, ISBN: 1844161560, 9781844161560, 764p.

Eisenhorn is an Inquisitor for the Imperium. Set apart by his psychic abilities, he roots out heretical and alien subversion, hunts down the enemies of the Empire, and metes out justice and death. Abnett is well known for adapting the popular *Warhammer 40,000* universe to novels and comics and fills this book with intrigue and adventure across an imaginative scattering of worlds and cultures. More impressively, Abnett also imparts an unusual believability to Eisenhorn's crew of outsiders and misfits. None of them fit within the strictures of Imperial society, yet each of them risks their lives and souls in the Empire's defense; perhaps they stay with Eisenhorn for the very loyalty and camaraderie that they cannot find anywhere else. This omnibus collection contains the novels *Xenos* (2001), *Malleus* (2001), and *Hereticus* (2002).

Asher, Neal

Gridlinked. <u>Agent Ian Cormac</u>. 2004 (2001). Tor, ISBN: 0765349051, 9780765349057, 423p.

A humanity arrayed across the Polity uses Runcibles—teleportation technology run by infallible A.I.s—to cross vast distances. Earth Central Security agent Ian Cormac investigates a Runcible accident that resulted in a number of deaths and ended terraforming on the planet Samarkand. Cormac's flagging humanity requires him to disconnect from the Polity's A.I.s but also deprives him of their resources. Worse, separatist terrorist Arian Pelter pursues Cormac with the murderous intent to avenge the sister Cormac killed. Asher successfully blends a gritty tone with a vast, awe-inspiring universe complete with powerful aliens and dangerous androids.

Cadigan, Pat

Dervish Is Digital. <u>Artificial Reality Division</u>. 2002 (2000). Tor, ISBN: 0312876564, 9780312876562, 230p.

Alternate reality has few limits and fewer boundaries—everybody lies, and everything's an illusion. Doré Konstantin attempts to police virtual space with a laughably small staff. Two of Konstantin's cases, one involving a casino in virtual Hong Kong and the other a cyberstalker, have a dangerous connection in Hastings Dervish, who abandoned his body and traded places with an artificial intelligence. Fans of police procedurals will enjoy Cadigan's sharp-witted detective and empathize with her frustration in performing an impossible job.

Castro, Adam-Troy

Emissaries from the Dead. <u>Andrea Cort</u>. 2008. Eos, ISBN: 0061443727, 9780061443725, 387p.

The AISource has created its own cylindrical and extremely toxic ecosystem filled with bizarre genetically engineered species. When one of the human colonists studying the habitat is murdered, the Diplomatic Corps assigns Andrea Cort the unenviable task of finding a scapegoat. They reason that no incriminating evidence must point to the A.I.s, because nobody could win a conflict against the powerful, disembodied minds. Cort, however, actually intends to solve the crime and discover the murderer's identity, regardless of the consequences. The bizarre environment alone will fascinate readers; coupled with a murder mystery and a deeply damaged, misanthropic protagonist, this series is sure to find a strong fan base and certainly deserved the Philip K. Dick Award.

Hammond, Warren

⇒ *Kop.* <u>Kop</u>. 2008 (2007). Tor, ISBN: 0765351366, 9780765351364, 336p.

Juno Mozambe is a corrupt cop in Koba, capital city of the Third-World planet Lagarto, a world where economic disparity and the constantly encroaching jungle lead to bitter daily struggles for survival. Juno's long-standing connections with the local crime cartel help keep some semblance of livability in Koba, but his supervisor Paul Chang just delivered some unwelcome news. Chang needs Juno to work a murder case that may lead to confrontation with the mayor and has assigned young, idealistic partner Maggie Orzo to help Juno. Hammond's portrayal of Lagarto's poverty and desperation is absorbing and he believably represents the necessity of corruption in Koba to achieve even the merest amount of justice.

Wagner, John, et al.

Judge Dredd: The Complete Case Files, **Vol. 1.** Judge Dredd. 2005. Rebellion, ISBN: 1904265790, 9781904265795, 336p. GN

After the Atomic Wars, humanity sealed itself away from the nuclear wasteland of the Cursed Earth into huge domed Mega-Cities. The Judges, law enforcement officers who act as judge, jury, and executioner, took over governance of Earth's surviving civilization. Most famous of Mega-City One's many judges is Judge Dredd; uncompromising in his enforcement of the law, fearless and upright, upholding his duty in every crisis, Judge Dredd is the law! Judge Dredd first appeared in the second issue of the British comics anthology *2000 AD* in 1977, a cop who's part soldier, part Dirty Harry, and part hero. Authors and artists use the *Judge Dredd* comic to tell an unbelievable variety of stories that include elements of science fantasy, action, adventure, war, cop drama, mystery, sociopolitical satire, and humor ranging from dark to absurd. Publisher Rebellion is reprinting the entire run of *Judge Dredd* from the beginning, and although they may be difficult to find in some areas, these graphic novels preserve an important slice of science fiction and comic history and are well worth reading.

Last Hopes and Chosen Ones: Saviors and Messiahs

Messianic stories may initially seem out of place in a book on science fiction, but in universes where psychic powers make prescience possible and time distortions occur too frequently for anyone's comfort, prophecies of liberators and fabled leaders become acceptable parts of the imaginative landscape. And the supposed redeemers have harder lives than most would think: one moment, they're trying to live normal lives, the next moment they find the weight of the world, perhaps the universe, on their shoulders. At best, they can expect intrigue to dog their every step; at worst, they become refugees, always on the run and dodging assassination attempts. These saviors inspire faith and hope, and perhaps their stories will awaken your empathy.

Herbert, Frank

Dune Messiah. Classic Dune. 1987 (1969). Ace, ISBN: 0441172695, 9780441172696, 329p.

> Paul Atreides is now emperor of a star-spanning Empire, yet for all his power he feels helpless, trapped by the horrific universal jihad and religious excesses carried out in his name. Able to see the future, Paul tries to steer humanity's destiny without destroying it. Yet even as he does so, elements within his own Empire seek to oust him, usurp his throne, and slay his family. This powerful follow-up to the science fiction classic *Dune* successfully and suspensefully continues the saga of the Atreides line.

Moorcock, Michael

⇒ *Behold the Man*. Karl Glogauer. 2007 (1969). Overlook, ISBN: 1585677647, 9781585677641, 144p.

> Karl Glogauer is a deeply troubled man, swamped by neuroses and insecurity. He finds the story of Christ's crucifixion fascinating and travels back in time to AD 28 seeking enlightenment, when John the Baptist discovers the lone traveler to the past. From there Glogauer becomes determined to locate Joseph and Mary and to meet Jesus Christ himself. But when Glogauer discovers the startling truth about the so-called messiah, he decides to change history forever. In this book (considered irreverent or blasphemous, depending on the reader), Moorcock pens a dark, iconoclastic story of the Christ.

Simmons, Dan

Endymion. Hyperion Cantos. 1996 (1995). Bantam, ISBN: 0553572946, 9780553572940, 563p.

The Rise of Endymion. Hyperion Cantos. 1998 (1997). Bantam, ISBN: 0553572989, 9780553572988, 709p.

> The canny poet Martin Silenus cares for the young Aenea until she enters the fabled Time Tombs. He selects Raoul Endymion to be her protector and mentor when she emerges, until such time as she comes into her destiny as the One Who Teaches. Meanwhile, a revived and ruthless Catholic Church, now the major power in human space, sends its operatives to hunt and kill the girl, lest her knowledge and revelations lead to the Church's downfall. Simmons completes his epic tale, begun in *Hyperion* and *The Fall of Hyperion*, and finally reveals the mysteries lurking in the shadows of this vast universe while meditating on themes of faith, free will, and predestination.

Tevis, Walter

The Man Who Fell to Earth. 1999 (1963). Del Rey, ISBN: 0345431618, 9780345431615, 209p.

> Thomas Jerome Newton, technological genius and wealthy businessman, is actually an alien. He came to gather the resources he needed to construct a spacecraft and transport the few remaining members of his people to Earth from their dying planet, Anthea. But when the U.S. government discovers Newton, its interference endangers his rescue mission. Tevis perfectly captures Newton's alienation and despair and holds up a mirror to humanity's pettiness.

Zelazny, Roger

Lord of Light. 2004 (1967). Eos, ISBN: 0060567236, 9780060567231, 296p.

> On a colonized world, a ruling elite enforces its will, using fantastic technology to assume the roles of Hindu gods. Sam, ousted from the pantheon, takes on the guise of a new Buddha to foment a revolution and end the gods' tyranny. In this Hugo Award–winning novel, Zelazny demonstrates his trademark ability to seamlessly blend the fantastical with science fiction and offers up an interesting view of religion as a vehicle for both oppression and liberation.

Play to Win: Gamblers and Game Players

These characters are serious about their games. The protagonists on this list need every ounce of ingenuity, cunning, skill, and luck that they can muster as they play for the highest stakes imaginable—including their lives. Do you have what it takes to sit across the table from them? Take the time to read these books and earn your boasting rights.

Banks, Iain M.

The Player of Games. <u>Culture</u>. 2008 (1988). Orbit, ISBN: 0316005401, 9780316005401, 405p.

> The Culture, a pampered utopia made possible and maintained by artificial intelligences, is no place for Jernau Gurgeh. Gurgeh is a gambler and game player of the highest order, and his boredom (and a little blackmail) lead him to the Empire of Azad. All status in Azad is decided by a grand three-dimensional strategy game. Game play incorporates tactics, strategy, and chance and reflects the perspective of the individual players, testing philosophies and political views before they are applied in practice. Best of all, the winner of the game becomes emperor. Banks uses the competition to

critically examine social structures that, in retrospect, seem more cutthroat and arbitrary than any game, all the while maintaining a gripping, involving psychological tension.

Brunner, John

The Squares of the City. 1991 (1965). Collier, ISBN: 0020175116, 9780020175117, 318p.

In the future, South America has a new paradise. Vados is the crown jewel of the continent, a shining achievement of urban perfection, but the planner Hakluyt finds himself a pawn in a much larger game of subliminal manipulation, intrigue, and class warfare. Ultimately, everything comes down to a game of chess . . . but not in any way you'll expect. Brunner's intricately structured novel will intrigue fans with its layers of strategy and political implications.

Burroughs, Edgar Rice

The Chessmen of Mars. <u>Barsoom</u>. 2009 (1922). BookSurge Classics, ISBN: 1594568545, 9781594568545, 354p.

The ferocious Martian people of Manator capture Tara, Princess of Helium and daughter of the famed Earthman John Carter and Martian princess Dejah Thoris. Gahan, heroic prince of Gathol, seeks to save her life and win her love. To do so, he must survive a deadly game of Jetan, a Martian chess game that uses live pieces—warriors who battle to the death. Self-styled historians of science fiction will find a rich vein of imaginative adventure in Burroughs's work, and as an extra bonus, lucky readers may find rules to Jetan in the appendix!

Dick, Philip K.

⇒ *The Game-Players of Titan.* 1992 (1963). Vintage, ISBN: 0679740651, 9780679740650, 215p.

Pete Garden is a Bluff player, one of the depopulated Earth's elite who gamble everything they own, including their spouses, on a regular basis. The alien Vugs, inhabitants of Saturn's moon, Titan, oversee the Earth and the game. When the Vugs transport Pete and his Bluff syndicate to Titan, they play the ultimate game against the telepathic aliens with the Earth as the prize. Philip K. Dick's surreal plots will delight fans who can lose themselves to the flow of the narrative and Dick's incredible and bizarre ideas.

Fawer, Adam

Improbable. 2005. William Morrow, ISBN: 0060736771, 9780060736774, 403p.

David Caine's poor gambling skills leave him in debt to the Russian mob, but his ability to calculate probabilities takes an incredible leap when he receives an experimental treatment for epilepsy. Suddenly, Caine is able to glimpse possible futures and soon discovers that the CIA wants control over his ability. Fawer's first novel crafts an exciting thriller around its science fictional premise and won the International Thriller Writers Award for best first novel.

Noon, Jeff

Nymphomation. 2000 (1997). Black Swan, ISBN: 0552999067, 9780552999067, 363p.

The future is awash with a miasma of advertising in the form of biotechnological blurbflies, many of which extol the AnnoDomino company's thrilling new lottery game, Domino Bones. Players buy dominos with constantly shifting faces; every Friday the faces become fixed and decide a winner. Daisy Love and Jazir Malik decide to peek at the heart of the lottery's code, an investigation that leads to a virus spread by the blurbflies and the frightening reality behind the game. Noon's twisted creativity gives a grotesque surreal glimpse of the mutating memes that drive faddish crazes.

Weird Science: Mad Scientists, Uncontrollable Creations

Some people say there's a fine line between genius and madness. For the characters on this list, that line is best represented by a lit fuse. Their obsession and intelligence enable them to unravel the secrets of the universe, but their efforts seem fated to result in destruction. Marvel at these scientists' achievements, but take your cue from Igor: when the lab assistant exits stage left, follow his lead.

Ellis, Warren, et al.

Doktor Sleepless, Vol. 1: *Engines of Desire.* 2008. Avatar, ISBN: 1592910556, 9781592910557, 216p. **GN**

Where is the future we were promised? Where are the flying cars? Where are the jet packs? Doktor Sleepless wants to know and intends to find out! Wealthy scientific prodigy, pirate DJ, and utterly bonkers, Sleepless releases mad science and bleeding-edge technology into the cultural underground of Heavenside. Sleepless rails against the future we got, with its crass commercialism, consumerism, and soullessness, rather than the one we dreamed of. Sleepless, however, has a covert agenda in using the city as his personal testing ground, but whether this new future is one of devastation or transhuman potential is anybody's guess. An interesting social commentary as well as an examination of the wonders of science that lie just around the corner, this graphic novel is sure to amaze and please.

Foglio, Phil, and Kaja Foglio

Girl Genius, **Vol. 1:** *Agatha Heterodyne and the Beetleburg Clank*. Girl Genius. 2001. Airship Entertainment, ISBN: 1890856193, 9781890856199, 87p. **GN**

In an age of industry driven by the achievements of mad scientists, Agatha Heterodyne is a student of Transylvania Polygnostic University, a prodigy born with the Spark that enables her and others like her to create wonders of technology. Unfortunately, Sparks also become raving lunatics when inspiration overwhelms them, but that's the price you pay for science! Alternately described as steampunk and gaslamp fantasy, *Girl Genius* is a comic that features action, romance, mad science, wondrous inventions, and more pulp adventure than an entire summer's worth of blockbuster movies. Even better, readers can enjoy the entire series for free at http://www.girlgeniusonline.com.

Shelley, Mary

⇒ *Frankenstein; or, the Modern Prometheus*. 2000 (1818). New American Library, ISBN: 0451527712, 9780451527714, 212p.

Shelley's masterpiece is perhaps the first modern science fiction novel, and features the first truly mad scientist. Victor Frankenstein rails against death and treats it like a disease to be cured. Uncovering secrets humanity was not meant to know, Frankenstein builds a hideous, misshapen creature out of corpses and brings it to life, only to be horrified at what he has wrought. The creature, however, escapes and makes its way into a world that will never accept it. Intelligent, cunning, and powerful, it hates its loneliness and demands a mate, but Frankenstein denies its desire and invites a horrific retribution. This story of science that goes beyond its creator's control is very readable; its theme remains timely, and it deserves its classic status.

Stevenson, Robert Louis

The Strange Case of Dr. Jekyll and Mr. Hyde and Other Tales of Terror. 2003 (1886). Penguin, ISBN: 0141439734, 9780141439730, 177p.

Dr. Jekyll, obsessed with humanity's dual nature of good and evil, pursues a chemical formula to separate these aspects within himself. He succeeds, and inadvertently releases his dark half, Mr. Hyde, upon an unsuspecting public. As Hyde's depredations become more heinous and his darker side grows in strength, Jekyll desperately searches for an answer to his dilemma. Stevenson's haunting depiction of the beast within still has the power to repulse and fascinate readers and has influenced a multitude of later creations, from novels like Stephen King's *The Dark Half* to comic book characters such as the Hulk and *Batman* villain Two-Face.

Wells, H. G.

The Invisible Man. 2005 (1897). Penguin, ISBN: 014143998X, 9780141439983, 161p.

Griffin, a mysterious stranger swathed in bandages, checks into the Coach and Horses Inn. He performs bizarre chemical experiments, shuns company, and only goes out at night, leading people to shy away from him out of suspicion and fear. Little do they know that the seemingly injured man, a former medical student and brilliant scientist, has discovered a chemical that renders him invisible! He attempts to enlist the aid of an old colleague, Kemp, to find a cure for his invisibility. When Kemp learns of the invisible man's megalomaniacal plans for his secret formula, he opposes Griffin and earns the madman's promise of vengeance!

Next to Godliness: Creators, Space Gods, and Self-Styled Deities

The concept of gods in fiction leads many people to think of fantasy literature, but science fiction has its share of divinities and supposedly higher beings. These "deities" are sometimes aliens with incredible powers or technologies who assert their dominance over less advanced beings, but just as often they are shams and pretenders, wizards in their own versions of Oz or mere mortals lost in hubris and megalomania. Whether their omnipotence is fact or feigned, it is typically insufficient insulation from change and transformation when these gods encounter mere mortals. To you, dear reader, I hold out these visionary tomes, fit offerings in the temples of Imagination and Wonder, in hopes that they elicit rapture and awe (or at least a good bit of fun).

Burroughs, Edgar Rice

The Gods of Mars. Barsoom. 2006 (1918). Townsend Library, ISBN: 1591940621, 9781591940623, 247p.

John Carter returns to Mars and encounters his green Martian friend, Tars Tarkas. Tarkas relates that Carter's long absence led his loved ones to believe the human hero dead. Tarkas and Carter's beloved red Martian princess, Dejah Thoris, made the pilgrimage to the supposed Martian paradise of the Valley Dor to be with him. The Valley, however, is a death trap ruled by the Therns, members of a white-skinned race who pose as gods of a religion designed to lure Martians to a life of slavery. The Therns in turn serve as prey for the black-skinned race of Martians called the First Born. Carter must escape and, with the help of his newfound son Cathoris and the First Born warrior Xodar, defeat the black Martians' withered, wicked queen Issus; failure ensures the heroes' deaths, and the death of Dejah Thoris as well. *The Gods of Mars* takes a surprisingly antagonistic and cynical view of religion while maintaining the thrills and adventure of Burroughs's planetary romance series.

Dick, Philip K.

Valis. 1991 (1981). Vintage, ISBN: 0679734465, 9780679734468, 241p.

Horselover Fat receives a communication from the heavens through a pink beam of light. Thereafter, Fat embarks on a quest for God, meaning, and the nature of reality. When he discovers the true nature of God, however, Fat (and the reader) may have difficulty dealing with the revelation. Readers interested in a considered exploration of the world's religions in the form of science fiction may enjoy Dick's quest for enlightenment.

Herbert, Frank

God Emperor of Dune. Classic Dune. 1987 (1981). Ace, ISBN: 0441294677, 9780441294671, 423p.

Leto Atreides rules as God Emperor—and has for millennia. A monstrous mutation, his body now resembles the great sandworms of Dune. Leto rules with an iron fist, making full use of the religious apparatus surrounding him, and enforces a state of peace and safety throughout his realm. However, even as the empire stagnates, Leto puts into motion his final schemes: a breeding program to free the human race and an object lesson for those who rule after him.

Simmons, Dan

Ilium. Ilium. 2005 (2003). Harper Torch, ISBN: 0380817926, 9780380817924, 731p.

The Greek gods have assembled on Mars's Mons Olympus, there to watch the Trojan War played out before them in all its gory detail. They have resurrected classics scholar Thomas Hockenberry to observe the war and report on any deviation from Homer's classic. But Hockenberry is a pawn in a dangerous game, for Aphrodite has enlisted his aid in assassinating her sister, Pallas Athene. Dan Simmons continues his tradition of grand-scale literary space opera and science fiction in *Ilium*, which was nominated for a Hugo Award.

Wells, H. G.

⇒ *The Island of Dr. Moreau.* 2005 (1896). Penguin, ISBN: 014144102X, 9780141441023, 139p.

A shipwrecked man, Edward Prendick, makes his way to a mysterious island where he meets Dr. Montgomery and the enigmatic Dr. Moreau. Prendick recalls that civilized society banished Moreau because of his hideous vivisection experiments and discovers that Moreau continues those same experiments in an attempt to grant beasts humanlike forms and intelligence. Moreau's megalomania goes beyond Frankenstein's mere invasion of God's purview; his vivisections amount to torture as a means to satisfy scientific curiosity. Moreau compounds his hubris by asserting himself as a God figure over his creations, complete with a Mosaic prophet communicating Moreau's Laws to the beast people, thus creating a tenuous situation that yields predictably disastrous results.

Zelazny, Roger

Isle of the Dead. 2001 (1969). Ibooks, ISBN: 0743434684, 9780743434683, 448p.

Francis Sandow is centuries old, and the only human to ever learn the psychic disciplines of the alien Pei'an. Sandow is a telepathic worldscaper: bound to the Pei'an god Shimbo, he can terraform planets with the power of his will. Upon receiving evidence that friends and enemies thought long dead are alive, Sandow finds himself drawn into conflict with Shimbo's ancient nemesis. The realistic personal perspectives of his protagonists balance Zelazny's big ideas and unparalleled world shaping. Fans who like permeable boundaries in their SF will enjoy Zelazny's science-fantasy blend. (Note: this edition also contains Zelazny's novel *Eye of Cat*.)

Real Heroes Wear Their Underwear on the Outside: Superheroes and Superhumans

Superheroes combine nobility and the concept of saviors with archetypes and powers of mythical gods. Whether paragons of virtue like Superman, or objects of terror like Batman, they serve to make their cities, worlds, and universes safe against every kind of bizarre and evil threat. As time went on, writers began taking these demigods out of the mythic mode and their more innocent (and naïve) contexts. Some attributed more realistic motivations and psyches to the vigilantes, while others plunged their characters into dark, bleak environments where little moral or ethical light falls. Both despite and because of this transformation, superheroes remain popular icons well into this new century, as the following titles demonstrate. If these tales inspire you, I've no doubt you'll read your way through this list faster than a speeding bullet.

Carey, Jacqueline

Santa Olivia. 2009. Grand Central, ISBN: 044619817X, 9780446198172, 341p.

A pandemic isolated Outpost 12, an area on the Texas-Mexico border. The only way to win your freedom is to beat the Army's best fighter. Fortunately for Loup Garron, she's got an edge. Loup's father was a genetically engineered "wolf man," and she inherited his heightened physical power and fearlessness. When Loup assumes the mantle of the town's patron saint, the oppressed citizens of Santa Olivia gain their own champion. Carey takes a moment away from epic fantasy to write a heroine who rights wrongs.

Grossman, Austin

⇒ *Soon I Will Be Invincible.* 2008 (2007). Vintage, ISBN: 0307279863, 9780307279866, 318p.

Doctor Impossible, genius mad scientist, is embarking on his latest attempt to conquer Earth by creating a new ice age to bring the world to its knees. With the planet's premier superteam, the Champions, away on a separate mission, novice superheroine Fatale works to pursue and capture Impossible. Underlying the classic comic book plot is Grossman's brilliant depiction of Impossible's midlife crisis, as the villain's reflection and introspection force him to consider all he could have done with his life and talents—curing illness, ending world hunger, becoming wealthy—instead of persistently trying to conquer Earth and getting beaten for his efforts. Ultimately, every reader will likely relate to Impossible's primary struggle with himself and his madness: the insanity of doing the same thing over and over again while expecting different results each time.

Kirkman, Robert, et al.

Invincible, **Vol. 1:** *Family Matters*. Invincible. 2007. Image Comics, ISBN: 1582407118, 9781582407111, 120p. **GN**

Mark Grayson has all the usual teen woes—school, job, lack of girlfriend, and, oh yeah, his dad's the world's greatest superhero! When Mark discovers that he's inherited his father's superpowers, he learns the joys and responsibilities that go with the mask.

Lackey, Mercedes, et al.

Invasion. <u>The Secret World Chronicle</u>. 2006. Available at http://www.secretworldchronicle.com/index.php

Lackey and her fellow writers, artists, and voice actors have created a fantastic series of free podcasts featuring superpowered action and flawed characters whom fans will relate to. Metahumans first appeared during World War II, and people with the powers of gods walk the Earth. The organization Echo employs metas for law enforcement duties and pays quite well. Their efforts are put to the test when the Nazi Thule Society launches a devastating first strike against Echo's facilities worldwide. What fiendish plot lies behind the attack? Go to the podcast Website and find out for yourself!

Martin, George R. R., ed.

Inside Straight. <u>Wild Cards</u>. 2008. Tor, ISBN: 0765357127, 9780765357120, 421p.

The popular <u>Wild Cards</u> series of shared-world books originated with a role-playing game campaign run by the series editor. An alien race known as the Takisians released a bioengineered virus on the genetically similar human race to test its ability to create superpowered mutations. Later dubbed the "Wild Card," the virus kills ninety percent of those exposed to it (called "drawing the Black Queen"); nine percent of the survivors mutate into horrific forms—Jokers—and one percent of its hosts become superhuman Aces. In the series, Martin and his fellow writers craft a realistic and believable alternate history forever altered by the Wild Card. In this relaunch of the series, the reality show *American Hero* features wild cards who perform for the camera; viewers support their favorites while voting others off the program. As the show progresses, some of the contestants unexpectedly learn what it means to be a hero. Fans of *Heroes* and *Watchmen* will find much to enjoy here.

Maxey, James

Nobody Gets the Girl. 2003. Phobos, ISBN: 0972002626, 9780972002626, 244p.

Richard Rogers was a normal guy with a wife and a comedy gig, but one morning he awoke in a strange place and discovered that he was invisible. A very apologetic Dr. Knowbokov explains that he is responsible for Rogers's condition. Feeling responsible, he offers Rogers a job helping the perhaps mad genius and his superhuman daughters save the world. Of course, Knowbokov really needs to change everything and everyone to fit his grand design in order to make his plan work, but that's a minor quibble, right? Maxey's humorous homage to comic book superheroics contains a thoughtful subtext on the responsibilities and potential pitfalls that power brings: if a person can save the world, should he do so regardless of the cost?

Mayer, Robert

Superfolks. 2005 (1977). St. Martin's Griffin, ISBN: 0312339925, 9780312339920, 231p.

Mild-mannered David Brinkley is actually the alien hero Indigo . . . or at least he used to be before he lost his powers. All the other superhumans are either retired or dead, and Brinkley is dealing with a midlife crisis when his powers mysteriously return. Now he needs to learn how to be a superhero all over again. Mayer's satire predates the more famous deconstructions and reenvisionings of the superhero genre with which readers may be familiar, including Alan Moore's *Miracleman* (a.k.a. *Marvelman*) and *Watchmen*, Kurt Busiek's *Astro City*, and Frank Miller's *The Dark Knight Returns*, and this work influenced many of them. Superhero fans take note: an obscure title important to comic book history is back in print!

Millar, Mark, et al.

The Ultimates, **Vol. 1:** *Super-Human.* The Ultimates. 2002. Marvel Comics, ISBN: 0785109609, 9780785109600, 160p. **GN**

Mark Millar and Bryan Hitch reestablish Earth's mightiest superteam in Marvel's Ultimate universe. Captain America, Iron Man, Giant Man, Wasp, and Thor battle to defend the world in a darker, post-9/11 world.

Moore, Alan, et al.

Watchmen. 1995 (1987). DC Comics, ISBN: 0930289234, 9780930289234, 413p. **GN**

The murder of a former costumed vigilante points to a conspiracy of frightening proportions. *Watchmen*, with its adult themes and thoughtful deconstruction of the superhero genre, helped to change the course of comics when Moore gave readers a glimpse into the fetishistic and sometimes fascistic psyches of men and women who, as a matter of course, put on costumes and beat people up. *Watchmen* also epitomizes classic science fiction: it postulates a point of departure—in this case, the transformation of a human scientist into the godlike Dr. Manhattan—and demonstrates how this single change affects culture, politics, science, and society. You may have seen the movie—be sure to read the graphic novel.

Morrison, Grant, et al.

⇒ All-Star Superman.

Vol. 1. 2008. DC Comics, ISBN: 140121102X, 9781401211028, 160p. **GN**

Vol. 2. 2009. DC Comics, ISBN: 1401218377, 9781401218379, 160p. `GN`

Alternate universes! Visitors from the future! Superpower serums! Cloning! Mad Science! When was the last time you saw all of these things and more in a single series? Grant Morrison and Frank Quitely take the most famous, iconic superhero and use all of the possibilities inherent in the genre and more to evoke a magnificent atmosphere of wonder. More important, they do so by celebrating the essence of Superman: the inherent nobility, strength, and hope the character embodies. Suitable for young readers as well as adults, these stories will delight your inner child, enable you to leave your cynicism behind, and remind you what it's like to dream again, and dream big!

Ridley, John

Those Who Walk in Darkness. Soledad O'Roark. 2005 (2003). Aspect, ISBN: 0446612022, 9780446612029, 376p.

Colorfully costumed superhumans in battle were a regular occurrence in the United States until a supervillain destroyed San Francisco. Now America has zero tolerance for metanormals. MTacs—metanormal tactical squads—have the dangerous job of hunting and killing any and all superhumans found in the United States. For Soledad O'Roark, being an MTac cop isn't simply a job, it's a vocation, and she makes every effort to exterminate the superpowered threat. When O'Roark's enthusiasm for her job leads her to kill a metanormal healer, her MTac team becomes the target of a psychic bent on revenge. Ridley writes O'Roark with an edgy nuance, creating a strong female protagonist with a very ugly and vicious prejudice against metanormal "freaks."

Sale, Tim, et al.

***Heroes*, Vol. 1.** Heroes. 2007. Wildstorm, ISBN: 1401217117, 9781401217112, 233p. `GN`

This graphic novel collects the first portion of online comics that tie in to the television program of the same name. Tim Sale and a host of other talented contributors flesh out the world of *Heroes* with new characters and stories that form a connective tissue that expands and elaborates on the television episodes. Fans of the series will recognize Sale's artwork from the show's fictional comic book, *9th Wonders*.

Schwartz, David J.

Superpowers. 2008. Three Rivers, ISBN: 0307394409, 9780307394408, 377p.

In 2001, five college friends awaken after a party and discover that they have superpowers. Following their best intentions, the quintet forms a team of heroes, the All Stars, and generally attempt to use their powers for the common good. They patrol their home of Madison, Wisconsin, foiling crimes and aiding people in trouble, but soon encounter the unexpected consequences of their superhuman abilities as they try to live ordinary and extraordinary lives side-by-side. As time inexorably approaches the fateful events of September 11, the young heroes' powers serve to delineate more clearly their too-human limitations. Schwartz does an admirable job of balancing incredible power with a believable and vulnerable voice.

On the Outside Looking In: Paranormal Pariahs

I don't think it's a coincidence that the age of adolescence seems to correspond with many fans' discovery of speculative fiction. At some point in life, just about everyone feels like an outsider, different and misunderstood. These authors capture that feeling and give it full form in characters that embody those emotions, beings with unbelievable abilities who cannot seem to fit into normal society. Some view average humanity with envy, and others with disdain, but because of their powers, which may alternately seem like gifts and curses, acceptance eludes these outcasts. Perhaps after reading their stories, you'll accept a few of them into your home.

Beresford, J. D.

The Wonder (a.k.a. *The Hampdenshire Wonder*). 1999 (1911). University of Nebraska Press, ISBN: 0803261624, 9780803261624, 297p.

Viktor Stott is deformed and physically weak, but intellectually astounding. He is a wonder, with an amazing memory, an intelligence that absorbs and comprehends the sum of human knowledge, and the ability to control others mentally. Unfortunately, he cannot relate to humanity, and much to Viktor's dismay, the only human who desires his company is the village idiot. The brilliance of the novel lies in the author's ruminations on how society might react to such a wunderkind, including Viktor's athletic father, a man who seems unable to accept his son.

Stapledon, Olaf

Odd John: A Story between Jest and Earnest. 1975 (1935). Garland, ISBN: 0824014375, 9780824014377, 191p.

This early novel is difficult to find but well worth reading. The story's eponymous character possesses incredible intelligence, and later develops telepathy. He quests to form a community of other mutants and metahumans like him. The most striking aspect of this novel is the proposition that beings with advanced intellects would have to develop their own morality to govern the actions of their kind and would owe no allegiance to normal humanity and its mores.

Sturgeon, Theodore

⇒ *More Than Human.* 1998 (1952). Vintage, ISBN: 0375703713, 9780375703713, 192p.

This masterpiece earned Sturgeon the International Fantasy Award in 1954. Several children with fantastic mental abilities—telepathic Lone, telekinetic Janie, the teleporting twins Bonnie and Beanie, the frighteningly brilliant Baby, and abused Gerry—are all drawn to one another as they form a new stage in evolution rooted in a psychic gestalt. Readers will appreciate these superhumans' struggle with the question of morality and their debt to humanity in relation to their survival.

Van Vogt, A. E.

Slan. 2007 (1946). Orb, ISBN: 0312852363, 9780312852368, 255p.

When a genetically engineered superhuman race called Slan demonstrate talents of telepathy and hyperintelligence, their role as humanity's helpers becomes subverted by the fears of normal people. When humans kill the mother of Slan child Jommy Cross, he becomes swept up in political machinations to undermine the dictator Kier Gray. Jommy may be the last hope of his race, but a confrontation with Gray yields a startling revelation. Van Vogt's depiction of humanity's attitude toward a race it created makes for a classic SF novel that continues to inform novels, comics, and blockbuster films.

Wylie, Philip

Gladiator. 2004 (1930). University of Nebraska Press, ISBN: 0803298404, 9780803298408, 332p.

Professor Danner experiments on his unborn child with unparalleled success. Young Hugo is superhumanly strong and bulletproof but must hide his special abilities from others. Hugo spends his life desperately trying to find a place for himself in our society, but his unusual nature only seems to lead him into one disaster and disappointment after another. The ambiguous, and perhaps depressing, ending may leave readers wondering if any good can come from being "special."

Life Sentences: Prisoners' Roll Call

In the novel *The House of the Dead*, Dostoevsky states, "The degree of civilization in a society can be judged by entering its prisons." Although the penal system's role is to confine, punish, and rehabilitate prisoners, convicts endure unimaginable and grueling conditions. Their experiences and struggles seem even more horrific and poignant if the prisoners are actually innocent or if the authorities that sentenced them are corrupt and unjust. Experience incarceration with these characters and consider their crimes and punishments for yourself.

Dietz, William C.

Prison Planet. 1999 (1989). E-Rights E-Reads, ISBN: 1585863262, 9781585863266, 196p.

The prison system doesn't care if Jonathan Renn is actually innocent. The authorities send him to a prison planet known as Swamp, the most salient feature of the world if you don't count the deadly creatures that live there. Renn must learn to fight, hunt, and kill in order to survive both the native wildlife and his fellow convicts. Fortunately, he has the help of his new friend, Marla, a cybernetic German Shepherd with a woman's mind. Renn intends to escape Swamp and, with a little luck and a lot of vengeance, find those responsible for his imprisonment.

Disch, Thomas M.

⇒ *Camp Concentration.* 1999 (1969). Vintage, ISBN: 0375705457, 9780375705458, 184p.

Louis Sacchetti is a poet, a pacifist, and a conscientious objector to America's war overseas. His views earn him imprisonment and a transfer to Camp Archimedes, run by General Humphrey Haast. The authorities administer an unusual compound to the inmates, a modified disease that drastically increases the recipient's intelligence but quickly destroys their bodies within months. The military wants its captive geniuses to invent new weapons to kill the enemy, but Sacchetti observes their obsession with alchemy and the secret of immortality. Disch uses Sacchetti's documentation of camp activities and ruminations upon morality to examine injustice and people's responsibility to do more than merely complain about or denounce it.

Eskridge, Kelley

Solitaire. 2002. Eos, ISBN: 0060088575, 9780060088576, 353p.

Ren Segura is a Hope, a child destined someday to represent her corporation-country of Ko. However, Segura learns a secret about her status, and a subsequent accident leads to her conviction for murder. Segura is stripped of her title and sentenced to eight years of virtual solitary confinement. Although Segura's imprisonment lasts only months in real time, her subjective torment leaves her drastically changed, and she must learn to rebuild herself and her life. This indictment of society's treatment of criminals, as well as its message of hope and healing, earned a Nebula nomination.

Hall, Sarah

The Carhullan Army (a.k.a. *Daughters of the North*). 2008 (2007). Faber, ISBN: 057123660X, 9780571236602, 224p.

As war spreads across the world, Britain becomes dependent on its relationship with the United States, and a tyrannical dictatorship takes power. Contraceptive devices are compulsory, a law that violates women's procreative rights. One woman, a dissident and soldier who calls herself Sister, describes the self-sufficient, Carhullan community of women to her captors. This collection of prison interrogations contains tales of violence, suffering, and ultimately hope and freedom.

Von Schlegell, Mark

Mercury Station. System. 2009. Semiotext(e), ISBN: 1584350717, 9781584350712, 287p.

Eddard Ryan, formerly a member of the Black Rose Army, serves out his prison sentence on the planet Mercury. The solar system's society collapses, but the prison continues its routine with computer precision. Ryan's comrade, the chrononaut Reginald Skaw, offers escape through time. After Skaw stages an explosion, Ryan awakens to find a fourteenth-century document that contains clues about what happened to his lover. Von Schlegell writes a complex plot that weaves between the past and present, blending both into a strange and unreal whole.

Getting the Job Done: Problem Solvers, Butt-Kickers, and Name-Takers

These novels are full of bounty hunters, suicide soldiers, and other characters who could tell you what they do for a living, but if they did, they'd have to kill you. The only people who know these operatives' names are either underworld crime lords or have security clearances containing colors you've never heard of. These are the people you call in when you have missions that are best described in terms of wetwork, complete deniability and extreme prejudice. In fact, these pages will self-destruct, so read them quickly.

Abnett, Dan, et al.

Sinister Dexter, **Vol. 1:** *Gunshark Vacation.* Sinister Dexter. 2004 (1995). Rebellion, ISBN: 1904265162, 9781904265160, 128p. **GN**

The sprawling supercity of Downlode lies across Europe like a chalk outline. Finnigan Sinister and Ramone Dexter are the best gunsharks (hit men) that money can buy, and they prove their rep time and again. These two stylish killers abide by a strict code of conduct and take out the worst criminals Downlode has to offer. Unfortunately for them, even their much-deserved vacation becomes an opportunity for violence and retribution. Abnett combines the action of a Chow Yun-Fat film and cynical humor with the kind of improbably zany and convoluted situations you'd find in a film cowritten by the Marx Brothers and Terry Gilliam.

Ennis, Garth, et al.

The Boys, **Vol. 1:** *The Name of the Game.* The Boys. 2008. Dynamite Entertainment, ISBN: 1933305738, 9781933305738, 152p. **GN**

When out-of-control superheroes carelessly and thoughtlessly kill his girlfriend, young Hughie Campbell is devastated, until one day a man named Billy Butcher comes to call. The Butcher hates the so-called superheroes, because their powers and irresponsibility are a deadly combination. Butcher leads a small covert team called The Boys, and it's their job to keep the supes in line or remove them permanently. Garth Ennis (writer of the acclaimed comic book series *Preacher*) and Darick Robertson (artist for *Transmetropolitan*) join forces on a graphic novel series filled with dark humor, ultraviolence, satire, and genuine humanity. Be warned, however—this comic's graphic depiction of violence and sexuality means it is most definitely not for children.

Roberson, Chris

The Dragon's Nine Sons. Celestial Empire. 2008. Solaris, ISBN: 1844165248, 9781844165247, 429p.

The Chinese arrived in Europe before Columbus ever set sail for the new world and established their cultural and military dominance on Earth. Centuries later, the Celestial Empire and the Aztec theocracy of Mexica vie with one another to control the stars. The Empire gives nine criminals and dissidents the choice of execution or an honorable suicide mission: fly a captured Mexica ship into enemy territory and destroy their base. Their situation becomes graver when the nine discover a prison full of Empire citizens who will soon become ritual sacrifices. Roberson's alternate future history is a playful and careful extrapolation of cultures to a cosmic stage, right down to the Aztec ships that require blood sacrifice to function.

Shepard, Joel

⇒ *Crossover.* Cassandra Kresnov. 2006. Pyr, ISBN: 1591024439, 9781591024439, 457p.

Cassandra Kresnov is an android soldier for the League; to make her more deadly, the League gave her the ability to think. Unfortunately for them, Kresnov thinks she'd rather have a normal life and escapes to the Federation, despite its prohibition against artificial life. She makes her way to the planet Callay, and although Kresnov would rather enjoy libidinous liaisons, she soon finds herself protecting Callay's president from assassination attempts. The combination of a strong female protagonist coupled with lots of violence and sexual escapades fuels this novel's appeal.

Williams, David J.

The Mirrored Heavens. Autumn Rain. 2009 (2008). Bantam Spectra, ISBN: 0553591568, 9780553591569, 416p.

The terrorist organization Autumn Rain destroyed the world's first space elevator and destabilized relations between the world's superpowers. Agents Claire Haskell and Jason Marlowe investigate the crime and hunt the perpetrators. They can't trust anyone, certainly not their bosses who want to maintain the international status quo, and not even themselves, as those same bosses may have tampered with the agents' memories. Williams sets forth a fast-paced science fiction techno-thriller that will keep fans of spies and specialists turning pages and coming back for more installments in the series.

Williams, Walter Jon

Hardwired. Hardwired. 2006 (1986). Night Shade, ISBN: 1597800627, 9781597800624, 257p.

After the devastating Rock War, when rival powers dropped asteroids on major cities from orbit, America is a Balkanized post-apocalyptic nightmare, and the survivors struggle to make lives for themselves. Cowboy, a former fighter pilot cybernetically hardwired into his vehicles and equipment, now smuggles goods across borders. Sarah is a cyborg assassin who works so that she and her brother can leave the Earth for space, where the wealthy and powerful dwell. When a job goes wrong, the two fight for their independence from the Orbitals that govern the planet. Williams blends furious action and elements of Westerns and post-apocalyptic elements into this classic cyberpunk novel without skimping on the invasive technology and even more invasive corporate interests that peppered the iconic 1980s subgenre.

Rebel Yell: Fighting the System

People can endure injustice and tyranny only so long before they resist. Some use weapons and take the battle to their oppressors; others use words that inspire idealism and bravery and point the way to a new and better world. The cost is always high for those who would throw off the chains of their conquerors, but perseverance and sacrifice may win the day. Freedom fighters unite, and read the books on this roll call of rebellion!

Doctorow, Cory

⇒ *Little Brother*. 2008. Tor, ISBN: 0765319853, 9780765319852, 384p.

Marcus, a.k.a. w1n5t0n, is a computer genius par excellence. He and his friends Van, Darryl, and Jolu decide to skip school one day and end up in the wrong place at the wrong time when terrorists attack San Francisco. Department of Homeland Security agents arrest the friends and subject the youth to harsh treatment. Upon release, the friends endure constant surveillance and don't dare tell anybody about their ordeal for fear of reprisal. Marcus, scared and frustrated with San Francisco's transformation into a technological police state, turns outrage into action and leads the fight against the DHS. Along the way, he learns the pains of rebellion and responsibility. In a novel that asserts the importance of individual liberty and explores outlets for righteous outrage, Doctorow reminds us that true rebellion is more than fighting against something: it's fighting *for* something.

Ellis, Warren, et al.

Transmetropolitan, Vol. 1: *Back on the Street*. Transmetropolitan. 2009 (1998). DC Comics, ISBN: 1401220843, 9781401220846, 144p. [GN]

Spider Jerusalem is a journalist for *The Word*. No, he's not one of those mouthpieces that spouts infobytes. He's a *real* journalist who searches for the Truth, and will go to any lengths to uncover it, no matter the consequences. This attitude pits Spider against religious institutions, corporate corruption, and political powerhouses, including the President of the United States himself. Working under contract and the deadline of his editor Royce, Spider works tirelessly to expose the abuses those with power heap upon those without it. Set in a world that's one part cyberpunk, one part transhumanist, and one part classic Hunter S. Thompson gonzo, *Transmetropolitan* delivers dark humor and vicious social commentary. Be warned, however: this graphic novel series is definitely for mature readers.

Fukui, Isamu

Truancy. 2008. Tor, ISBN: 0765317672, 9780765317674, 429p.

The tyrannical Mayor and his enforcers, the Educators, run a repressive totalitarian system that indoctrinates students. Arrayed against them is the Truancy, students who refuse to submit to the Mayor's regime. Tack is a struggling student until the day his sister dies in a battle between Educators and Truancy. Tack blames the reckless rebels for her death and infiltrates the Truancy, seeking vengeance; instead, he comes to identify with their cause. The author began writing this criticism of the educational institution when he was in his early teens, making his resulting success even more impressive.

Heinlein, Robert A.

The Moon Is a Harsh Mistress. 1997 (1966). Orb, ISBN: 0312863551, 9780312863555, 382p.

The lunar colony houses Earth's dissidents and criminals and their descendents. Earth depends on the colony's hydroponically grown wheat, but the sentient computer Mike predicts food shortages, riots, and disaster on the moon in a few years if Earth continues increasing its demands. Soon the lunar citizens begin a revolution to win their independence from Earth and establish a new society. Heinlein's tale of rebellion communicates interesting implications for the consequences of colonization, even as he uses history to model the birth of a new nation.

Rosen, Selina

Chains of Freedom. Chains. 2001. Meisha Merlin, ISBN: 1892065428, 9781892065421, 391p.

Persuasive and charismatic political prisoner David Grant flees his captors and runs into RJ, an elite soldier and guerilla resistance fighter. RJ and Grant form the core of a rebel group determined to take on a totalitarian galactic regime, the oppressive Reliance. Small battles accumulate into greater victories, as word spreads about an opposition movement that dares to speak out about justice and freedom. Rosen writes hard-hitting action sequences and hair's-breadth escapes that drive the narrative to a satisfying conclusion. Subsequent novels, *Chains of Destruction* and *Chains of Redemption*, continue the series.

Smarter Than the Average Alien: Cunning Characters and Rakish Rogues

A knowing smirk, a confident swagger, and a cunning mind characterize the colorful personalities that populate these books. Their arrogance is bound to lead to harrowing adventures, but readers will enjoy watching these devil-may-care scoundrels live up to their (mostly accurate) reputations.

Harrison, Harry

Adventures of the Stainless Steel Rat. Stainless Steel Rat. 1987. Ace, ISBN: 0441004229, 9780441004225, 402p.

"Slippery" Jim diGriz, a.k.a the Stainless Steel Rat, is a rakish, roguish master criminal with a conscience. When the government catches up to him, they make him an offer he can't refuse and draft the crafty con man into the Special Corps. When he tracks down the deadly Angelina, a woman whose cunning nature matches his own, it's love at first sight for our antihero. These humorous, short reads are long on adventure—I'm surprised nobody's turned them into films yet! If one can forgive minor inaccuracies and anachronisms in scientific extrapolation—including punch-card computers—these novels will reward the reader's time with quick wit and humorous exploits. This omnibus edition contains the novels *The Stainless Steel Rat* (1961), *The Stainless Steel Rat's Revenge* (1970), and *The Stainless Steel Rat Saves the World* (1972).

Mitchell, Sandy

Ciaphas Cain: Hero of the Imperium. Ciaphas Cain. 2007. Black Library, ISBN: 1844164667, 9781844164660, 756p.

Ciaphas Cain, commissar in the Imperial forces in the *Warhammer 40,000* universe, is considered a hero by many, although that's mostly a result of Cain's uncanny ability to survive being in the wrong places at the worst times. Despite his best efforts to enjoy the bounty of his reputation while doing as little real fighting as possible, no matter where Cain travels or finds himself stationed, Chaos and peril are sure to find him. Mitchell's witty and inwardly cowardly commissar is a perfect counterpart to Dan Abnett's stoic Ibram Gaunt (from the Gaunt's Ghosts series). Cain's frank and humorous ongoing internal monologue delightfully complements the stories' intense action. This omnibus contains the novels *For the Emperor* (2003), *Caves of Ice* (2004), and *The Traitor's Hand* (2005).

Moore, C. L.

Northwest of Earth. <u>Northwest Smith</u>. 2008. Planet Stories, ISBN: 1601250819, 9781601250810, 220p.

Northwest Smith is a roguish pilot, drifter, and smuggler who roams the solar system seeking dishonest work and adventure. Along the way, he and his Venusian companion Yarol encounter alien gods, primitive civilizations, and ancient ruins galore. C. L. Moore made a big name in the pulp adventure magazines, and fans of Han Solo, *Cowboy Bebop*, or Joss Whedon's *Firefly* and *Serenity* may enjoy this complete collection of Moore's <u>Northwest Smith</u> stories.

Morrison, Robbie, et al.

Nikolai Dante, **Vol. 1:** *The Romanov Dynasty*. <u>Nikolai Dante</u>. 2004. Rebellion, ISBN: 1904265200, 9781904265207, 185p. **GN**

In the twenty-seventh century, Imperial Russia controls a vast empire. Tsar Vladimir rules with absolute ruthlessness. His only rivals to power are the Romanov Dynasty and their weapons crests, technology that grants Romanov scions with incredible powers. Nikolai Dante, the scoundrel and thief who claims he's "too cool to kill," discovers his illegitimate Romanov heritage when he accidentally bonds with a weapons crest. Intrigue abounds as he comes to know his newfound family, although responsibility doesn't curb his swashbuckling and lusty adventures.

Telepaths, Psychics, and Psionics, Oh My!

Some say that science fiction authors envy the fantastical and use psychic powers as a cheat, a way to keep magic in their tales without calling it such. On the other hand, the possibility that accessing the brain's untapped potential may allow for bizarre abilities is an intriguing and attractive prospect and allows for a variety of interesting personal, psychological, and societal explorations and extrapolations. If people knew that you could read their minds, how might they react toward you? Even more significantly, how might your responses change toward others? Would you respect their privacy, or use your abilities to manipulate them? And how would the authorities uncover and monitor such activities and abilities? Psychic gifts represent the ultimate triumph of mind over matter. And yes, their inclusion allows for some pretty cool powers, too. It's a win-win!

Asimov, Isaac

Foundation and Empire. Foundation. 1991 (1952). Spectra, ISBN: 0553293370, 9780553293371, 320p.

After the Foundation manages to avoid an Imperial invasion, its position seems secure. It appears that no force in the universe can derail the plan Hari Seldon formulated for the preservation of civilization and the course of a new Empire in Asimov's *Foundation*. Seldon's grand design, however, is based on the principles of psychohistory; it factors in the vast statistical probabilities of humanity as a whole, not individual actions. A hidden psychic, known only as the Mule, uses his potent abilities to derail Seldon's plan. He intends to take over the Foundation and then discover the location of the only power that can rival his: the hidden Second Foundation. This second installment of Asimov's Foundation series injects suspense and tension into the stories with an unknown variable that endangers the scientific endeavor of building a better world.

Bester, Alfred

The Demolished Man. 1996 (1953). Vintage, ISBN: 0679767819, 9780679767817, 243p.

Telepaths, called peepers for their ability to look into others' minds, have changed all aspects of society, especially law enforcement. A premeditated murder seems impossible to pull off, until somebody succeeds. Wealthy businessman Craye D'Courtney is dead, and the most likely suspect is D'Courtney's rival, Ben Reich. But telepathic officer Lincoln Powell still has to collect evidence and prove Reich's guilt the old-fashioned way. This book won the first Hugo ever awarded; it is an exemplary novel that effectively demonstrates how a single alteration can transform an entire world. The novel even includes a handy and frighteningly catchy rhyme to stymie telepathic intrusion, just in case you need one.

Brown, Eric

Necropath. Bengal Station. 2008. Solaris, ISBN: 1844166023, 9781844166022, 414p.

Although many novels depict telepathy as a remarkable gift, Brown's protagonist struggles with his talent. Jeff Vaughan works at the spaceport Bengal Station as an inspector, where his troubling telepathic ability proves useful. While investigating drug shipments, Vaughan runs afoul of a dangerous cult and its alien god. Vaughan is a believably cynical and distant protagonist, as one might expect given how his telepathy reveals people's true thoughts and strips away any pretense of civility, but Brown manages to render him in a sympathetic light.

Dick, Philip K.

Ubik. 1991 (1969). Vintage, ISBN: 0679736646, 9780679736646, 216p.

Glen Runciter runs an anti-psychic security agency, a lucrative business in a world where powerful people have secrets to keep and are nervous and paranoid about telepaths gaining access to them. In the course of a routine mission, an explosion kills Runciter. As his team speeds to get his remains to cryogenic storage, they soon notice that reality is coming unraveled. Time seems to flow wrong, and they keep receiving bizarre messages from their dead boss, including advertisements for the only thing that can save them: the aerosol spray Ubik. Dick's vision of corporate telepaths blends with his talent at undercutting the reader's sense of reality to create a suspenseful, surreal experience.

Ellis, Warren

FreakAngels, **Vol. 1.** 2008. Avatar, ISBN: 1592910572, 9781592910571, 144p.
GN

In a flooded, postapocalyptic London, the psychic FreakAngels dwell in Whitechapel. The cause of a catastrophe that shook the world, most of these psychic youth use their abilities to care for their adopted home and make life bearable for the others who live there. The disaster set technology back more than a century, but the FreakAngels keep food growing and develop steam-powered vehicles to maintain a semblance of civilization. However, an exiled FreakAngel, banished for breaking the psychics' law against mind control, sends an assassin on a mission of vengeance and begins a new period of uncertainty and fear. This ongoing webcomic can be read for free at http://www.freakangels.com.

Foster, Alan Dean

Flinx Transcendent. Pip and Flinx. 2009. Del Rey/Ballantine, ISBN: 0345496078, 9780345496072, 398p.

Foster's latest and final installment in this classic series that spans nearly four decades ties up loose ends from previous novels and gives the main characters a great send-off. Flinx is a roguish empath who, accompanied by his minidragon, Pip, roams the universe and manages to find trouble wherever he goes. He assembles an alliance and seeks out a powerful weapon to defeat the Great Evil that threatens the universe, all the while avoiding the fatal attention of the nihilistic Order of Null.

King, Stephen

Firestarter. 2003 (1980). Signet, ISBN: 0451167805, 9780451167804, 401p.

When Andy and Vicky McGee volunteered for an experiment in college, they didn't expect to gain psionic abilities, nor did they anticipate that the procedure would alter their genetics and grant their child powers as well. Charlie McGee is a pyrokinetic, able to start fires with her mind, but she possesses little control over her ability. When the government agency that sponsored the college experiments, known as the Shop, discovers Charlie's talents, they attempt to capture and study her. Many readers will be familiar with King's work, and Charlie's story of power and flight to freedom will resonate with fans of *X-Men* and similar stories.

Otomo, Katsuhiro

Akira, **Vol. 1.** Akira. Translated by Yoko Umezawa, Linda M. York, and Jo Duffy. 2000. Dark Horse, ISBN: 1569714983, 9781569714980, 359p. **GN**

Young Kaneda and his biker gang stumble upon a shriveled child in the ruins of Old Tokyo. When the military shows up to take possession of the child, they also take Kaneda's friend, Tetsuo. The Japanese government researches the incredible psychic abilities of select children, and all speak in awe of their most powerful subject, Akira. As Tetsuo's powers grow, his personality warps and twists; he becomes obsessed with Akira and sets himself up as a tyrant. Kaneda's guilt over losing Tetsuo and his desire for the rebel Kei leads to a final confrontation with his old friend. The animated movie adapted from Otomo's sprawling epic was pivotal in introducing much of the United States to Japanese animation. Otomo explores rebellion and authority, abuse of power, politics, transformation, and transcendence in this classic comic. Akira was originally published in Japan from 1982 to 1990; Dark Horse's collected editions contain the entire epic in six volumes.

Smith, E. E.

First Lensman. Lensman. 1997 (1950). Old Earth, ISBN: 1882968107, 9781882968107, 306p.

The benevolent Arisians and vile Eddorians continue their eons-old war for control over the universe. The Arisians bequeath the Lens, a crystal that allows its owner to tap latent telepathic powers, to the incorruptible Virgil Samms. Samms forms the Galactic Patrol to police space, protect the innocent, and defend civilization. The Lensman novels are seminal science fiction, and Smith's ideas fertilized a host of well-known later works, including the Green Lantern Corps, *Star Wars*, and *Babylon 5*. Although some readers may find the starkly black-and-white morality to be simplistic, many young readers and inner children will thrill to the adventures of Smith's noble and heroic characters.

Vinge, Joan D.

⇒ *Psion.* Cat. 2007 (1982). Tor, ISBN: 076530340X, 9780765303400, 364p.

Cat's unusual, dilated eyes mark him as only half human. Alone, he struggles to survive on the streets until the authorities capture him. A psionic research center takes an interest in the young boy and trains him to use his telepathic abilities. The institute intends to use him as a tool to capture the powerful psychic criminal Quicksilver, but Quicksilver wants Cat to join him in his schemes. It's easy to see why the American Library Association voted *Psion* as one of its best books for young adults as the teen protagonist deals with discrimination, street life, and tough moral choices.

To Infinity and Beyond: Heroes of High Adventure

It seems like there's always been a shortage of larger-than-life heroes in our world, but science fiction never lacked for them. They'll cross the bitter cold of space, encounter strange alien races, discover ancient civilizations in overgrown jungles, survive tortuous crossings in desert wastelands, defend themselves against monstrous beasts, bring justice to oppressed peoples—all before lunch! At their best, they exemplify courage, give us hope to overcome our own limitations, and enable us to believe that we can be more than what we are. Hoist a glass to these mighty heroes, peruse these pages, and transport yourself to times of high adventure!

Brackett, Leigh

The Secret of Sinharat and *People of the Talisman.* Eric John Stark. 2007 (1964). Planet Stories, ISBN: 1601250479, 9781601250476, 240p.

Eric John Stark, gunrunner and warrior, is a human raised by the natives of Mercury. He infiltrates the rebels of the Martian Drylands to end a revolution and discovers the secret of the ancient Martian race of Ramas. Still hungry for adventure, he travels to the polar regions of Mars to return a stolen artifact and soon leads the defense of the city against invading hordes. Forget everything science tells you about our solar system and enjoy the thrill of pulp adventure! Leigh Brackett, perhaps better known now for her work on the script of *The Empire Strikes Back,* pens tales of adventure, romance, and exotic locales that will please fans of Robert E. Howard, Edgar Rice Burroughs, and similar scribes.

Green, Simon R.

Deathstalker: Being the First Part of the Life and Times of Owen Deathstalker. Deathstalker. 1995. Roc, ISBN: 0451454359, 9780451454355, 523p.

Aristocrat Owen Deathstalker is nothing like his namesake; while he is an accomplished martial artist, he'd much rather continue as a historian than "death" anything. Unfortunately, for reasons completely unknown to Owen, the mad Empress Lionstone declared him an outlaw. On the run and desperate for allies, Deathstalker discovers that he must live up to his name, lead a rebellion, and restore the decadent empire to its former glory. Readers looking for witty adventure and swashbuckling space opera will enjoy this wild romp through Deathstalker's universe.

Harrison, Harry

Deathworld. Deathworld. 2005 (1960). BenBella, ISBN: 1932100415, 9781932100419, 456p.

Jason dinAlt is a gambler and scoundrel; his ability to manipulate probability means that he has luck on his side. Bored with life, he travels to the deadly world of Pyrrus, where every type of flora and fauna seems intent on killing the human colonists. Intrigued by the oppressed "grubbers" who live outside the colony city, dinAlt learns the reason behind Pyrrus's hostility toward the newcomers, but he may not survive long enough to tell anyone! Harrison's smart protagonist sets a fast pace and finds adventure amid a sea of savagery.

Kline, Otis Adelbert

The Swordsman of Mars. Swordsman of Mars. 2008 (1933). Planet Stories, ISBN: 160125105X, 9781601251053, 160p.

Daredevil thrill-seeker Harry Thorne has faced every adventure Earth can offer. Bored and depressed, he accepts the unusual offer to telepathically trade bodies with a Martian warrior. Soon Harry is hurtling through an array of adventures, from slavery in the baridium mines to sword fighting and enjoying the company of Martian princesses—quite a cure for ennui! Kline was a contemporary of Edgar Rice Burroughs, and with that esteemed author one of the early voices of planetary romance stories.

Nowlan, Philip

Wings over Tomorrow: The Collected Science Fiction of Philip Francis Nowlan. 2005. Wildside, ISBN: 0809510952, 9780809510955, 425p.

Although few may recognize Nowlan's name today, his character, Anthony "Buck" Rogers, appeared in pulp magazines, radio dramas, comics, movie serials, and television and helped to popularize science fiction and make it a part of the mass consciousness. In addition to Nowlan's lesser-known works, this book collects the Buck Rogers stories, including his first: *Armageddon 2419 A.D.* Rogers, a World War I veteran, awakens from suspended animation to a world where he uses his skills to help free a future America from foreign oppression. Like other early pulp fiction stories, sensibilities of race and gender in these works do not mesh with modern views, but those who enjoy adventure fiction and the pulps of the late 1920s or who are avid SF historians will benefit from reading this book.

Raymond, Alex

Alex Raymond's Flash Gordon, **Vol. 1.** <u>Flash Gordon</u>. 2004. Checker, ISBN: 097416643X, 9780974166438, 98p.

Meteors bombard the Earth, and Dr. Zarkov is determined to discover the cause of this threat. He kidnaps two innocent survivors of a plane crash, "Flash" Gordon and Dale Arden, believing them to be spies. The three ride in Zarkov's rocket ship to the planet Mongo, the source of the meteors. There the trio encounter the despot Ming the Merciless and engage in a variety of adventures in fantastic, exotic locales such as Arboria, Tropica, and Frigia and meet bizarre hybrid peoples with the attributes of lions, hawks, sharks, and other animals. These early, infectiously imaginative swashbuckling comic strips originally competed with the Buck Rogers franchise; they remain a delight to the eyes and senses and transport readers to a time and place of grand adventures.

Smith, E. E.

Triplanetary. <u>Lensman</u>. 2009 (1934). Cosmos, ISBN: 0843959495, 9780843959499, 352p.

The ancient, noble, enlightened Arisians oppose the plots of the evil Eddorians, who intend to conquer the universe. The Eddorians have been instrumental in causing many calamities and destructive disasters upon Earth, but the Arisians see humanity as the perfect means to breed a race of superbeings, psionic protectors capable of defeating the Eddorians. Conway Costigan, a member of the Triplanetary military service, stumbles across this billions-year-long conflict as he pursues the space pirate Gray Roger in his quest to bring the vicious criminal to justice. Smith's <u>Lensman</u> series defines space opera with its vast scope, simpler morality, and high-stakes science fiction adventure. This prequel to the series kicks off a foundational story in SF history.

Stirling, S. M.

The Peshawar Lancers. 2003 (2002). Roc, ISBN: 0451458737, 9780451458735, 482p.

In 1878, a meteor swarm devastated the Northern Hemisphere and forced the British Empire to abandon its island and emigrate to its colonies. Nearly 150 years later, Captain Athelstane King serves his queen and country by combating Russian spies and foiling assassinations and deceptions meant to weaken the empire. Fans of Rudyard Kipling, H. Rider Haggard, and similar adventure writers will enjoy high adventure, the political intrigue of the Great Game, and the authentic air to Stirling's reimagined future.

Vance, Jack

⇒ *Planet of Adventure*. <u>Tschai</u>. 1993. Tor, ISBN: 0312854889, 9780312854881, 541p.

Adam Reith crashes onto the exotic and deadly planet Tschai and encounters the world's varied denizens in four adventures: *City of the Chasch* (1968); *Servants of the Wankh*, a.k.a. *The Wannek* (1969); *The Dirdir* (1969); and *The Pnume* (1970). Much to Reith's dismay, all humans on Tschai are either slaves or servants. Reith inspires others to join forces and follow his dream of freedom from their oppressors, but escape means acquiring or building a ship, a goal that drives Reith across the length and breadth of the planet. In his travels, he survives harrowing adventures, horrific monsters, and fellow humans who idolize their masters. He even manages to avoid becoming a museum piece for scholarly study. Fans and newcomers alike will enjoy the author's witty style.

You Wanna' Live Forever?: Second Chances, Lengthy Life Spans, and Immortal Agendas

The possibility of renewed life, even immortality, is a fascinating concept. Alchemists sought for the secret to the philosopher's stone, and ever since science and science fiction have toyed with the notion of cheating death. Some characters have cause to regret their researches—just ask Victor Frankenstein—but some marvel at what humanity could accomplish, particularly if our best and brightest minds could continue shining indefinitely. These novels imagine the possibility of immortality and what that gift would mean sociologically and individually. (For me, it would mean a lot more time to read!)

Anderson, Poul

The Boat of a Million Years. 2004 (1989). Orb, ISBN: 0765310244, 9780765310248, 470p.

Fans of both historical and science fiction will enjoy this book for its vivid descriptions and the depth of its characters, elements that secured Hugo, Nebula, and Promethean Award nominations. Across the centuries, from the distant past to the far future, certain humans discover their immortality; although they can be killed, they cease aging, never seem to fall ill, and heal fully from all but the most severe injuries. As they collect and relate lifetimes of experience, they must also hide their true nature from others, and adapt to the continuing loss of loved ones. Over time, the immortals find companionship and understanding in one another and, estranged from humanity, leave Earth to explore the stars together.

Bova, Ben

The Immortality Factor. 2009. Tor, ISBN: 0765305259, 9780765305251, 480p.

Science fiction is the funhouse mirror we hold up, not to the future but to the present. At a point in history when debate rages over stem cell research, Bova's novel is timely indeed. Arthur Marshak has discovered the secret of organ and limb regeneration; even more important, the new organs can be grown within the patients' own bodies. This announcement leads to a severe social backlash in the form of sensationalist journalism and political and religious opposition. Even worse, Marshak's own brother is speaking out against the breakthrough, because the expensive procedure is prohibitive for all but the very wealthy. As Marshak appeals to a U.S. science court to determine the fate of his procedure, Bova adds courtroom drama to the ongoing problem of interference with scientific progress.

Brown, Eric

Kethani. 2008. Solaris, ISBN: 184416473X, 9781844164738, 311p.

Many of us enjoy discussing the big news of the day, kvetching about or extolling events in equal measure. Brown taps this tendency brilliantly by filtering the most unbelievable event through the voices of everyday people. The Kethani offer immortality to humanity in the form of implants that resurrect the recipients. A group of friends that meets regularly at the pub shares drinks and discuss how this incredible possibility affects their lives. From their perspective, the reader sees how our entire species changes and transforms in response to the aliens' gift.

Hamilton, Peter F.

Misspent Youth. 2008 (2002). Del Rey/Ballantine, ISBN: 0345461649, 9780345461643, 403p.

Jeff Baker created the datasphere and revolutionized information technology. Rather than seeking wealth by copyrighting it, he made it a free gift to the world. Decades later, scientists recognize his humanitarian gesture by offering him an experimental procedure that will return the genius to the prime of life. The world expects Baker to use his new lease on life to make another incredible breakthrough. Unfortunately, his rejuvenation only serves to strain relationships with his family and friends.

Sawyer, Robert J.

Rollback. 2007. Tor, ISBN: 0765311089, 9780765311085, 320p.

Thirty-eight years ago, Dr. Sarah Halifax made successful first contact with an alien race. At eighty-seven years old, she has just received a second message, but given her age, she may not have enough time to decode and continue her correspondence. When Sarah is offered a radical life extension technique called rollback that will return her body to its early twenties, she demands that her husband, Don, be given the same treatment. But while Don's rollback is successful, Sarah's is not. This novel, nominated for a Hugo Award, successfully explores the ethics of science that grants a second chance and its personal effects on the recipient's life and relationships, while simultaneously delivering on its theme of peaceful alien contact.

Sterling, Bruce

⇒ *Holy Fire*. 1996. Spectra, ISBN: 0553099582, 9780553099584, 326p.

Mia Ziemann lives in a society where the possibility of radical life extension treatments creates a permanent upper class gerontocracy. Having lived a conventional, approved, unadventurous if accomplished life, the nonagenarian opts for the treatment and gains the body of a twenty year old again. She then renames herself Maya, escapes to Europe, and begins to live life passionately, exuberantly, and unapologetically among disenfranchised artists and freethinkers, people who, according to society's standards, are undesirables ineligible for the treatment. Sterling uses Maya's experiences to challenge views of medical life extension and considers the morality of using such technology as he envisions a world with new definitions of haves and have-nots.

Zelazny, Roger

This Immortal (a.k.a. . . . *And Call Me Conrad*). 2004 (1966). Ibooks, ISBN: 0743497848, 9780743497848, 176p.

A devastated postwar Earth becomes a tourist attraction for aliens. Conrad Nomikos has been hired to act as a tour guide and bodyguard for the Vegan Myshtigo, who is supposedly writing a travelogue but may be sizing Earth up for purchase. Zelazny firmly established his reputation by winning the Hugo Award for this early achievement.

Beyond Laika and Ham: Futuristic Fauna

Humans treat the animals we share the Earth with in a variety of manners, from loving to thoughtlessly cruel. The following authors envision worlds where said treatment has radical consequences. Will we grant animals sentience so that their companionship becomes intellectual as well as emotional? Will we continue to experiment on and abuse them until they turn on us? Take a look at what the future may bring, but be warned— Dr. Dolittle isn't on this list!

Boulle, Pierre

Planet of the Apes. 2001 (1963). Ballantine, ISBN: 0345447980, 9780345447982, 268p.

Three individuals testing a faster-than-light ship land on a habitable planet. There they discover a society of evolved apes that rule over a savage humanity. The apes use their humans for hunts and medical experiments, but one of the crew, Ulysse, convinces the apes that he is intelligent. As he investigates the apes' society, Ulysse discovers the origins of their civilization. Boulle's classic science fiction novel has spawned many movies, but fans may be interested in the fact that the film *Planet of the Apes* has a different ending than the book.

Brin, David

Startide Rising. <u>Uplift</u>. 1995 (1983). Bantam, ISBN: 055327418X, 9780553274189, 458p.

In an intergalactic civilization divided between patrons and biologically uplifted client species (a procedure that grants the clients sentience), humanity is unique in that it has no patron species, a fact that prejudices many older races against it. Fortunately, humanity had already uplifted both chimpanzees and dolphins before they made contact with aliens and thus have patron status. In *Startide Rising*, the human and uplifted crew members of *Streaker* discover an ancient fleet of ships that may belong to the Progenitors, the mythical first patrons. They try to take samples back to Earth, but when other races learn of the find, they attack *Streaker* to acquire the fleet's location for themselves. Brin's <u>Uplift</u> books are a must-read foundational series, and this particular novel won both the Hugo and Nebula Awards.

Ellison, Harlan, and Richard Corben

Vic and Blood: The Continuing Adventures of a Boy and His Dog. 2003. Ibooks, ISBN: 0743459032, 9780743459037, 128p. **GN**

Long after the Cold War gave way to World Wars III (III.1, III.2, and III.3 to be exact) and IV, the blasted irradiated wastelands make survival difficult for those still living aboveground. Vic, a young man without the benefit of education, civilization, or morals, wanders the world's rubble with his telepathic dog, Blood. When Vic receives an invitation to one of the downunders—underground cities that survived the blast—he abandons Blood. Unfortunately, the subterranean city has only one use for Vic, so he escapes to rejoin his canine companion. This edition contains Ellison's three stories about Vic and Blood—"Eggsucker," "A Boy and His Dog," and "Run, Spot, Run"—as well as famed comic artist Richard Corben's adaptations of all three tales.

Koontz, Dean

Watchers. 2003 (1987). Berkley, ISBN: 0425188809, 9780425188804, 487p.

Former soldier Travis Cornell encounters a strangely intelligent dog that he names Einstein. He discovers that Einstein is one of two results of government experimentation; the other, called the Outsider, is a violent creature intent on killing his canine "brother."

Morrison, Grant, et al.

⇒ *We3*. 2005. DC Comics, ISBN: 1401204953, 9781401204952, 104p. **GN**

In this touching and heartbreaking story, the government experiments on animals and turns them into cybernetically enhanced killing machines. When the project ends, the military decommissions the three pets and orders their disposal. Unable to bear their destruction, their trainer releases the three animals. The remainder of this graphic novel portrays the dog Bandit, the cat Tinker, and the bunny Pirate running, fighting for their freedom, and sacrificing themselves for one another as they struggle to find a place called home. This surprisingly powerful graphic novel addresses animal rights, employs rather graphic violence, and may leave you questioning which characters seem most human.

Norton, Andre

Beast Master's Planet. Hosteen Storm. 2005. Tor, ISBN: 0765313278, 9780765313270, 363p.

Hosteen Storm is a Beast Master. He served Earth in its war against the Xik, aided by his telepathically linked team of genetically altered animals. Earth is dead, and Storm tries to lead a new life as a herder and animal handler on the planet Arzor, but the past won't stay buried. Andre Norton, also known as the Grand Dame of SF, is receiving more attention recently as her works come back into print. This omnibus collects her early novels *The Beast Master* (1959) and *The Lord of Thunder* (1962).

Chapter Three

Setting

Memorable characters need someplace to enact their dramas, undergo their trials, and experience their adventures, and exciting stories need a stage. Without a doubt, the science fiction genre offers the grandest stages. In this chapter, readers will encounter a panorama of astounding settings that far surpass the status of mere backdrop. Some of these books describe lost worlds of grave peril and astonishing beauty, while others take readers far into a future of remarkable possibility or devastating horror, and many do both. Fans can even venture into the past to periods only encountered in history lectures, times that may be familiar or altered beyond all recognition. Some of the scenery found here may be familiar from movie and video game franchises, while others are entirely novel (pardon the pun). In fact, the setting of a narrative can be so attractive, so amazing, so fascinating that it becomes a shadow character within the story. Certainly, readers readily form attachments to fictional places and develop a fondness for them that lasts throughout entire series. Fortunately, fans never truly need to leave their favorite settings—they have only to open their beloved books to once again visit these second homes.

Empires of Every Sort: From Tyrannies to Benevolent Dictatorships

I have always been fascinated by the tendency of imagined future civilizations to adopt systems of government that herald to periods of history centuries before the creators of these galaxy-spanning sovereignties wrote their stories. In and among the various republics and federations are a variety of monarchic and feudal empires ready to shed their light and impose their rule across space. Perhaps authors were simply fascinated by various eras in Earth's history and wanted to incorporate particular elements from those times into their stories. Maybe the grand epics of the literature of the past put indelible marks on authors writing space opera, the grand epics of the future. Or maybe the authors concluded that centuries of technological development might not be proof against powerful people exalting themselves. In any event, enjoy these grand tales of empires-to-be, with all their adventure, intrigue, and fodder for postcolonial criticism.

Herbert, Frank

Dune. Classic Dune. 1990 (1965). Ace, ISBN: 0441172717, 9780441172719, 535p.

> A vast empire rules space with an iron fist. It balances precariously between the noble houses and their aristocracy, the religious and genetic manipulations of the Bene Gesserit sisterhood, and the Spacing Guild that holds the monopoly on interstellar travel. All these factions' machinations revolve around the desert world of Arrakis, also known as Dune. Hissing sands cover nearly the entire deadly arid planet, and leave no hint of green plant or blue water. Dune is home to desert nomads and monstrous sandworms that can swallow vehicles whole. It is also the only source of the spice melange, the most important commodity in the universe. Melange extends life and is necessary for interstellar travel. House Atreides governs Dune in the name of the Emperor, but when vicious Machiavellian plots, covert warfare, and betrayal destroy the Atreides family, young Paul Atreides flees into the desert. Taken in by the militant and rebellious Fremen, Paul must come to terms with the fantastic abilities he acquires and decide if he is the Fremen's prophesied Messiah or something even greater. *Dune* is a fantastic example of space opera and was ecologically thoughtful before such awareness became common in SF. It also won the Hugo and Nebula Awards.

Judson, Theodore

   The Martian General's Daughter. 2008. Pyr/Prometheus, ISBN: 1591026431, 9781591026433, 253p.

   Readers who enjoy Roman history, as well as fans of the film *Gladiator*, should run right out and get a copy of this novel. The vast and Romanesque Pan-Polarian Empire rules a considerable portion of the world, as well as other planetary colonies. General Peter Justice Black has led its armies to victory on numerous occasions and was instrumental in securing its power. But when the Emperor Mathias dies, his mad son Luke Anthony becomes a vicious tyrant. Justa Black, the Martian general's brilliant illegitimate daughter, compiles a record of the events of her father's life and through her eyes we see the height and fall of an empire.

Lucas, George, et al.

   Star Wars Trilogy. Star Wars. 2004. Ballantine, ISBN: 0345475828, 9780345475824, 720p.

   A long time ago, in a galaxy far, far away . . . . The tyrannical Empire controls the galaxy with an iron fist. A despotic emperor rules its forces with the aid of his disciple, the Sith Lord Darth Vader. A desperate Rebellion opposes the Empire's domination. But on a small desert world called Tatooine, farm boy Luke Skywalker learns of his prestigious heritage as the son of a great Jedi Knight. The Jedi were once the galaxy's peacekeepers and wielders of the mystical Force, before the Empire destroyed their order. Luke must train to achieve his full potential and earn the title of Jedi, but doing so means facing the powerful Vader and the Emperor himself. Lucas's science fiction adventure is a genre classic, and fans of the movies will likely thrill to these accounts of Skywalker and his allies. This omnibus edition contains the novelizations of *A New Hope* (1976), *The Empire Strikes Back* (1980), and *Return of the Jedi* (1983).

Moeller, Christopher

   Iron Empires, Vol. 1: *Faith Conquers*. Iron Empires. 2004. Dark Horse, ISBN: 1593070152, 9781593070151, 160p. **GN**

   The Iron Empires, known for the mechanical battlesuits called Irons, vie for power after the fall of the Human Federation. The Void, an area formerly under Federation control but now lost to civilization, forms the boundary of these factions. The Vaylen, wormlike aliens that infest and dominate human hosts, slowly subvert the remaining bastions of galactic civilization. Trevor Faith arrives on Hotok to take command of its garrisons and discovers a disordered and indolent population. Unwilling to see the planet fall into Vaylen hands, he bolsters its defenses and prepares its citizenry for war. SF fans will be delighted that Dark Horse republished this excellent comic from

1994 when they see Moeller's art, as his lush visuals bring the Iron Empires to vivid life. Dark Horse also republished the second Iron Empires volume, *Sheva's War*.

Talbot, Bryan

Heart of Empire: The Legacy of Luther Arkwright. Luther Arkwright. 2007 (2001). Dark Horse, ISBN: 1593077262, 9781593077266, 296p. **GN**

In a British Empire on an alternate Earth, Queen Anne's oppressive rule incites rebellion. The pope, enraged by Britain's independence of Catholic rule, schemes to place Anne's kingdom under papal authority. Victoria, daughter of Anne and the psychic posthuman Luther Arkwright, struggles with her awakening abilities even as she quests in search of her dead brother. When Victoria encounters her father, they discover the corruption at the empire's heart. Fans of Michael Moorcock's Jerry Cornelius and other multiverse stories will enjoy this sequel to *The Adventures of Luther Arkwright*, especially Talbot's criticism of the terrible cost necessary to perpetuate an empire.

Vinge, Joan

The Snow Queen. Snow Queen. 2001 (1980). Warner, ISBN: 0446676640, 9780446676649, 434p.

Two clans, the Summer and the Winter, rule the planet Tiamat. The cycle is determined by a nearby black hole that permits trade and travel with the rest of the galactic Hegemony. During the technologically progressive Winter rule, the Snow Queen reigns. Her people hunt the mer, intelligent sea-dwelling creatures that Winter uses to create an immortality drug. Summer rule forbids mer hunts and demands a return to a more technologically primitive existence. But the Snow Queen Arienhrod is reluctant to relinquish power and implants her embryos into Summer women in hopes that a clone will continue her reign. Young Moon, however, has no intention of continuing the Queen's dynasty and competes to win the title of Summer Queen for herself.

Westerfeld, Scott

⇒ ***The Risen Empire.*** Succession. 2008 (2003). Tor, ISBN: 0765319985, 9780765319982, 352p.

The Killing of Worlds. Succession. 2008 (2003). Tor, ISBN: 0765320525, 9780765320520, 336p.

The Risen Empire patterns itself after ancient Egypt, a civilization that revered and respected its dead. The Risen, also known as Grays, are humans exalted by a process that grants immortality, living dead that rule over eighty worlds. They govern in conjunction with a mortal senate, many of whom rankle at the societal stasis imposed by the Risen. The Empire vies with the

Rix, cybernetic nemeses that chose another path for humanity and serve the cause of artificial intelligences. When the Rix capture the Emperor's sister, the heroic Captain Laurent Zai attempts to rescue her, but the Emperor will do anything, even sacrifice an entire world, to prevent the Rix from learning the secret of the Grays' immortality. Westerfeld made a big noise with this pair of novels that marry the rollicking pulp adventure of space opera to more contemporary visions of extrapolated future technology. Space opera fans, take note!

Pioneering Spirit: Colonies

When I was a child, I was firmly convinced that there would be colonies on the moon, Mars, and space stations within my lifetime. As an adult, I am firmly convinced that the only reason we don't have colonies spread out across the solar system is that no country wants to be the first to fund the next United States of America. The U.S. started out as thirteen small colonies, after all, and look what happened! In addition, colonialism is a word that leaves a bad taste in the mouths of many people, and with good reason, as inequality and tensions between countries and their territories often lead to violence. Considering that these same tensions crop up in the novels on this list, it seems that even authors who envision humanity's future cannot foresee a time when we care more about exploration than power, politics, and exploitation.

Bova, Ben

Moving Mars. 2007 (1993). Tom Doherty Associates, ISBN: 0765318237, 9780765318237, 448p.

> The human colony on Mars is a fractious mix of squabbling factions. The Binding Multiples function as familial economic powerhouses that determine the course of Martian politics. Parent planet Earth, fearing the discoveries made by Martian scientists, seeks to impose its will upon its unruly neighbor. Casseia Majumdar navigates the treacherous political divisions between Earth and Mars as her friend, Charles Franklin, discovers a means of accessing the underlying programming of the universe and manipulating space and time. Together, they break free of Earth's influence and permanently change the fate of the red planet. Bear complements a keen sense of political intrigue and suspense with an incredible representation of the fundamental nature of the universe, a superb feat that gained him the Nebula Award.

Heinlein, Robert A.

Farmer in the Sky. 2008 (1950). Baen, ISBN: 1439132771, 9781439132777, 290p.

Bill Lerner accompanies his family when they leave an overcrowded Earth to join a colony on Ganymede, one of Jupiter's moons. The cramped environs of the transport ship, the *Mayflower*, highlight the difficulties of space travel. Ganymede is even less hospitable; its low-pressure atmosphere, volcanic surface, and deadly moonquakes make farming even more arduous than on Earth. Heinlein successfully transfers early American frontier life to outer space, and this novel, aimed at juvenile readers, remains an excellent read despite the intervening decades. *Farmer in the Sky* is the epitome of science fiction stories that get young readers excited about science.

Roberts, Adam

⇒ *Gradisil.* 2007 (2006). Pyr, ISBN: 1591025389, 9781591025382, 551p.

In a saga that spans generations, the Gyeroffy family discovers a means to propel craft using Earth's magnetic field. Over time, a colony forms in low Earth orbit, the Uplands, free from the laws and strictures of terrestrial nations. When the United States attempts to take control of the Uplands and impose its will, Gradisil Gyeroffy leads the colonists in revolution. Fans of historical fiction, as well as readers who fondly remember Golden Age SF, will find much to enjoy in this future-historical novel of nation-building, politics, and betrayal.

Robinson, Kim Stanley

The Martians. Mars. 1999. Bantam, ISBN: 0553574019, 9780553574012, 434p.

Kim Stanley Robinson's epic Mars trilogy (*Red Mars*, *Green Mars*, and *Blue Mars*) covers the founding and fate of the human colony on the fourth planet. By contrast, this fourth book serves as the perfect end cap to the series and gives readers glimpses of life on the colonized world using vignettes, history, poetry, scientific journals, a Martian constitution, and a treatise about baseball in non-Terran conditions. Readers will feel like amateur archaeologists and historians combing through documents to better understand life in this new civilization. Robinson even includes a few alternate universe visions of the Mars colony and portrays different ways events could have played out on the formerly red planet.

Scalzi, John

The Last Colony. Old Man's War. 2007. Tor, ISBN: 0765316978, 9780765316974, 320p.

The Colonial Union offers veteran soldiers John Perry (from *Old Man's War*) and Jane Sagan (from *The Ghost Brigades*) leadership of a new colony, ominously named Roanoke. The protagonists soon find themselves in the center of a difficult physical and political landscape. The Union traps the colonists on the planet and forbids them the use of advanced technology, restricting them to basic tools and machinery. Perry must confront opposition to his leadership as creatures that resemble werewolves prey upon the settlers. Worst of all, the Union is using the settlement as a political goad against the alien Conclave, a union of races who forbid colonization by anyone other than its members. Caught between two superpowers, Perry and Sagan have to negotiate a political balance while surviving a hostile world.

The Grass Is Always Greener: Alternate Earths, Parallel Universes

Parallel universes and alternate Earths are a longtime staple of science fiction. Sometimes these new worlds are recognizably similar to our more familiar surroundings despite certain historical changes. Other times, the parallel universes are radically different, essentially alien realms. Some may conflate certain parallel universe tales with alternate history and time travel stories, and they do seem to be similar outgrowths of the same core concept—fans of one subgenre may enjoy all three! Take a step across the boundaries that divide related worlds into the universes next door and see.

Asimov, Isaac

The Gods Themselves. 1990 (1972). Spectra, ISBN: 0553288105, 9780553288100, 293p.

Asimov's setting remains balanced between our own universe and another with different physical laws. In ours, a world hungry and desperate for cheap energy siphoned from a parallel reality accepts the discovery of the Electron Pump and ignores the danger posed by this technological Trojan horse. The universe next door is home to a three-gendered alien race. Their universe is slowly dying; they must siphon energy from our universe or face extinction, even though their process will cause our sun to go nova. On both sides of the divide, leaders refuse to sway from their courses of action while objectors argue against certain doom.

McAuley, Paul

⇒ *Cowboy Angels.* 2008 (2007). Gollancz, ISBN: 0575082232, 9780575082236, 408p.

McAuley's novel's mixture of espionage and science fiction features adventures across alternate Americas. In the vast swathe of these other

Americas, only one boasts the title of America the Real. This particular America has Turing Gates, devices that allow access to alternate histories and realities called sheaves, including Americas without human civilization, or where the pro-Nazi movement established itself as a major influence, or where Nixon actually became president! (Wait, that last one sounds familiar.) The Real used the gates to conduct Cold War operations and aid alternate Americas on various sheaves until President Jimmy Carter called an end to the program. But former Company agent and Cowboy Angel Adam Stone reenters the Great Game when his one-time partner goes rogue with a plot to change all histories, including that of the Real.

McDonald, Ian

Brasyl. 2007. Pyr, ISBN: 1591025435, 9781591025436, 357p.

Three different Brazils play host to a reality-spanning conspiracy. In the present, television producer Marcelina Hoffman makes her way through a prismatic and raucous Rio. In 2032, Sao Paulo is a garish cyberpunk cityscape, although with better music than that typically found in most futuristic urban jungles, where streetwise fixer Edson can fall in love with a quantum computing hacker. And in 1732, Jesuit Luis Quinn delves into the dark heart of Brazil's forests to find a rogue priest. McDonald immerses his readers in Brazil's language and music and thoughtfully provides a glossary for those brave enough to take the trip.

Melko, Paul

The Walls of the Universe. 2009. Tor, ISBN: 0765319977, 9780765319975, 384p.

Paul Melko describes a universe where a wondrous device allows its user to visit alternate Earths. The traveler, John Prime, steps into a world similar to the reality he left behind so that he can start over. He cons his local double, John Rayburn, into taking the device and exploring other worlds. Prime intends to use his technical and cultural know-how to introduce new fads and get rich. Unfortunately, other travelers covet the wondrous device for their own nefarious ends. Melko writes a novel big on ideas, adventure, and comedy and confirms that the grass is most definitely not greener on the other side.

Metzger, Robert A.

Picoverse. 2002. Ace, ISBN: 0441008992, 9780441008995, 389p.

The test of a new fusion reactor has the remarkable side effect of creating a picoverse, an extremely tiny alternate universe where time moves far more quickly than ours. But the creation of one picoverse has a cascading effect, and the researchers must discover how to keep all of creation from collapsing. In doing so, they discover some interesting facts about our own universe. A delightful alternate reality romp with action and good humor, this novel netted a Nebula nomination.

Norton, Andre

Crosstime. Crosstime. 2008. Baen, ISBN: 1416555293, 9781416555292, 361p.

Blake Walker's unusual flashes of insight lead him to prevent a murder. He soon discovers that parallel Earths with variant histories exist alongside our own, all of them separated by the thinnest of margins and each hinging on a vital divergence from the others. Blake is soon out of his depth as he races across parallel worlds to prevent a dangerous psychotic from an alternate Earth from conquering our own world. This omnibus edition contains the novels *The Crossroads of Time* (1956) and *Quest Crosstime*, a.k.a. *Crosstime Agent* (1965).

Rucker, Rudy

Mathematicians in Love. 2006. Tor, ISBN: 076531584X, 9780765315847, 364p.

Rucker depicts a universe where the fundamental structure is so stable that mathematicians Bela and Paul, working under the genius Roland Haut, discover they can predict future events from patterns of seemingly unrelated phenomena. Theoretically, one could use snowfall to predict winning lottery numbers . . . or future elections? But a conservative Heritagist president, who won the election by dishonest means and used a war on terror to increase and solidify his power base, learns about these universal dynamics and wants to use the science to further his agenda. Bela uses his knowledge to escape the Heritagists and steps outside our universe to a higher realm, a realm where bizarre aliens, including calculating insects, decide to perform mathematical experiments on Bela's home. Rucker writes thinly masked political commentary and social satire in a bizarre mathematical comedy that keeps readers laughing, albeit nervously, as they start wondering about the reality we live in.

Sawyer, Robert J.

Hominids. Neanderthal Parallax. 2002. Tor, ISBN: 0312876920, 9780312876920, 444p.

Ponter Bodditt is a brilliant scientist experimenting with quantum physics. He is also a Neanderthal in a world where *Homo sapiens* never achieved dominance who finds himself accidentally transported to our world. The more he learns about *Homo sapiens,* the more horrified he becomes with our overpopulated, polluted, violent society. The Neanderthals of Ponter's world live in harmony with their planet and breed violence out of their species, but his society is far from perfect. The Neanderthals favor security and crime prevention over privacy, and their legal system puts the burden of proof on the accused—a distressing matter for Ponter's partner when he finds himself charged with the scientist's murder and has no idea how to prove his innocence! Sawyer's look at humanity through alien, if kindred, eyes, won a Hugo Award.

Talbot, Bryan

The Adventures of Luther Arkwright. <u>Luther Arkwright</u>. 2007 (1997). Dark Horse, ISBN: 1593077254, 9781593077259, 216p. **GN**

Luther Arkwright is a psychic spy, assassin, and agent for an organization that monitors events across parallel worlds. His adventures lead him to an Earth where the sun never set on Cromwell's England and the monarchy never returned to power. But even as Royalist rumblings promise another vicious and bloody English Civil War, both Cromwell's Puritan forces and those loyal to the crown serve as proxies in an even larger conflict between Arkwright's supervisors and the nihilistic Disruptors. *The Adventures of Luther Arkwright* is one of the most underappreciated and important graphic novels in the English language. Although Talbot's comic demands a bit of mental work, readers' efforts will reap rich rewards from a story that influenced the likes of Warren Ellis and Alan Moore.

Turtledove, Harry

Gunpowder Empire. <u>Crosstime Traffic</u>. 2004 (2003). Tor, ISBN: 0765346095, 9780765346094, 286p.

Earth solves its scarcity problem by trading and acquiring resources from parallel timelines and neighboring alternates. The Solter family spends much of its time in an alternate Earth where Agrippa never died, and as a result the Roman Empire endured. Turtledove does an excellent job of evoking life in a Roman frontier city during peacetime and war; the teen protagonists Jeremy and Amanda deal with difficulties ranging from Roman bureaucracy to slavery and worse when the machine permitting travel between worlds breaks down and leaves them stranded during an invasion.

Williams, Walter Jon

Implied Spaces. 2008. Night Shade, ISBN: 1597801259, 9781597801256, 265p.

Aristide is a computer programmer turned swordsman exploring an artificial multiverse. Massive orbital A.I.s, prevented from achieving sentience, create pocket universes that are accessible by wormholes. Humanity populates these subcreated worlds, our species having a kind of immortality using backup minds that can be downloaded into new bodies. Humanity's achievements, however, also lead to ennui. Aristide alleviates his boredom by exploring the artificial universes' implied spaces, bits of the worlds whose existence is implied due to the intentionally created features of those worlds. As Aristide travels the pocket realities with his talking cat Bitsy and his blade Tecmessa, a sword-cum-wormhole, he discovers a threat that could end the multiverse he helped create. Williams creates a wildly imaginative adventure blending singularity SF with the insanely magnificent multiverse-spanning backdrops reminiscent of Roger Zelazny.

Wilson, Robert Charles

Mysterium. 1994. Bantam, ISBN: 0553569538, 9780553373653, 276p.

When the U.S. government sets up a research facility outside of the town of Two Rivers, Michigan, to study an unusual artifact, their experiments transport the entire town to an alternate reality—an Earth where Gnostic Christian fundamentalists rule the land. When the Proctors, the government's religious police, invade Two Rivers, they take over the town and make a discovery in its library that astounds them: the secret to the atomic bomb. Now all they need is a convenient place to test the weapon. Wilson won the Philip K. Dick Award for this tense and thrilling novel of displacement.

The Road Not Taken: Alternate History

Alternate history authors postulate a difference in how events actually played out in our past and extrapolate changes that difference may lead to. This wonderful experiment in what-if epitomizes the term "speculative," hence the category's fit as a subgenre of science fiction. Judging from the sheer number of alternate history books available, I daresay it's also one of the most popular SF subgenres—check out some of the books on this list and discover why!

Birmingham, John

Without Warning. 2009. Ballantine, ISBN: 0345502892, 9780345502896, 516p.

A vast energy field engulfs the United States of America and kills every animal and human inside it. A world without the U.S. quickly destabilizes as alliances shift and countries make their newfound power felt. Birmingham's removal of the U.S. from the world stage is an intriguing thought experiment, and the resultant chaos he describes seems frighteningly believable.

Chabon, Michael

The Yiddish Policemen's Union. 2007. HarperCollins, ISBN: 0007149824, 9780007149827, 432p.

In response to Nazi persecution of Jews, the United States establishes a temporary Jewish settlement in Alaska, saving many lives. As the protagonist,

Meyer Landsman, investigates a murder in the hotel where he lives, Chabon portrays a community faced with its imminent dissolution and no nation state to call home. The bleak landscape and mood blends well with the noir stylings of the story. This novel earned its author the Nebula Award.

Dick, Philip K.

The Man in the High Castle. 1992 (1962). Vintage, ISBN: 0679740678, 9780679740674, 259p.

After the Allies lost World War II, Japan and Germany proceeded to conquer the world and divided the United States between them. Now the two superpowers seek a decisive advantage over each other. Meanwhile, a mysterious novelist, known only as the man in the high castle, writes the book *The Grasshopper Lies Heavy,* a proscribed work depicting a world where the Axis lost the war. Philip K. Dick's alternate reality within an alternate reality gives hope to both the characters and the reader, hope that people can change the world from what it is and help it become what it should be.

Ellis, Warren, et al.

Ministry of Space. 2005. Image Comics, ISBN: 1582404232, 9781582404233, 96p. **GN**

Toward the end of World War II, the United States launched Operation Paperclip, an attempt to forcibly liberate Germany's greatest scientific minds and enlist their service. But what if Great Britain had been one step ahead? Sir John Dashwood convinces Winston Churchill to direct funds toward Britain's new Ministry of Space, a move that technologically and militarily places the island nation ahead of every other country on Earth. In his later years, however, the British government calls Dashwood to account when it learns the source of the ministry's funding. The author writes a bittersweet tale of humanity taking its place among the stars that celebrates our drive and determination while simultaneously castigating our faults. Ellis creates a world where England prevails, but old prejudices and injustices continue.

Goonan, Kathleen

In War Times. 2007. Tor, ISBN: 0765313553, 9780765313553, 348p.

Soldier Sam Dance lost his brother to the attack on Pearl Harbor. As World War II progresses, he trains as a code breaker and encounters Hungarian physicist Dr. Eliani Hadntz. She believes that physics can be applied to biology to remove the human tendency toward violence and gives Sam plans for a device that will realize her goal. Sam and his friend Al Winklemeyer soon discover that their love of jazz aids in their research: the improvisational thinking necessary for the music form also attunes them to quantum possibilities as they attempt to derail the timeline from its present destructive course and steer it toward Hadntz's vision of a better future. Goonan riffs on music appreciation, theoretical physics, and utopian vision in a story full of hope.

Roberts, Keith

Pavane. 2000 (1968). Millennium, ISBN: 1857989376, 9781857989373, 288p.

The assassination of Queen Elizabeth stymies the growth of Protestantism, and the Catholic Church dominates much of the Western world well into the twentieth century. Technological development suffers under the Church's restrictions and the common people's restlessness hints at the possibility of rebellion. Roberts's classic is one of the pillars of alternate history fiction—fans and scholars of the subgenre should seek out this sequence of stories.

Robinson, Kim Stanley

The Years of Rice and Salt. 2003 (2002). Bantam, ISBN: 0553580078, 9780553580075, 763p.

Imagine a world where the Black Death devastated Europe's population and Asian and Middle Eastern cultures, societies, and religions come to dominate the globe. Buddhism and Islam thrive unopposed by Christianity, and different empires arise to colonize the new world. This brilliant novel provides a captivating retelling of the last six hundred years, a panoramic alternate history that earned a Hugo nomination.

Silverberg, Robert

Roma Eterna. 2004 (2003). Eos, ISBN: 0380814889, 9780380814886, 449p.

Silverberg sets his tale in a world where the Jews never escaped Egypt, Christianity never took root, and the Roman Empire endured well into the future. From early in the city's history, here dated according to the Roman calendar year A.U.C. (*ab urbe condita,* "from the founding of the city") rather than A.D. or C.E., Silverberg offers a series of vignettes, each focusing on a different emperor through Rome's tumultuous history. Alternate historians will enjoy following the Roman Empire through its foreign and civil wars, secessions and imperial successions, and discoveries of science and the new world as Rome takes its first steps among the stars.

Turtledove, Harry

In the Balance. Worldwar. 1995 (1994). Ballantine, ISBN: 0345388526, 9780345388520, 565p.

During the violence of World War II, humanity suddenly has a greater concern as aliens strike with atomic weapons and advanced technology. Suddenly, despite their animosity, Axis and Allies must band together and present a unified front against the hostile invaders. Turtledove, best known for his alternate history novels, believably presents famous historical personalities, and his military and strategic research is dead-on.

Walton, Jo

Farthing. 2007 (2006). Tor, ISBN: 076535280X, 9780765352804, 320p.

In the years following World War II, in a world sideways to our own, Britain enjoys a lasting peace thanks to its treaty with Germany, an agreement arranged by the "Farthing set." During a dinner party, one of the set is murdered, found with a dagger pinning a Star of David to his chest. Two characters guide us through the mystery: Inspector Carmichael of Scotland Yard, and Lucy, a daughter of the set whose Jewish husband stands accused of the murder. As they investigate and navigate dangerous social and political waters, the novel portrays how easily a society can slip into fascism. This intriguing coupling of mystery and alternate history was nominated for the Nebula award.

Westerfeld, Scott

⇒ *Leviathan*. 2009. Simon Pulse, ISBN: 1416971734, 9781416971733, 448p.

Westerfeld's latest novel reenvisions World War I in a way that fans will be buzzing about. Deryn dresses like a boy so she can join the British military and serve on a Darwinist airship, a carefully crafted bioengineered warcraft made of animals that forms a bizarre ecosystem. On the other side of the conflict, the murder of young Alek's parents sparks the wide-ranging war. As the last prince of the Austrian line and son of Archduke Ferdinand, Alek must hide from the Clankers who would ascend to dominion with their diesel and steam-powered weaponry, including tanks that move on two legs. Keith Thompson's incredible illustrations supplement Westerfeld's words and bring this new twentieth century to life.

(After) the End of the World As We Know It: Apocalypse Tomorrow

In the aftermath of World War II, humanity realized that it could conceivably destroy the entire Earth and end all life on the planet. During the Cold War, and in the years that followed, a variety of authors faced this horror head-on and wrote a number of tales in which nuclear warfare turned our world into a hellish wasteland. With the advances of science, particularly nanotechnology and biotechnology, and the degradation of the environment, the post-apocalypse subgenre is enjoying something of a revival. Although few today believe that anything could survive an all-out nuclear war, the new vehicle *du jour* for human fear and stupidity seems to be the bioengineered plague. Enjoy what's left afterward!

Braziel, James

Birmingham, 35 Miles. 2008. Bantam, ISBN: 055338502X, 9780553385021, 292p.

Humanity's irreparable damage to the ozone layer turns the American South into a desert wasteland. Killing heat and deadly unfiltered sunlight force the remaining humans to hide during the day and travel during downpours. The government pays the migrants to do useless mining labor, possibly to keep them from becoming refugees and straining the remaining "Saved World," as the damage slowly creeps further every year. Yet despite having two visas out of the South, Mat refuses to leave Alabama with his wife. Environmental and literary science fiction fans will enjoy Braziel's cautionary tale; history buffs will appreciate the novel's reflection of the 1930s Dust Bowl era with its ecological disaster and discrimination against the poor and disenfranchised.

Brooks, Max

⇒ *World War Z.* 2007 (2006). Three Rivers, ISBN: 0307346617, 9780307346612, 342p.

A terrible virus sweeps the world and causes the hungry dead to rise. As the plague spreads, humanity becomes an endangered species. Israel closes its borders to the rest of the world, Cuba becomes a haven for refugees, and U.S. citizens must retake their country one foot at a time. These are the stories of the survivors of the Zombie War, their recollections, reminiscences, their fears and hopes, and, ultimately, the story of humanity's victory. For fans of Romero's films and *28 Days Later*, this intelligent, insightful, humorous, satirical, disturbing, and hopeful book about the world beyond the apocalypse is a work readers will remember long after they finish it.

Butler, Octavia

Parable of the Sower. <u>Parable</u>. 2000 (1993). Warner Books, ISBN: 0446675504, 9780446675505, 345p.

Lauren Olamina is an eighteen-year-old African American woman who experiences the world with a hyperempathy—when another hurts, Olamina feels the pain as if it were her own. Olamina's world in 2025 is riven by ethnic strife, disease, and economic and ecological collapse. When pyromaniac savages overrun her suburban enclave, she escapes and joins with other refugees to form a fledgling faith called Earthseed that emphasizes hope and community, a faith that may give humanity a second chance. This tale continues in *Parable of the Talents*.

Dick, Philip K.

Dr. Bloodmoney; or, How We All Got Along after the Bomb. 2002 (1965). Vintage, ISBN: 0375719296, 9780375719295, 298p.

After the bombs drop, a bizarre cast of characters learns to survive after the fall of civilization. Their communities contain mutants who, warped by radiation, possess paranormal abilities. The psychotic Bruno Bluthgeld holds himself responsible for the atomic strike. Walt Dangerfield orbits the Earth in a satellite; the atomic bombs interrupted the next stage of his trip, so he keeps in contact with the world via radio. Dr. Stockstill, the psychiatrist, helps to treat those disturbed by this unexpected turn of events. And the telekinetic phocomelus Hoppy Harrington has dangerous designs on Marin County. Readers in general, and fans of *Dr. Strangelove* in particular, will revel in the absurdity, paranoia, and will to power that radiate off of every page.

Forstchen, William R.

One Second After. 2009. Forge, ISBN: 0765317583, 9780765317582, 350p.

A nuclear weapon detonates high over the United States and produces an electromagnetic pulse that disables every electronic device in America. A small North Carolina town suddenly finds itself bereft of electricity. There's no refrigeration, no communications, and no utilities. The roads are choked with stranded cars, refugees come pouring in from every direction, and there are no vehicles to supply food and medication. Society collapses, neighbors turn on neighbors, and gangs with guns begin taking what they want. In the midst of this chaos, John Matherson, a history instructor with two daughters, bands the town together, focuses on community survival, and leads the panicked population in defense against a vicious and barbaric gang. Forstchen writes a chilling and convincing tale that warns its readers to be prepared for disaster.

Johnston, Antony, et al.

Wasteland, **Book 1:** ***Cities in Dust.*** Wasteland. 2007. Oni, ISBN: 1932664599, 9781932664591, 160p. **GN**

A century after the legendary disaster known only as the Big Wet, Earth is a barren desert burned dry by a pitiless sun. Technology belongs to the past, and in what was once America small outposts of humanity continue their hardscrabble attempts at survival. When the telekinetic wanderer Michael comes to the small settlement of Providence, vicious mutants attack the town. In the aftermath, the survivors make their way to the thriving city of

Newbegin, unaware that its leader, Marcus, has begun a program of vicious religious persecution.

MacLeod, Ken

The Sky Road. <u>Fall Revolution</u>. 2000 (1999). Tor, ISBN: 0312873352, 9780312873356, 291p.

This novel hinges on two settings to bring its story to fruition. In the first, a Balkanized world boasts a motley assortment of small nations each with its own ideology—anarchist, socialist, conservative, capitalist, green, religious, and a whole gamut of others. In the midst of this fragmented political landscape, Myra Godwin-Davidova heads the International Scientific and Technical Workers Republic, the faction with the world's last cache of nuclear weapons. But a rival state, the Sino-Soviet Union, threatens to conquer the world. Centuries later, young Clovis lives in a nearly utopian Scotland thanks to the actions of the legendary and revered Deliverer, Myra. In this peaceful, pastoral landscape, computer technology is markedly absent. When Clovis's lover Merrial becomes tempted by technology of the past, the pair uncovers forbidden knowledge. The author's leftward-leaning politics interweave brilliantly with scientific extrapolation, and MacLeod's deft handling of technological and societal what-ifs earned him a Hugo nomination.

Matheson, Richard

I Am Legend. 2007 (1954). Tor, ISBN: 0765318741, 9780765318749, 317p.

Robert Neville is the last man on Earth. Los Angeles is a ghost town by day, quiet and deserted. But at night the dead rise and assault Neville's lonely home, the last bastion of humanity. Every night his once-normal neighborhood fills with the shrieks and mocking laughter of vampires who were once his friends and neighbors. Wracked by despair and loneliness, Neville refuses to succumb. Instead, he spends his time studying the vampire phenomenon and hunts the undead while they sleep. In time, Neville becomes a legend, the monster they come to fear. *I Am Legend* is one of the best early stories that uses science to explain and demystify the supernatural without defanging it.

McCarthy, Cormac

The Road. 2006. Alfred A. Knopf, ISBN: 0307265439, 9780307265432, 241p.

A man and his son walk the ash-strewn streets of a bleak, gray, burnt-out landscape at the end of the world. They stumble through dead fields and abandoned cities, without the time or the luxury to speculate on the cause of the devastation, since every day is a struggle to survive, to find food and shelter as they hope to reach better climes. As they travel through the wasteland, avoiding bandits and cannibals, their journey reflects a theme of walking the knife-edge between succumbing to horror and daring to hope. McCarthy won a well-deserved Pulitzer for this work, and I'm delighted to say that I can even recommend the film to fans of the novel.

Pfeffer, Susan Beth

Life as We Knew It. Moon Crash. 2008 (2006). Harcourt, ISBN: 0152061541, 9780152061548, 347p.

An asteroid strikes the moon with cataclysmic effects on the Earth. The moon shifts orbit, causing earthquakes, tsunamis, volcanic eruptions, massive flooding, and a terrible loss of life. Miranda, a high school student, soon discovers that the necessities of survival, including stockpiling food and rationing, require harsh decisions. As winter sets in and the utilities fail, she cycles through despair, determination, and hope. Pfeffer's excellent book for teens realistically portrays both the effects of a global catastrophe and a young woman's maturation in difficult circumstances.

Sargent, Pamela

The Shore of Women. 2004 (1986). BenBella, ISBN: 1932100369, 9781932100365, 469p.

Long after a nuclear war, men and women live in segregated communities. The women inhabit walled cities and command advanced technology, while the men scrabble to survive in primitive conditions. To maintain control over men, the women set up a false religion that serves to deify them and give them complete control over procreation. When a city banishes Birana and condemns her to live in the harsh wilderness, she meets the man Arvil, and they learn that neither is what the other expected.

Stewart, George R.

Earth Abides. 2006 (1949). Ballantine, ISBN: 0345487133, 9780345487131, 345p.

Isherwood Williams returns from his mountain cabin to discover that civilization has ended. Immune to the disease that wiped out most of humanity, Isherwood builds a small community with other survivors. Over time, a world not dominated by humanity reverts to nature as utilities eventually fail and amenities become scarce. Domesticated animals become wild or die; likewise, formerly civilized men and women must learn to adapt to the demands of this new world. Although Isherwood tries to preserve the knowledge, science, and values of civilization, the survivors' descendents turn to a simpler, more primitive lifestyle based on immediate needs and survival. It would be difficult to overestimate Stewart's influence on the post-apocalypse subgenre of SF. He incorporates thoughts on ecology, anthropology, religion, and community building into a rich tale of humanity's continued survival that is also haunted by great loss. Take the time to read this rewarding eulogy for civilization.

Stirling, S. M.

Dies the Fire. Emberverse. 2005 (2004). Roc, ISBN: 0451460413, 9780451460417, 573p.

A mysterious and sudden change in physical laws eliminates modern technology; all electrical devices fail, and gunpowder inexplicably becomes useless. Planes fall from the skies, communications break down, and the central government collapses. Humanity begins forming small communities in an effort to survive as people compete for the remaining, rapidly dwindling resources, and rule of law gives way to "might makes right." Portland, Oregon, becomes a medieval kingdom when a former history professor uses his knowledge to arm and organize criminals and gangs into a terrible army. Michael Havel, a former Marine, guides, protects, and forges survivors into a formidable band, while Wiccan priestess Juniper Mackenzie leads a strong, independent, practical and spiritual commune. Readers should note that, while Stirling's series begins with books of life after the fall of modern civilization, some of the more recent novels in the series seem to take a more fantastic turn.

Vaughan, Brian K., et al.

Y the Last Man, Vol. 1: *Unmanned*. Y the Last Man. 2003. DC Comics, ISBN: 1563899809, 9781563899805, 126p. GN

When a devastating plague strikes worldwide, Yorick and his trained monkey, Ampersand, find themselves the last male mammals on Earth. The world's female population must now adapt to the utterly changed ecological, political, and social realities of a post-male world. As most of the technical, scientific, medical, and military fields, as well as high political offices, consisted primarily of men, civilization and governments fall into chaos. Worse, with men gone, the human race is in jeopardy of becoming extinct. Responses to the plague vary, from an Amazon cult that believes the plague was a judgment on men, to a female troupe of entertainers who keep hope alive. Vaughan and artist Pia Guerra people their comic with fully realized characters and imagine a believable world without men as it struggles to define itself and avoid simplistic utopianism in favor of a more realistic conception of humanity.

Wilson, Robert Charles

Julian Comstock: A Story of 22nd-Century America. 2009. Tor, ISBN: 0765319713, 9780765319715, 413p.

Long after the age of oil, plague, and economic collapse, America is no longer a secular society—it turned away from heretics like Darwin to embrace the Dominion church. President Deklan Comstock is the dictatorial ruler of twenty-second-century America, a nation that looks to the nineteenth century for its technology and mores. The paranoid president had his brother killed to secure his regime, and his nephew Julian fights in Labrador against the Dutch. When Julian's friend Adam Hazzard pens tales of the younger Comstock's wartime adventures, he inadvertently launches the unwilling Julian into the limelight. Wilson balances his bleak portrait of postfall America with a light tone that provides a charming and humorous touch to the narrative.

Zelazny, Roger

Damnation Alley. 2001 (1969). Ibooks, ISBN: 0743413172, 9780743413176, 192p.

In the years following nuclear war, the nation of California receives word that Boston is suffering from a terrible plague. Convict Hell Tanner is offered a pardon if he's willing to drive across the sprawl of wasteland that used to be the United States and brave the dangers of mutants, savage storms, and worse in order to deliver a vaccine. Zelazny offers up an interesting pulp adventure with a hero whose drive offers salvation to others and redemption for himself.

All This and World War Too!: Axis, Allies, and Alternate Endings

The only thing history buffs enjoy more than discussing history is discussing how history could have gone differently, and one favorite point of divergence is World War II. The authors featured in this section consider how the war would have progressed given a twist in events, although these twists range from the plausible to the impossible to the deeply strange. Readers should be prepared for anything from alternate military tactics to wormholes to—dare I say it—Godzilla. (See? I told you it was deeply strange!) How these differences affect the outcome of the war is anybody's guess, and these authors' specialty.

Birmingham, John

Weapons of Choice. Axis of Time. 2005 (2004). Ballantine, ISBN: 0345457137, 9780345457134, 483p.

Because of an experiment with wormhole technology, the USS *Hillary Clinton* and its support group travels from 2021 to the year 1942, just as Admiral Spruance and his fleet prepare to battle the Japanese navy at the Midway Atoll. A misunderstanding leads to an initial clash between the twenty-first-century forces and Spruance's ships. As a result, the Battle of

Midway never occurs and the Allied victory in World War Two is no longer certain. Birmingham's depictions of battles will have readers turning pages so fast they risk combustion, but he also ably portrays the culture clash between characters in the navies of 2021 and 1942.

Conroy, Robert

1945. 2007. Ballantine, ISBN: 0345494792, 9780345494795, 432p.

After the bombing of Hiroshima and Nagasaki, Japan prepares to capitulate to America's ultimatum. When Japanese fanatics halt Emperor Hirohito's surrender to Allied forces, they provoke a long and deadly land war in Japan. Conroy portrays Truman's political struggles and General Douglas MacArthur's violent land battles with equal aplomb and takes readers on a rather grisly and realistic tour of duty.

Gingrich, Newt, and William R. Forstchen

Pearl Harbor: A Novel of December 8th. <u>Pacific War</u>. 2009 (2007). St. Martin's, ISBN: 0312943393, 9780312943394, 400p.

Days of Infamy. <u>Pacific War</u>. 2009 (2008). Griffin, ISBN: 0312560907, 9780312560904, 400p.

In *Pearl Harbor* the authors posit the consequences of Admiral Yamamoto personally leading the famous attack and causing even more devastation than the battle yielded in our history. *Days of Infamy* continues the storyline, as Yamamoto continues his attacks on Oahu, tracks down the absent American aircraft carriers, and engages in deadly conflict with U.S. Admiral Halsey. The team of Forstchen and Gingrich has written a number of acclaimed alternate history stories since the mid-1990s, many of which are popular with fans of the subgenre. These novels represent their recent efforts, and World War II buffs will enjoy the books' action, historical accuracy, and plausibility.

Morrow, James

⇒ *Shambling Toward Hiroshima.* 2009. Tachyon, ISBN: 1892391848, 9781892391841, 170p.

At the tail end of World War II, the conflict in the Pacific drags on, but the Japanese refuse to surrender. The U.S. military's top-secret Knickerbocker Project could bring the war to a rapid close by releasing mutated, giant fire-breathing reptiles upon Tokyo, but conscientious scientists have raised objections. In its hour of need, the military turns to monster movie actor Syms Thorley. Uncle Sam wants Thorley to dress up in a rubber suit and devastate a movie set designed to resemble Tokyo. The United States will invite high-ranking Japanese officials to view the movie and, if Thorley is convincing enough, hopefully frighten the enemy into surrender. Can

Thorley's performance end the war and prevent even greater loss of life? Morrow continues a fantastic tradition of satire with a story that connects wartime espionage with Godzilla by way of *Dr. Strangelove.*

Priest, Christopher

The Separation. 2005 (2002). Old Earth, ISBN: 1882968336, 9781882968336, 338p.

> Jack and Joe Sawyer, twin brothers with the same initials, go their separate ways and lead very different lives during World War II. From their competition in the 1936 Olympics, one becomes a military pilot, the latter works for the Red Cross. Their innocuous actions, small choices, and determined decisions lead to big changes, as Britain makes peace with Germany, and the United States continues a war across the world. But years later, a historian's effort to research facts from an obscure reference to "J. Sawyer" reveals a bizarre confusion of alternative histories. Priest's careful weave of lives and strange turns of events won both the British Science Fiction Award and the Arthur C. Clarke Award.

Turtledove, Harry

Hitler's War. 2009. Del Rey, ISBN: 0345491823, 9780345491824, 496p.

> Turtledove is arguably the best-known alternate history writer, and he shows off his skill in this book. In *Hitler's War,* he examines the consequences of reversing Prime Minister Neville Chamberlain's policy of appeasement. Without the Munich Agreement, Hitler begins his war in 1938 by invading Czechoslovakia. This earlier date also means that World War II begins in parallel with the ongoing Spanish Civil War, now led by a still-living Nationalist General Sanjurjo. Turtledove spends plenty of time in the trenches with his soldiers, who form only a portion of a massive cast of characters—readers may have to test their memory a bit to keep track of all of them.

The Big Picture: Vast Realms

Science fiction is renown for the scope of its settings, vast tapestries of space inhabited by humans, aliens, mutants, robots, sentient starships, galactic empires, corrupt republics, and noble federations. (Try saying that five times fast.) Given such a broad canvas, it's no easy task to fill it. Some authors rely on suggestiveness, giving the readers just enough detail to let them fill in the blanks and see the whole with their imaginations. Other authors seem to populate, quantify, and define every inch of their universes with an array of interesting cultures, races, civilizations, and breathtaking wonders. These novels satisfy that yearning to travel and explore a universe burgeoning with marvels. Pick one up, and begin a journey best described as an odyssey.

Banks, Iain M.

Consider Phlebas. Culture. 2008 (1987). Orbit, ISBN: 031600538X, 9780316005388, 527p.

Banks presents readers with a dizzying array of settings, including a massive, deserted world crafted in the shape of an orbital ring and its island housing an apocalyptic cannibal cult; a gambling tournament that manipulates the players' emotions and takes the lives of the gamblers' proxies; and a dead world preserved by a godlike alien intelligence. Against this backdrop, an interstellar war rages between the fanatical Idirans, with their religious, cultural, and evolutionary hierarchy, and the manipulative Culture, where sentients live lives of peace and fulfillment, catered to (or enslaved) by powerful artificial intelligences called Minds. When a young Mind escapes capture by the Idirans, the enigmatic Horza leads a ragtag band of mercenaries to capture it. But one of the Culture's Special Circumstances agents intends to recover the Mind first. Banks helped define the New Space Opera subgenre with this groundbreaking series; if you're ready to get hooked on an expansive new universe, start here.

Blish, James

Cities in Flight. Okies. 2005. Overlook, ISBN: 1585676020, 9781585676026, 591p.

Thanks to antigravity engines (spindizzies) that permit faster-than-light travel, entire cities launch from Earth and take to the stars. Blish's stories follow our species' freedom from oppressive regimes and the evacuation of a planet exhausted in resources and potential. From there, humanity explores the galaxy, foils alien plots, and lives to the end of time to see the end of the universe. This omnibus edition contains the following books: *They Shall Have Stars*, a.k.a. *Year 2018!* (1956); *A Life for the Stars* (1962); *Earthman Come Home* (1956); and *The Triumph of Time*, a.k.a. *A Clash of Cymbals* (1958).

Cherryh, C. J.

Downbelow Station. Company Wars/Alliance-Union Universe. 2008 (1981). Daw, ISBN: 0756405505, 9780756405502, 426p.

The Earth-based Company is responsible for much of humanity's space exploration. It built a chain of stations as it expanded outward into space, including Pell Station, also known as Downbelow. The rebel Union, a coalition of colonies, refuses to bow to the Company's control, which results in a vicious war with the space stations and merchant traders caught in the middle. *Downbelow Station* becomes the focal point for a star-spanning conflict between massive spacefaring factions in Cherryh's Hugo Award–winning novel and is a good introduction to the Alliance-Union Universe that hosts many of her other books.

Farmer, Philip José

To Your Scattered Bodies Go. Riverworld. 1998 (1971). Ballantine, ISBN: 0345419677, 9780345419675, 220p.

Famous explorer Sir Richard Francis Burton finds himself miraculously resurrected, nude, hairless, and in his prime alongside every human being who ever lived. They awaken in an unusual, idyllic, almost Edenic world situated along a river millions of miles long. Metallic tubes attached to their wrists provide food, water, cigarettes, and other needs. Welcome to Riverworld! Ever the adventurer, Burton decides to explore the length of the river, ultimately hoping to learn the reasons behind humanity's second chance and the intelligence that created the magnificent Riverworld. A treat for history buffs, a pulp adventure, a philosophical exploration, and a mystery all in one, this novel won the Hugo Award while keeping readers on their toes. The remainder of the series includes *The Fabulous Riverboat*, *The Dark Design*, *The Magic Labyrinth*, and *Gods of Riverworld*.

Hamilton, Peter F.

The Reality Dysfunction. Night's Dawn. 2008 (1996). Orbit, ISBN: 0316021806, 9780316021807, 1108p.

Six hundred years from now, the human race expands across space in two primary factions: the Adamists with their mechanistic culture, nanotechnology, and religious dogma; and the Edenists, biotechnological telepaths. Both factions work together in a Confederation along with a number of nonaligned settlements. Against this star-spanning cultural backdrop, a starship pilot investigates the ruins of an ancient civilization and comes across a record that cites something called the Reality Dysfunction as responsible for the settlement's destruction. As energy beings from another dimension begin possessing humans, the Reality Dysfunction comes to threaten the entire Confederation. Hamilton's Night's Dawn series is massive in scope (and page count) and will keep fans of longer series well satisfied.

Kenyon, Kay

⇒ *Bright of the Sky.* The Entire and the Rose. 2007. Pyr, ISBN: 1591025419, 9781591025412, 453p.

Pilot Titus Quinn lost his family in an accident that left him stranded in another universe, a place called the Entire created by the alien Tarig. The Entire is enclosed by massive storm walls and divided into five primacies managed by proxies, all connected by the hyperspatial River Nigh. The tall, bronze-skinned Tarig rule over a miscellany of races, including the humanoid Chalin, who borrow their culture from ancient China; the four-footed Hirrin, who cannot tell lies; and the massive, telepathic Inyx, mounts who bond with blinded riders. Quinn returns to reclaim his family, only to discover that while a few years have passed for him, a decade has passed in the Entire. Worse, the Entire has designs on our universe, and Quinn needs to warn the Earth of its impending doom. Kenyon has crafted a science fiction story that reads like the best blend of planetary romance and fantasy, with an exotic world that enchants like few others. Action, adventure, and romance await in the Entire.

Vinge, Vernor

A Fire upon the Deep. <u>Qeng Ho</u>. 1993 (1992). Tor, ISBN: 0812515285, 9780812515282, 613p.

> Vinge takes the concept of the Singularity, a point beyond which an intelligence will be created that is beyond human understanding, and gives it spatial dimensions. He creates a galaxy with zones of space, each having distinct limits on intellectual and technological progress. A group of researchers from the Beyond discovers a computer archive from the Transcend, where the greatest intelligences dwell. They inadvertently release a being called the Blight, a malign entity that spreads its influence by enslaving other intelligent minds. The researchers' escape ship becomes stranded on a low technology, medieval world with dog-like beings called the Tines. Meanwhile, another group from the Beyond travels to the Tine world to find the researchers, hoping to discover information on how to overcome the Blight. Vinge's unique setting with its strict intellectual boundaries and his thoughtful conception of the alien Tines with their gestalt pack minds combined to win the Hugo Award.

Sealed Systems: Enclosed Spaces

The following books depict societies confined to close quarters, many of them on generation ships taking very long journeys. (No faster-than-light travel here!) Authors may use these unusual circumstances to poke at society's innards and examine our own world in comparison and contrast with these microcosms. When these civilizations find themselves in desperate straits, stress on the system can lead to even more curious dilemmas. Enjoy these chronicles of claustrophobic communities!

Aldiss, Brian W.

Non-Stop (a.k.a. *Starship*). 2005 (1958). Overlook, ISBN: 1585676837, 9781585676835, 241p.

As a vast generation ship glides through space, its inhabitants forget their origins. They live brief and savage lives in remnants of a society distorted by time. Roy Complain of the Greene tribe joins Marapper the Priest on his journey of discovery to the legendary realm of Forwards. As they explore their world and its various sections, they seek to gain control over their home. Aldiss writes convincingly about the degeneration of the ship's population even as he fascinates the reader with his bizarre vision of the world within the craft.

Bear, Elizabeth

Dust. Jacob's Ladder. 2008. Bantam, ISBN: 055359107X, 9780553591071, 342p.

When the injured Sir Perceval recognizes the young servant Rien as her half-sister, the pair set forth on a quest to save their world. This fantastical feudal society, however, is actually a damaged generation ship settled next to a sun about to go supernova. The Exalt nobles, bluebloods both figuratively and literally thanks to the nanotech running through their veins, lord their status over the mundane Means. Angels evolved from an A.I. oversee the world and compete with one another for power. Unless Rien and Perceval succeed in their mission and unite the angels and Exalts in a common purpose, their squabbling will lead to the destruction of their entire civilization. Bear uses nearly every fantasy trope known, adds the elements of medieval romance, and uses Clarke's Third Law to good effect in this delightful genre mix.

DuPrau, Jeanne

⇒ *The City of Ember*. Ember. 2008 (2003). Yearling, ISBN: 0385736282, 9780385736282, 270p.

Ember is a city shrouded by eternal night, with only electric lights to fend off the darkness. The citizens do not know their history, have lost the knowledge of making electricity and fire, and believe that nothing exists outside their city. Over two centuries have passed since the founding of Ember; its supplies dwindle, and the generator is breaking down. Two young citizens, Lina Mayfleet and Doon Harrow, find an old document that leads them to the truth behind the city's founding and the discovery of what lies in the Unknown Regions beyond.

Gloss, Molly

The Dazzle of the Day. 1998 (1997). Tor, ISBN: 031286437X, 9780312864378, 254p.

As humanity anticipates the death of Earth, a group of Quakers boards an ecologically self-sufficient generation ship and departs their home. Gloss's novel records the life of this community as its seekers struggle against despair in their search for a new planet.

Heinlein, Robert A.

Orphans of the Sky. <u>Future History</u>. 2001 (1963). Baen, ISBN: 0671318454, 9780671318451, 209p.

The *Vanguard*'s original mission as an expedition ship is ancient and forgotten history thanks to the crew's internal conflict and the loss of scientific knowledge. Old truths have faded into legend as the so-called scientists perform the ship's duties in the same way priests perform religious rituals. For the inhabitants, the ship is their whole world, a realm divided between the muties and the humans. When Hugh Hoyland views the universe outside the ship's windows, he spreads the truth about the ship and endeavors to complete its mission. Heinlein's classic was originally published in two installments in 1941 and helped establish the generation ship tale.

Russo, Richard Paul

Ship of Fools. 2001. Ace, ISBN: 0441007988, 9780441007981, 370p.

The massive *Argonos* wanders aimlessly through space. Bartolomeo Aguilera, advisor to the Captain, is uncomfortable with existence aboard ship: most of the population forms an underclass that works to maintain the ship and support the power of a privileged few. When the *Argonos* receives a signal from a colony world, the crew members want to colonize the planet themselves rather than remain in perpetual servitude aboard the *Argonos*, but then they find the remains of slaughtered inhabitants and a mysterious alien craft nearby. Russo won the Philip K. Dick Award for this creepy and claustrophobic novel that holds a magnifying glass up to a confined society.

Dreams (and Nightmares) of a Red Planet: Martian Fantasies

Few celestial bodies have held as great a fascination for humanity as the planet Mars. Since astronomer Percival Lowell declared that the red planet's features included canals, which others misinterpreted as an implication that world once hosted intelligent life, authors have populated Earth's neighbor with savage civilizations, ancient empires, lost cities, and noble dynasties. Even when the assumptions of intelligent life fell by the wayside in view of better examination, writers decided to claim and conquer the red planet for humanity just as nations decided against such expenditure. Someday people may walk in the red sands, but until then, you can read these books and dream of Mars.

Arnold, Edwin Lester Linden

Gullivar of Mars. 2003 (1905). University of Nebraska Press, ISBN: 0803259425, 9780803259423, 193p.

Lieutenant Gullivar Jones wishes to escape from the mediocrity of Earth and ends up on a magic carpet ride to Mars. The hedonistic Hither folk and their would-be conquerers, the barbaric Thither people, inhabit Mars' red sands and traverse its extensive canals. Gullivar, meanwhile, bumbles his way through a series of exciting adventures involving ancient races, princesses, and wars, before returning to marry his fiancé. Arnold's work established the tropes that inspired a host of later authors, but Gullivar himself is rather humorously inept compared to subsequent adventure heroes, and the tale is laced with a sharp, satirical poke at colonialism and assumptions of racial superiority.

Bova, Ben

Mars Life. 2008. Tor, ISBN: 0765317877, 9780765317872, 432p.

The remnants of a Martian civilization and Earth's fractious political environment serve as a backdrop to this book by Ben Bova. Ancient ruins prove the existence of a Martian society, but Earth's governments, overwhelmed by a failing environment, see little profit in continuing exploration, and religious conservatives condemn the expedition as a blasphemous hoax. The discovery of a Martian fossil challenges the accepted religious dogma and brings matters to a head. The story's emphasis on pushing the cause of science to the fore above political concerns and religious objections makes for controversial and interesting discussion.

Bradbury, Ray

The Martian Chronicles (a.k.a *The Silver Locusts*). 1984 (1950). Bantam Spectra, ISBN: 0553278223, 9780553278224, 181p.

Humans eager to explore, find new opportunities, or escape Earth begin colonizing Mars. The telepathic Martians, however, are not inclined to welcome the newcomers. Time after time, the Martians halt the humans' colonization efforts, only to be devastated by human disease. The colonists show little regard for their new home, its native inhabitants, or its ecology. Bradbury's contribution to science fiction cannot be overestimated, a fact demonstrated by this collection of stories the author loosely weaves into a novel. By turns eerie, surreal, haunting, and nostalgic, these stories compose a literary masterpiece.

Burroughs, Edgar Rice

A Princess of Mars. Barsoom. 2007 (1917). Penguin, ISBN: 0143104888, 9780143104889, 186p.

When civil war veteran John Carter is set upon by Indians, he stumbles into a cave and is somehow transported to the planet Mars. Called Barsoom by its inhabitants, Mars is a unique blend of civilization and savagery. Four-armed Green Martian tribes lie scattered across the sands, while technologically adept Red Martians live in shining cities. Because of the low Martian gravity, Carter is unbelievably powerful compared to its native inhabitants. He quickly rises in prominence among both Green and Red Martians, rescues the beautiful Princess Dejah Thoris, and leads his comrades to war! Burroughs is a prime author of adventurous SF and a powerful influence on later writers in both science fiction and fantasy. This novel is a must-read for SF fans for its historical importance, its impact on the genre, and its fantastic pulp action.

Haldeman, Joe

Marsbound. 2008. Ace, ISBN: 0441015956, 9780441015955, 296p.

Carmen's family wins an opportunity to help colonize Mars! It's a fantastic opportunity, although she's got to leave behind everything else she loves. While walking, Carmen suffers a fall. Injured and unable to radio for aid, Carmen receives help from a tentacled, potato-headed alien, part of a race that has already settled the red planet. First contact between the two species becomes tense when a plague and mysterious signals from space cast doubts upon the aliens' intentions. Haldeman writes honestly of the trying, difficult, and dangerous aspects of space travel and living in a hostile environment, while simultaneously charming fans with an optimistic story suitable for younger readers and adults.

Lewis, C. S.

Out of the Silent Planet. Space Trilogy. 2003 (1938). Scribner, ISBN: 0743234901, 9780743234900, 158p.

Taken captive on Earth, Elwin Ransom awakens on a spacecraft bound for Mars. Ransom escapes his captors and explores the beautiful and strange world of Malacandra, the inhabitants' name for their planet, with its eerily and impossibly tall, slender plant life and strange inhabitants. He encounters members of each of the planet's races, including the thin and towering seroni, the otter-like hrossa, and the industrious pfifltriggi, and marvels at their harmonious existence. Lewis's Mars is an unfallen world, and its peaceful societies stand in marked contrast to Earth's contentious and violent peoples.

Moorcock, Michael

City of the Beast (a.k.a. *Warriors of Mars*). Kane of Old Mars. 2007 (1965). Planet Stories, ISBN: 1601250444, 9781601250445, 157p.

Brilliant physicist Michael Kane transports himself to Mars of the distant past, a place of exotic beauty and peril that the natives call Vashu. Kane falls in love with Princess Shizala of the city of Varnal and soon after battles the gigantic blue-skinned Argzoon and embarks on a quest to rescue his beloved. Moorcock, best known for his cycle of Eternal Champion stories, seems to have written the Kane novels as a pulp love letter to the works of Edgar Rice Burroughs. This story and its sequels, *Lord of the Spiders* and *Masters of the Pit* (a.k.a. *Blades of Mars* and *Barbarians of Mars*, respectively) redeem the term "escapism."

Robinson, Kim Stanley

Red Mars. Mars. 1993 (1992). Spectra, ISBN: 0553560735, 9780553560732, 572p.

John Boone leads a team of scientists known as the First Hundred to Mars. Unfortunately, humans take their penchant for conflict with them into space. Boone struggles with a love triangle, even as his fellow scientists debate on maintaining the ecological soundness of Mars versus terraforming the red planet. Sadly, hopes for a new society crumble under the weight of old ideologies. A new anti-aging drug allows these original visitors to observe through the long years as voracious capitalist corporations push to exploit Martian resources, and the colonists rebel against Terran authority. This contemplation of strife-ridden human nature won the 1993 Nebula Award and spawned two subsequent novels, *Green Mars* and *Blue Mars*, as well as a collection of novellas and short stories titled *The Martians*.

Stirling, S. M.

⇒ *In the Courts of the Crimson Kings*. 2008. Tor, ISBN: 0765314894, 9780765314895, 304p.

The space race between the United States and its Cold War socialist rival nations results in the discovery of life on nearby planets. Although in decline, the ancient Tollamune Empire rules Mars, and archaeologist Jeremy Wainman gains permission to study its civilization and cities. When he discovers an artifact that identifies his guide, Martian Teyud za-Zhalt, as an heir to the Martian dynasty, plotters seeking to usurp the Tollamune emperor's throne attempt to capture Teyud to further their plans. Stirling's homage to exotic and adventure-filled planetary romances continues in this volume.

The Final Frontier: Space Westerns

When SF authors envisioned humanity spreading across the stars, perhaps inevitable comparisons to the migration across the American frontier began to crop up in their stories. In time, the science fiction and Western genres merged even further, combining cowboys with starships and a grand frontier full of danger, adventure, and opportunity. Get set to explore these wide open spaces, but be sure to strap on your blaster.

Boxleitner, Bruce

Frontier Earth. Frontier Earth. 2001 (1999). Ace, ISBN: 0441007945, 9780441007943, 322p.

Macklin wanders into Tombstone in 1881 with a bad case of amnesia. He manages to befriend the Earps and face off against the Clantons at the OK Corral, even as a pair of aliens hunts him down. If only Macklin could remember why! This entertaining book from Boxleitner (who played the character John Sheridan from the series *Babylon 5*) is a fun crossover between genres.

Kibuishi, Kazu

Daisy Cutter: The Last Train. 2005. Viper Comics, ISBN: 0975419323, 9780975419328, 153p. **GN**

Daisy Kutter is bored stiff since she left behind her life of crime. An invitation to rob a train guarded by security robots is exactly the distraction she needs. Kibuishi's simple, sharp art adds spice to his weird Western tale.

Nightow, Yasuhiro

⇒ *Trigun*, **Vol. 1**. Trigun. 2003. Dark Horse, ISBN: 1593070527, 9781593070526, 360p. **GN**

Vash the Stampede, also known as the Humanoid Typhoon, is a walking disaster—wherever he goes, entire towns and settlements suffer unbelievable damage. Meryl Strife and Milly Thompson, two agents from Bernardelli Insurance, set out to discover the truth about this legendary figure. They discover that Vash is actually a pacifist gunfighter pursued by bounty hunters greedy for the reward on his head. Nightow's comic steampunk Western takes a decidedly serious and more science fictional turn as the series progresses, when readers learn about Vash's secrets, the truth about the colonies on planet Gunsmoke, and Vash's vicious brother, Knives. *Trigun* is a manic, magnificent, and highly satisfying read that continues into a second volume, then progresses through a second series titled *Trigun Maximum*.

Resnick, Mike

Santiago: A Myth of the Far Future. <u>Birthright Universe</u>. 2002 (1986). Tor, ISBN: 0812522567, 9780812522563, 376p.

　　　Santiago is a wanted man across the known galaxy. His crimes are legendary, and the bounty that the outraged Democracy puts on his head is appropriately impressive. Where there are bounties, there are bounty hunters—individuals skilled or desperate enough to take up the challenge and hunt down the outlaw. Join these sinners and killers as they search the Frontier for Santiago.

TenNapel, Doug

Iron West. 2006. Image Comics, ISBN: 1582406308, 9781582406305, 160p. GN

　　　Outlaw Preston Struck becomes a reluctant hero when he stumbles across a bizarre threat. A strange artifact fell from the sky and is churning out robots with the intent of taking over California. TenNapel's wacky premise fuels a charming adventure complete with a wise shaman, a saloon gal with a heart of gold, and Sasquatch. Trust me—TenNapel makes it work.

Whedon, Joss, et al.

Serenity: Those Left Behind. <u>Serenity</u>. 2007. Dark Horse, ISBN: 1593078463, 9781593078461, 96p. GN

　　　Joss Whedon brings back Captain Malcolm Reynolds and the crew of *Serenity* for an adventure that bridges the events between the television series *Firefly* and the feature film *Serenity*. During the Unification War, the Browncoats and the Alliance fought the bloody Battle of Sturges over a crate of money that was never recovered. Mal and the crew pursue the cash and encounter old enemies.

Prehistoric Peril: Hollow Earths and Lost Lands

　　　In an era before satellite photography, scientists and explorers set forth to discover all the wonders the Earth held. In those days, the possibility of discovering lost lands, both on and within the Earth, could still command the imagination. Put on your pith helmet and set forth to map unknown and untamed worlds. They might even name a new species after you!

Burroughs, Edgar Rice

At the Earth's Core. <u>Pellucidar</u>. 2000 (1922). University of Nebraska Press, ISBN: 0803261748, 9780803261747, 296p.

　　　Companions David Innes and Abner Perry test a drilling device that delivers them into a prehistoric world at the center of the Earth. They encounter savage beast-men and become slaves of the reptilian Mahar in their struggle for freedom. In time, David returns to the surface world to deliver this story before venturing back beneath the planet's crust. Originally published in serial form in 1914, Burroughs's fantastical tale was based on an equally fantastical theory.

Burroughs, Edgar Rice

The Land That Time Forgot. 1999 (1924). University of Nebraska Press, ISBN: 0803261543, 9780803261549, 428p.

This novel allegedly has its origin in a manuscript found in a thermos that floated to civilization on ocean currents. The author, Bowen Tyler, arrives at the isle of Caprona and discovers a prehistoric land its natives call Caspak. As Bowen and company progress along the island's main river, they realize that the creatures and vegetation they encounter change in accordance with successive epochs of evolution. Burroughs's magnificent adventure continues with *The People That Time Forgot* and *Out of Time's Abyss*, also contained in this edition.

Doyle, Arthur Conan

The Lost World. Professor Challenger. 2007 (1912). Penguin, ISBN: 0141033770, 9780141033778, 263p.

Journalist Ed Malone interviews Professor Challenger about his outrageous claims of discovering creatures believed extinct for millennia. Challenger invites Malone to join his next expedition to South America with Professor Summerlee and adventurer Lord John Roxton. In the Amazon basin, the journalist learns that Challenger's claims are true, as the explorers encounter dinosaurs and resolve a war between primitive humans and ape-men. Those familiar with Doyle's most famous creation, Sherlock Holmes, will discover the author's versatility in this thrilling journey.

Lovelace, Delos, et al.

King Kong. 2005 (1932). Underwood, ISBN: 1887424911, 9781887424912, 150p.

Filmmaker Carl Denham leads his crew to the fabled Skull Island, a savage land populated by gigantic beasts and prehistoric monsters, and discovers the massive ape called Kong. He returns to civilization with the creature, only to have the giant gorilla break free in New York City. This classic tale of beauty and the beast also criticizes civilization's hubris as it despoils the natural world for nothing more than fame and entertainment.

Rucker, Rudy

The Hollow Earth: The Narrative of Mason Algiers Reynolds of Virginia. 2006 (1990). MonkeyBrain, ISBN: 1932265201, 9781932265200, 234p.

Mason Algiers Reynolds, a Virginia farm lad, encounters Edgar Allan Poe, and the two voyage to the Antarctic. At the South Pole, they find the entrance to the Hollow Earth, a realm with strange gravity, bizarre creatures, and H. P. Lovecraft's Great Old Ones.

Verne, Jules

⇒ *Journey to the Center of the Earth.* <u>Voyages Extraordinaires</u>. Translated by Frederick Amadeus Malleson. 2009 (1864). Engage, ISBN: 1926606191, 9781926606194, 260p.

Professor Liedenbrock and his nephew Axel discover a code in an old manuscript. Axel deciphers the message, which tells of an entrance to the center of the Earth at a volcano in Iceland. Liedenbrock, Axel, and their guide Hans descend into the subterranean realm. As they go deeper into the Earth's strata, they encounter a host of prehistoric creatures that correlate with each stratum's layer in geologic time. Verne's extraordinary voyage imparts a wealth of information as it entertains the reader.

Industrial Revolutions: In Which Are Found "Punk" Settings of the Clock, Steam, Diesel, and Gear Varieties, with Occasional Appearances of Victorianesque Variants, Valiants, and Villains

The wheels of industry featured a fantastic push for mechanization and modernization, accompanied by a dawning awareness that the fruits of economic and technological progress are not always positive. Nevertheless, the Age of Steam and its sister subgenres fascinate fans of fashion and science fiction alike. These works feature rebellion, nobility, inequality, style, and, perhaps most prominently, creatively bizarre science, technology as it might have developed with a proper nudge in the right direction.

Blaylock, James P.

The Adventures of Langdon St. Ives. <u>Langdon St. Ives</u>. 2008. Subterranean, ISBN: 1596061707, 9781596061705, 470p.

Langdon St. Ives, Victorian dilettante, inventor, and adventurer, embarks on a series of rip-roaring adventures and battles against his nemesis, Ignacio Narbondo, as chronicled by St. Ives's faithful friend Jack Owlesby.

See the dead return to an unholy semblance of life! Marvel to alien aircraft! Feel the oppressive heat of the jungle! Smell the rich pipe smoke in exclusive clubs! Nowhere is beyond the reach of this intrepid voyager as St. Ives scours the dark corners of the Earth and travels into space and across vast epochs of time. As an added bonus, discover bizarre and uncanny scientific uses for carp! This volume contains four short stories and two novels (*Homunculus* [1986] and *Lord Kelvin's Machine* [1992]) detailing St. Ives's exciting and hazardous enterprises and will mystify, enchant, and enrapture fans of Victorian adventure and steampunk.

Di Filippo, Paul

The Steampunk Trilogy. 1997 (1995). Four Walls Eight Windows, ISBN: 1568581025, 9781568581026, 354p.

Di Filippo captures the language and spirit of the Victorian era and pulp adventure in a series of uncanny adventures, with the delightful addition of select and salacious naughty bits! Imagine the lascivious Queen Victoria replaced by a transformed nymphomaniac amphibian! Thrill to Lovecraftian weirdness in the colonies! Join poets Walt Whitman and Emily Dickinson on their lusty adventures in other dimensions on a ship utilizing occult science! If you have a penchant for the weird and wonderful reimagining of times past, you must read *The Steampunk Trilogy*!

Gibson, William, and Bruce Sterling

The Difference Engine. 1992 (1990). Bantam, ISBN: 055329461X, 9780553294613, 429p.

Steam technology coexists with Charles Babbage's difference engine, and England enters the Industrial and Information Ages simultaneously! Appearances by actual historical figures abound, including Lord Byron's daughter Ada Lovelace, as the authors weave a tale that highlights a considerable and coherent achievement at building an alternate history. Readers who need a little help with the variations in history, references, and slang should take a look at Dr. Eileen Gunn's supplement to the novel, *The Difference Dictionary*, at http://www.sff.net/people/gunn/dd.

Lansdale, Joe R.

Zeppelins West. <u>Ned the Seal</u>. 2001. Subterranean Press, ISBN: 193108100X, 9781931081009, 168p.

Lansdale pens a bizarre rollicking adventure incorporating pulps, comics, early SF, and Western dime novels. Buffalo Bill's Wild West Show, including Wild Bill Hickok, Annie Oakley, Sitting Bull, and a bodiless Buffalo Bill (whose head survives in a jar thanks to a curious solution of pig urine), travels far and wide by zeppelin to entertain kings and emperors. Along the way, they encounter Frankenstein's monster, Oz's Tin Man, Captain Bemo, and the mysterious Dr. Momo and his bestial creations. Lansdale uncorks his mojo and unleashes a most outrageous gonzo tale upon an unsuspecting public. If you're tired of the same-old in speculative fiction, Lansdale has a cure for what ails you.

Moorcock, Michael

A Nomad of the Time Streams. <u>Oswald Bastable</u>. 1995. White Wolf, ISBN: 1565041941, 9781565041943, 423p.

As in many of Moorcock's novels, the protagonist is an aspect of the Eternal Champion, a person who is transported throughout the multiverse to serve as an agent of balance between the forces of Law and Chaos. Captain Oswald Bastable, the eponymous nomad, finds himself transported from 1902 through time and into alternate histories in which Great Britain never lost its military superiority, airships rule the skies, and the colonies never asserted their independence. Through these adventure stories, Moorcock skillfully considers the effect technology has on society, the ramifications of colonialism and imperialism, and racism in the twentieth century, all without preaching or overshadowing his story (a feat at which far too many authors fail). This omnibus contains the novels *The Warlord of the Air* (1971), *The Land Leviathan* (1974), and *The Steel Tsar* (1981).

Pagliassotti, Dru

⇒ *Clockwork Heart.* 2008. Juno, ISBN: 0809572567, 9780809572567, 390p.

Taya is an icarus, a flying messenger with wings made of the lighter-than-air metal ondium. She soars above Ondinium, a city guided by punch-card computers and strictly divided by caste. When she rescues members of the Exalted caste, she encounters the two brothers Alister and Cristof; Alister moves in the rarified realm of politics, while Cristof renounced his caste but became a master programmer. Cristof's current program, Clockwork Heart, predicts happy marriages but may have attracted the attention of the Torn Cards, terrorists who would bring down the Great Engine and reshape society. Pagliassotti's first published novel features a fantastic fusion of a courageous heroine, down-to-earth romance, and bizarre steampunk technology.

Peters, S. M.

Whitechapel Gods. 2008. Roc, ISBN: 0451461932, 9780451461933, 374p.

Machines rule the Whitechapel district of London. Gold Cloaks, Black Cloaks, and Boiler Men maintain and enforce the order imposed by the mechanical gods Mama Engine and Grandfather Clock. Even worse, a plague is sweeping through the streets, a disease that converts people's bodies to clockwork horrors. Years ago, the Great Uprising failed to free humanity from the gods' tyranny, but a second one may succeed if the resistance can secure the ultimate weapon they need. Unfortunately, that weapon rests within the heart of Whitechapel itself. This imaginative novel evokes the feel of *The Matrix* in Victorian London and may be of interest to fans of steampunk (clockpunk?) and speculative alternate history.

Reeve, Philip

Mortal Engines. Hungry City Chronicles. 2004 (2001). HarperCollins, ISBN: 0060082097, 9780060082093, 373p.

After the Sixty-Minute War consumed the Earth, some cities followed the principles of Municipal Darwinism and mobilized their metropolises. The Traction City of London, like others of its kind, stalks, devours, and assimilates other mobile burgs along the Great Hunting Ground (formerly Europe). Arrayed against the mobile cities is the Anti-Traction League, safe behind their Shield Wall. But the Mayor of London has plans to use an ancient weapon of destruction, MEDUSA, against the League. When young apprentice historian Tom Natsworthy finds himself stranded on the Hunting Grounds, he becomes swept up in the war. Reeve's tale about dwindling resources and civilizations that repeat the mistakes of the past will win over many teen and adult fans.

Merchandizing Tomorrow:
Media Universe Tie-Ins

Many fans' first encounters with science fiction were television and film series such as *Star Trek* and *Star Wars*. These days, the magnificent graphics and complexity of SF video games are a major draw to the genre. Enjoy the following tie-in fiction that elaborates established canon and breaks new ground in established universes.

Abnett, Dan, et al.

Doctor Who: The Story of Martha. Doctor Who. 2008. BBC, ISBN: 1846075610, 9781846075612, 239p.

At the end of the revived Doctor Who's third series, the evil Master held the heroic Time Lord in his grasp. During those dark days, Martha Jones roamed the Earth and kept humanity's hope and faith alive. Abnett turns his hand toward one of the most beloved of Britain's pop icons, and his fellow authors add additional untold adventures of the Doctor and Martha in this volume.

Allston, Aaron

⇒ *Star Wars: Fate of the Jedi,* **Book 1:** *Outcast.* Star Wars. 2009. Del Rey, ISBN: 0345509064, 9780345509062, 318p.

Many science fiction fans are familiar with the Star Wars universe, but the landscape has changed a bit since the battle over Endor in *Return of the Jedi.* The galaxy is reeling from a civil war. The Galactic Alliance has replaced the New Republic, and blames Luke Skywalker for the recent chaos. With Luke in exile and the Jedi under suspicion, a new era of turmoil faces the Jedi Knights in this series of novels.

Buckell, Tobias

Halo: The Cole Protocol. Halo. 2008. Tor, ISBN: 076531570X, 9780765315700, 358p.

The alien Forerunners built massive halos in space, giant rings with their own ecosystems that also served as weapons against the Flood, a parasitic species of aliens. Thousands of years later, the United Nations Space Command (UNSC) and its cybernetic supersoldiers fight a desperate war against the Covenant, a theocratic and technologically advanced enemy determined to destroy humanity. To protect the Earth, the UNSC enacts the Cole Protocol, the destruction of any data that could lead the Covenant to Earth. Buckell adds his considerable talent to expanding the canon of the popular Halo video game universe.

Foster, Alan Dean

Star Trek. Star Trek. 2009. Pocket, ISBN: 143915886X, 9781439158869, 274p.

The United Federation of Planets consists of a variety of member worlds whose races and species send starships into space to explore new worlds and discover the wonders of the universe. But threats abound, and enemies from the future disrupt the entire timeline. James T. Kirk, Mr. Spock, and the crew of the starship *Enterprise* receive a complete makeover that revitalizes the franchise and frees it from past continuity without completely dismissing or discarding what came before—an incredible achievement. Foster's novelization of the film captures the spirit of the previous and new incarnations as the *Enterprise* crew boldly goes forth to new adventures.

Foster, Alan Dean

Transformers: The Veiled Threat. Transformers. 2009. Del Rey/Ballantine, ISBN: 0345515927, 9780345515926, 281p.

Giant robots from the planet Cybertron come to Earth to search for the source of machine life, the All-Spark. The existence of these alien machines redefines politics and power and changes the world forever as the benevolent Autobots aid humanity in its efforts to repel the malevolent Decepticons. In the aftermath of the events in the first *Transformers* film, Megatron's second-in-command, the vicious Starscream, enacts his own plot to destroy the heroic Optimus Prime. The giant robots you loved in cartoon form are back on the big screen and in these novels. Fans of the films will want to read Foster's novel, as it bridges the time between the first two movies.

Traviss, Karen

Gears of War: Aspho Fields. Gears of War. 2008. Del Rey/Ballantine, ISBN: 0345499433, 9780345499431, 385p.

The planet Sera is the source of a potent power source and home to a human colony. It is also host to the ferocious Locust Horde that inhabits its subterranean realm. The Coalition of Ordered Government is the last legitimate human authority on Sera, and its Delta Squad takes the most dangerous assignments in our species' war for survival. Traviss elaborates on the time set before the first installment of this video game franchise. She writes movingly about the history and long friendship between Marcus Fenix, protagonist of the game and novel, and Fenix's comrades, Dominic and Carlos Santiago. The battle at Aspho Fields leads to the death of one of the trio and later battles only serve as a reminder of that fateful day.

Zahn, Timothy

Terminator Salvation: From the Ashes. Terminator. 2009. Titan, ISBN: 1848560869, 9781848560864, 318p.

The machine intelligence Skynet launched a nuclear holocaust in an effort to destroy humanity. Men and women scrabble in the ruins of their former civilization and struggle against the cybernetic Terminator robots, Skynet's mobile killing machines. The Resistance movement, led by John and Kate Connor, fights against humanity's extinction and rages against the machines. Meanwhile, a young Kyle Reece, the man who will one day go back in time, and father John Connor scratch and scrape to survive. Zahn's novel connects the films *Terminator 3: Rise of the Machines* and *Terminator Salvation*.

Savory Settings: Bars, Restaurants, and Diners

Taverns and restaurants are meant to be places of good cheer, a respite from the road and a place to come in out of the cold. Alcohol sets tongues to wagging, and the presence of good company often leads to sharing news and telling stories. Just so, these books offer tales of the tallest varieties told in some of the finest establishments science fiction has to offer. Pull up a chair and have a pint on me!

Adams, Douglas

The Restaurant at the End of the Universe. <u>The Hitchhiker's Guide to the</u> <u>Galaxy</u>. 1995 (1980). Ballantine, ISBN: 0345391810, 9780345391810, 245p.

Arthur Dent and the crew of the *Heart of Gold* continue their mad adventures from *The Hitchhiker's Guide to the Galaxy*. Our heroes (and I use that term as loosely as possible) manage to make their way to Milliways, the Restaurant at the End of the Universe. All one has to do is deposit a penny sometime in the present (compound interest will take care of the diner's fee) and travel through time to get an excellent meal and watch the universe die. From there, the group travels to ancient Earth and discovers another key in the mystery to the ultimate question of life, the universe, and everything. (The answer is still 42.)

Anderson, Kevin J., ed.

Tales from the Mos Eisley Cantina. <u>Star Wars</u>. 1995. Bantam, ISBN: 0553564684, 9780553564686, 387p.

If you've ever seen the first *Star Wars* film (*Episode IV: A New Hope*), then you already know that the cantina scene is one of the most memorable ever filmed. In a relatively short span of time, George Lucas presents viewers with an amazing array of alien races, a tantalizing taste that suggests the vastness of his created universe. (And hey—alien lounge music!) But did you ever find yourself thinking, "There, that blue guy. What's his story?" Well Kevin J. Anderson and a variety of other authors tell us the tales of the cantina's patrons, from a stormtrooper's story to the band's tale. We even learn about Greedo's past before Han shot first. Come on in to this wretched hive of scum and villainy, sip your drink, and hear the stories of experienced spacers. Just keep your blaster handy—I hear it's a rough place.

Brust, Steven

Cowboy Feng's Space Bar and Grille. 2003 (1990). Orb, ISBN: 0765306646, 9780765306647, 297p.

Who is Cowboy Feng? Everybody wonders, nobody knows, but this time-and-space-hopping restaurant, with excellent Jewish cuisine and an Irish house band, seems to barely be keeping one jump ahead of destruction. For some unknown reason, it always seems to arrive in vicinities that soon suffer nuclear attacks. Fortunately, the Grille has heroic inhabitants who may be the galaxy's best hope against a wide-spanning conspiracy. Stop in at Cowboy Feng's for Irish music, heroism, and the best matzo ball soup you'll ever taste.

Niven, Larry

⇒ ***The Draco Tavern.*** 2006. Tor, ISBN: 0765347717, 9780765347718, 316p.

First contact with the alien chirpsithra leads to the construction of a Siberian spaceport at Mt. Forrel. Rick Schumann sees an excellent business opportunity and builds the Draco Tavern to cater to the wide variety of extraterrestrial visitors once word gets around that Earth is open for business. As you might expect, anywhere refreshments flow freely, so do stories, and Niven offers up a host of vignettes and brilliant gems for readers to enjoy.

Robinson, Spider

Callahan's Crosstime Saloon. Callahan's. 1999 (1977). Tor, ISBN: 0812572270, 9780812572278, 205p.

Mike Callahan runs the bar that bears his name and caters to the most bizarre clientele in this or any dimension. Aliens, time travelers, and even a talking dog all patronize the bustling saloon and think of it as a home away from home. Pull up a barstool, have a glass of your favorite poison, and listen to the sob stories, tall tales, and novel narratives of the customers. And if you stick around long enough, you'll even get to see how a listening ear and a thoughtful word can save the world. Robinson spins yarns with humor and empathy in this unforgettable start to a beloved series that spans nearly three decades.

Unplanned Obsolescence: Exploring Posthumanity and Peeking Beyond the Singularity

The transhumanist movement envisions a future in which technology boosts the human mind and body far beyond its current potential into realms that are currently the stuff of, well, science fiction. Imagine a world without illness, infirmity, and even death. Technology could change our species to the point where we are no longer recognizable as human—hence, posthuman. We won't go into this bright future alone, however. Machine intelligence, and perhaps posthuman intelligence as well, may achieve Singularity, a point beyond which their thought processes become incomprehensible to the merely human. It sounds like a bright future, doesn't it? But humanity has a disturbing knack for twisting dreams into nightmares. Which scenario sounds more likely to you?

Egan, Greg

Diaspora. 1998. HarperPrism, ISBN: 0061052817, 9780061052811, 290p.

The descendents of humanity exist in a variety of forms. Some still cling to the flesh and live on Earth, while others take on android forms or transform themselves into computer consciousnesses. When a stellar collision bathes the Earth in gamma rays, posthumanity ranges outward to explore the greater universe.

Melko, Paul

Singularity's Ring. 2008. Tor, ISBN: 076531777X, 9780765317773, 316p.

An artificial ring circles the Earth, a monument to the Singularity, when most of humanity formed a collective consciousness and disappeared. The remainder of humanity produces children in pods, multiple individuals who function together as a unit, almost a single being. Apollo Papadopulos, a pod of five youth, is training to become captain of a starship. Several training "accidents" lead the pod to suspect sabotage.

Rucker, Rudy

Hylozoic. Hylozoic Era. 2009. Tor, ISBN: 0765320746, 9780765320742, 334p.

After the events of *Postsingular*, humanity's minds are all connected to one another and everything is alive. Yes, *everything*. The posthuman condition attracts the attention of a variety of aliens who long to exploit humanity, whether through bizarre real estate deals or by using us as a power source. Fortunately, Rucker's protagonists manage to find their way through this minefield of bizarre multidimensional madness.

Stross, Charles

Accelerando. 2005. Ace, ISBN: 0441012841, 9780441012848, 400p.

Successive generations of the Macx family accelerate humanity's development toward, through, and beyond the Singularity point. Along the way, they discover nonhuman intelligences, virtual economic entities using sentients as currency, and discover the answer to the Fermi paradox: why humanity hasn't had contact with alien civilizations despite the fact that they should be out there somewhere. This book consists of nine separate stories that offer a delightful romp through extrapolations of science and geekspeak. It won the Locus Award, was nominated for the Hugo Award, and can be downloaded for free at http://www.accelerando.org.

Stross, Charles

⇒ *Singularity Sky*. 2004 (2003). Ace, ISBN: 0441011799, 9780441011797, 337p.

The twenty-first century saw the birth of the Eschaton. An incredible entity with godlike power, the Eschaton scatters humanity among the stars and denies them the use of technology that could threaten it. Many years later, the oppressive New Republic keeps advanced technology from its citizens and rules with an iron fist, until one day, on Rochard's World, the sky starts raining telephones. An advanced civilization known only as the Festival offers literally anything the people desire in exchange for entertainment. Stross mixes space opera, intrigue, geeky technological obsession, and interesting sociopolitical thought experiments in this Hugo Award–nominated novel that portrays the social and political chaos that results when humanity meets its posthuman kin.

We Shall Think for You: Dystopian Dilemmas

The word "dystopia" refers to a society in which, through totalitarianism or decay, conditions are repressive, oppressive, and horrific. Dystopian literature often serves to warn its readers of the frightening, if extreme, consequences should society follow a given course of action. Sadly, dystopias do not confine themselves to the printed page, although we can hope that these warnings may turn us away from further examples in our own world.

Bradbury, Ray

Fahrenheit 451. 1988 (1953). Ballantine, ISBN: 0345342968, 9780345342966, 199p.

> In the world of *Fahrenheit 451*, society rejects the printed word. After all, reading leads to thinking, and thinking leads to disharmony and unhappiness. The firemen burn books for the good of everyone, and the citizens devote themselves to their wallscreen televisions. (Prophetic, huh?) But when fireman Guy Montag encounters a woman who decides to burn with her books rather than live without them, his curiosity is piqued. It is interesting to note that the author has clearly stated that his book is not about censorship, but rather how television can supplant the place of books in society. That said, the world Bradbury presents certainly seems dystopian, even if the oppression is accepted from within rather than imposed from without.

Huxley, Aldous

Brave New World. 2006 (1932). Harper Perennial Modern Classics, ISBN: 0060850523, 9780060850524, 259p.

> The World State of Huxley's novel mass-produces people in laboratories and factories, altering the development of embryos to fill society's castes (a nice play on words that simultaneously evokes the concepts of social classes and industrial molds). Children are born in hatcheries and raised in conditioning centers to eradicate individual bonds and promote emotional attachment to the state. Bernard Marx is an outcast whose short stature is considered inappropriate to his Alpha caste level. Bitter and resentful, Bernard travels with a Beta caste woman, Lenina, to a reservation of "savages" whose religion and familial ties mark them as the antithesis of World State society. He discovers John, the child of a World State citizen, and brings him back to civilization as a curiosity for others to gawk at. John,

however, cannot reconcile himself to what he considers as the decadence and depravity of the World State. Huxley's novel is a vicious satire of social engineering, and clearly demonstrates how utopian ideals can lead to dystopian reality.

Miller, Frank, et al.

Give Me Liberty. Martha Washington. 1992 (1990). Dark Horse, ISBN: 0440504465, 9780440504467, 216p. **GN**

In 1996, the United States is a country in turmoil. The nation forcibly segregates areas like Cabrini-Green, cutting off these regions of poverty from the rest of the nation, and grants Native Americans their former territories, zones that prove to be radioactive and poisoned. Even the government stands divided against itself, as the Surgeon General and the preserved brain of the former president attempt to form a separatist state. The rest of the world is equally tumultuous and absurd, as burger barons fight corporate wars to expand their cattle ranches in the rainforests of South America. Follow Martha Washington's journey through this bizarre landscape as she progresses from student to psychiatric patient to soldier and discovers betrayal and friendship in her nation's conflicts. Only Frank Miller, creator of *300* and *Sin City*, could write this sharp, humorous political and social satire that skewers everyone's sacred cows on the same kebab.

Orwell, George

⇒ *Nineteen Eighty-Four* **(a.k.a. *1984*).** 2003 (1949). Plume, ISBN: 0452284236, 9780452284234, 339p.

Winston Smith is an employee of the Ministry of Truth in the government of Oceania. The ostensibly comforting reminder that "Big Brother Is Watching You" is pervasive throughout London, and the Party motto proudly declares that "War is Peace, Freedom is Slavery, Ignorance is Strength." In Oceania, ubiquitous two-way telescreens constantly broadcast Party propaganda and enable the Thought Police to spy on the nation's citizens. The state modified the English language to control how Oceania's citizens think. Even history is mutable, as Winston Smith spends his days rewriting it, changing records, modifying photographs, and deleting all proof of the existence of undesirables. Smith struggles against the domination of his mind and keeps a secret journal of the Party's inconsistencies, lies, and crimes. But is it only a matter of time before Winston Smith learns to love Big Brother? Nineteen Eighty-Four is perhaps the most well-known and well-crafted works of dystopian literature in the English language and is as relevant now as when it was first published.

Peek, Ben

Black Sheep. 2006. Prime, ISBN: 0809562634, 9780809562633, 333p.

After a ferocious war over culture and race, the United Nations makes multiculturalism a crime and segregates all cities into African, Asian, and Caucasian zones. Isao Dazai, a recent immigrant to Asian-Sydney, Australia, dares to find the beauty in other cultures. He hides his discontent with the system and distrust of authority until his desire to find like-minded individuals leads to his arrest and Assimilation. The state brutally strips Dazai of his identity, gives him a number instead of a name, and bleaches his skin a cold white that brands him as a permanent outsider. In time, Dazai discovers his betrayer and begins the slow crawl to reclaiming himself. Peek takes fear of the other and extrapolates a world where multiculturalism becomes heresy and ideology enforces the ultimate identity politics.

Zamyatin, Yevgeny

We. 2006 (1924). Modern Library, ISBN: 081297462X, 9780812974621, 203p.

Zamyatin imagines a One State that organizes its country according to mathematical principles and dehumanization. The state assigns men and women with designations rather than names and requires them to dress identically to one another to eliminate differentiation. The government even mandates legal requisition forms to determine opportunities for sexual activity, rather than leaving liaisons to desire, lust, or love. Scientist D-503, a rocket ship designer, details the beauty of the OneState in a journal intended for first contact with extraterrestrials. But not all men and women share his views; his involvement with a member of the Mephi resistance movement leads D-503 to question the foundations of his beliefs and his society. This early dystopian novel set the standards, structure, and even visual palate for later works in this vein and will appeal to readers with a taste for the bleak, as well as those interested in foundational works.

You Got Your Chocolate in My Peanut Butter!: Fantastical SF

Fantasy and science fiction share a rather large cross-section of fans. Nevertheless, some SF readers enter into sputtering conniptions when they glimpse shiny metal technology coupled with magic and dragons. I, on the other hand, have always been delighted by well-written genre blends. If any sufficiently advanced technology is indistinguishable from magic, then I applaud efforts to add a bit of wizardry to the mix, efforts that result in fantastic books like the novels on this list!

Bear, Elizabeth

All the Windwracked Stars. Edda of Burdens. 2009. Tor, ISBN: 0765318822, 9780765318824, 368p.

Ragnarok happened. The Light and the Tarnished battled on the last day, with only three survivors: Muire, the valkyrie who fled the field of battle; the valraven steed Kasimir; and Mingan, the Grey Wolf. Over two millennia pass, human civilization rises and falls, and the planet Valdyrgard is slowly dying. Its last city, Eiledon, is maintained by the efforts of its despot, the Technomancer. Muire vows to save the last people, but Mingan returns with a more final solution in mind. Bear blends Norse mythology and extremely advanced technology into a science fictional Edda that SF fans can recommend to their fantasy-reading friends.

Delany, Samuel R.

The Einstein Intersection. 1998 (1967). Wesleyan University Press, ISBN: 0819563366, 9780819563361, 135p.

Alien visitors inhabit the radioactive ruins of an abandoned Earth and act the parts of our legends and archetypes, from ancient myths to pop culture icons. Lo Lobey, an Orpheic hero, vows to confront Kid Death to reclaim his love. As his journey and quest progress, the reader is treated to a beautiful, bizarre, alien view of humanity cobbled together from the stories and myths that we leave behind.

McCaffrey, Anne

The Dragonriders of Pern. Pern. 1988. Ballantine, ISBN: 0345340248, 9780345340245, 820p.

Discover a world where courageous men and women form bonds with dragons and work together to prevent the destruction of their people from an enemy that threatens to annihilate all of them. The inhabitants are the descendents of interstellar colonists, the dragons they ride are the result of genetic manipulation, and the enemy they face is a bizarre spore called Thread that periodically descends upon the planet and destroys organic matter. Anne McCaffrey's planet Pern is a perfect example of the drive to blend the elements of fantasy and science fiction into a unified whole, complete with adventure, romance, and memorable characters. This volume in the series The Dragonriders of Pern includes the books *Dragonflight* (1968), *Dragonquest* (1971), and *The White Dragon* (1978), introducing readers to the society and world of Pern's protectors and stories that have delighted fans for decades.

Okorafor, Nnedi

The Shadow Speaker. 2009 (2007). Jump at the Sun/Hyperion, ISBN: 1423100360, 9781423100362, 352p.

Decades ago, the nations destroyed one another with nuclear weapons, and the Peace Bomb altered the world forever. The Great Change warped the animals and plants, opened ways to other worlds, and blessed some, called metahumans, with uncanny powers. Young Ejimafor Ugabe can speak to shadows, and they urge her to make the long journey to participate in talks of lasting peace with the nearby world of Ginen. Okorafor deftly blends mutation, magic, and Muslim and African culture into a rich mélange, a unique treat for the senses and the imagination.

Robson, Justina

⇒ *Keeping It Real*. <u>Quantum Gravity</u>. 2007 (2006). Pyr, ISBN: 1591025397, 9781591025399, 337p.

In the year 2015, the quantum bomb ruptured the boundaries between dimensions and opened contact between humanity and magical dimensions. Robson's blend of magic and technology allows cyborg agent Lila Black to rub shoulders with an elf rock musician, while protecting him from fanatical members of his own race. What happens when a realm of science meets demons, fey, and other denizens of mythical fantasy? Action, romance, transformation, and transcendence!

Williams, Liz

Snake Agent. <u>Detective Inspector Chen</u>. 2008 (2005). Night Shade, ISBN: 1597801070, 9781597801072, 375p.

Detective Inspector Chen is a Singapore cop and mystic whose expertise includes dealing with supernatural incursions. He performs his duties in an engaging and exotic futuristic China that interacts regularly with the celestial and infernal bureaucracies of Heaven and Hell, and features bodhisattvas, gods, devils, ghosts, and demons. In fact, the Underworld has its own police force; Chen's infernal counterpart, the demon Zhu Irzh, works with him to investigate why the ghost of a dead girl isn't in Heaven where she belongs. Williams's absorbing blend includes fantasy, science fiction, Chinese folklore, and a touch of Hong Kong cinema aesthetics to keep readers investigating along with her protagonists, so it's very fortunate that fans can continue to the series with *The Demon and the City*, *Precious Dragon*, *The Shadow Pavilion*, and *The Iron Khan*. Go read them all right now!

Zelazny, Roger

Creatures of Light and Darkness. 1970 (1969). Avon, ISBN: 0380011220, 9780380011223, 192p.

In a far-flung universe, Anubis and Osiris reign over the Houses of Death and Life. Anubis unknowingly resurrects an old power, a being who can travel the galaxies, bring down both gods, and restore order to the universe. Zelazny puts Clarke's Third Law to good use as he evokes a setting that blends the Egyptian mythos with advanced technology.

Chapter Four

Mood

When I work with patrons who are looking for new books to read, I sometimes ask them what kinds of books they're in the mood for. The desired novel may need to match the patron's frame of mind, like when one glowering young woman informed me that she didn't want to read anything "happy and sappy." Other patrons may desire to alter their current mood by reading a book, such as when they seek a scary read or a humorous novel. And some patrons want to recapture the feeling they experienced when they first discovered the genre many decades before. Peruse these emotionally oriented lists whenever you're in the mood for an interesting book.

Humor in a Vacuum: Universally Funny Fiction

Have you ever read a book and come across a passage so hilarious that you began laughing uncontrollably, such that everybody within earshot turned toward you with looks of confusion, concern, and apprehension? (Bonus points if you've done so in church.) These are the books SF readers turn to when they need a touch of mirth, and many of these stories will elicit chuckles, guffaws, and belly laughs from their readers. Some are absurdly over-the-top, others slyly humorous with sharp satirical jabs. If you're looking for comedy, you've come to the right place.

Adams, Douglas

⇒ *The Ultimate Hitchhiker's Guide to the Galaxy.* The Hitchhiker's Guide to the Galaxy. 2002. Del Rey, ISBN: 0345453743, 9780345453747, 815p.

Arthur Dent tours the universe with companions Ford Prefect (who thought automobiles were Earth's dominant life-form), fellow human Trillian, depressed android Marvin, and Zaphod Beeblebrox, the two-headed president of the Galaxy. On the way, readers will encounter the foul Vogons; discover the answer to life, the universe, and everything; learn the secret purpose of the Earth; decipher the final thoughts of a bowl of petunias; and read God's Final Message to His Creation. This groundbreaking and progressively mislabeled trilogy—the omnibus edition contains five novels (*The Hitchhiker's Guide to the Galaxy* [1979], *The Restaurant at the End of the Universe* [1980], *Life, the Universe, and Everything* [1982], *So Long, and Thanks for All the Fish* [1984], and *Mostly Harmless* [1992]) and a short story ("Young Zaphod Plays It Safe") —adds levity and joy to the SF genre. The series is required reading within the genre and perhaps the best choice for introducing readers to SF. Perusers will also discover entries from the eponymous guide sprinkled throughout the text that give colorful and helpful information, including the usefulness of Babel fish, the potency of a Pan-Galactic Gargle Blaster, and the great value and importance of knowing where your towel is.

Armstrong, John

Grey. 2007. Night Shade, ISBN: 1597800651, 9781597800655, 240p.

Michael and Nora, two young fashionistas in love with each other and their shared sense of style, live in a world of Darwinian corporate culture. When an attempted assassination ends their plans to marry, Michael eschews an alternate arranged pairing and his father's wishes and embarks on a Shakespearean scheme to reunite with Nora. Michael's encounter with his long-lost mother reveals the dark secret that underlies his colorful existence and forces him to choose between worlds. *Grey* is for fans that enjoy sharp, scathing cultural satire that targets our obsession with status and media.

Asprin, Robert

Phule's Company. Phule's Company. 1990. Berkley, ISBN: 044166251X, 9780441662517, 232p.

The novel begins with the court-martial of wealthy scion Captain Willard J. Phule. Phule's transfer to the Alliance's Space Legion comes with the dubious command of Omega Company, the worst dregs and losers the military has to offer. Phule uses his business sense to turn Omega into an elite fighting force and earns the enmity of Phule's nemesis, General Blitzkrieg. As Blitzkrieg sends Omega on increasingly difficult missions intended to wipe out the group, Asprin entertains with puns and the Company's improbable, almost ridiculous, successes. This long-running series reads like Monty Python meets *The Dirty Dozen* and continues with *Phule's Paradise* (1992), *A Phule and His Money* (1999), *Phule Me Twice* (2000), *No Phule Like an Old Phule* (2004), and *Phule's Errand* (2006); the latter four installments were cowritten with Peter J. Heck.

Frost, Toby

Space Captain Smith. Chronicles of Isambard Smith. 2008. Myrmidon, ISBN: 1905802137, 9781905802135, 320p.

The British Empire continues its questionable efforts to civilize and defend the known universe in the twenty-fifth century from the horrific insectoid Ghasts. Space Captain Isambard Smith represents the empire's finest example of inane heroism in his space-faring pseudo-Victorian/Edwardian society. With a rather mad crew consisting of an alien headhunter, an android former sex servant, and a hamster, he must retrieve Rhianna Mitchell and return her to the safety of the empire before either the Ghasts or the Edenite religious zealots can capture her. Frost's novel reads a bit like a wonderful SF version of George MacDonald Fraser's Flashman books and is followed by two more of Smith's adventures: *God Emperor of Didcot* and *Wrath of the Lemming Men*.

Mitchell, E.

The Amazing, Incredible, Shrinking, Colossal, Bikini-Crazed Creature from the Public Domain. 2009. Outskirts, ISBN: 1432703013, 9781432703011, 124p.

Mitchell's hilarious homage to 1950s sci-fi films is an excellent addition to the annals of humorous SF. Her deadpan verbal wordplay gives new life to mad scientists, mutants, monsters, creatures, and every strange subject of the old flicks.

Scalzi, John

The Android's Dream. 2007 (2006). Tor, ISBN: 0765348284, 9780765348289, 396p.

In the Common Confederation of sentient species, humanity is a minor player compared to many others, including the alien Nidu, who communicate by scent. When an Earth delegate kills his Nidu counterpart with gastric vulgarity, both governments begin to rattle sabers. The Nidu offer one chance at renewed peace: Earth must offer a sheep of the rare Android's Dream breed to be used in the aliens' upcoming ceremony. This demand heralds a mass extermination of the breed by parties opposed to the Nidu. Ex-soldier, hacker, and diplomat Harry Creek finds the last sample of Android's Dream DNA in the most unlikely place—the genetics of pet-store owner Robin Baker. As members of both militaries use excessive and potentially terminal force in their attempts to foil Harry's mission, Creek also contends with the knowledge that sheep used in the Nidu ceremony are typically sacrificed, something neither he nor Robin wants to happen. Scalzi amuses readers with both lowbrow humor and political satire and thrills fans with astounding action sequences.

Smith, Michael Marshall

Only Forward. 2000 (1994). Bantam/Spectra, ISBN: 0553579703, 9780553579703, 341p.

Stark is a detective in The City, where the quirky Neighborhoods each reflect a peculiar bent in their inhabitants' personalities. For example, in Colour, the surroundings change to coordinate with your outfit, and in the Action Centre, workaholics and overachievers intent on gaining status can do so nonstop. Stark must track down a kidnapped actioneer and rescue him from Stable, where the inhabitants think they're the last survivors of a terrible war. Their travels lead through Red, an outlaw demilitarized zone that would frighten most cyberpunk dystopias into hiding, and ultimately to a realm where you can confront your worst nightmare. Smith's novel reads like a bizarre travelogue of over-the-top SF tropes, but his absurd humor leads to some thoughtful introspection, a careful balance that earned the Philip K. Dick Award.

Willis, Connie

To Say Nothing of the Dog. 1998 (1997). Bantam, ISBN: 0553575384, 9780553575385, 493p.

The formidable Lady Schrapnell is obsessed with the restoration of Coventry Cathedral. To this end, she demands the aid of time-traveling historian Ned Henry, who must go back through the centuries and discover the whereabouts of the bishop's bird stump. Ned, suffering from time lag thanks to all the trips he endures, travels to the nineteenth century and discovers an alteration to the space–time continuum caused by fellow time traveler Verity Kindle. Will he correct the error before its effects permanently alter the future? And just where and what is the bishop's bird stump anyway?! Willis's witty send-up of Victorian fiction, particularly Jerome K. Jerome's *Three Men in a Boat*, will keep readers in stitches.

Zakour, John, and Lawrence Ganem

The Plutonium Blonde. <u>Zach Johnson</u>. 2001. Daw, ISBN: 0756400066, 9780756400064, 342p.

Zachary Johnson is Earth's best (and last) private eye. With gadgets aplenty and a smart-aleck computer built into his brain, there's no case Johnson can't crack. But when B. B. Starr hires him to find her homicidal android double, Johnson may need to plan early and pick out a burial plot. The double-crosses and plot twists are nearly as plentiful as the action and humor. Fans will find that it takes more than an android dame to put Johnson down, as the series is currently seven books and counting.

Marvin's Pick List: Books to Read When Happiness Is Overrated

Some books are powerful mood-lifters, the stories you read when you want uplifting, happy, humorous, and life-affirming endings. The books on this list are not that kind. These are the books that Douglas Adams's terminally depressed android Marvin keeps stored in his internal memory. These are the books you read when you need an antidote to giggling people in love, sunflowers, and greeting cards. If you put one of these novels next to a bottle of antidepressants, the pills may spontaneously combust. Yes, they're those kinds of books, because, let's face it, sometimes you want to have your pessimism confirmed and feel justified in your misanthropy. So, being the considerate fellow I am, I designed this list just for you. I know you'll enjoy them, sneering all the while you read.

Ballard, J. G.

The Drowned World. 2006 (1962). Harper Perennial, ISBN: 0007221835, 9780007221837, 175p.

The events in Ballard's haunting and dreamlike novel take place after solar radiation has caused the ice caps to melt and returned the world to a prehistoric ecology. Vivid dreams afflict several researchers exploring what was once London, and the team soon begins acting more primitively as their surroundings transform their consciousnesses. Whether readers see the transformations as adaptive assimilations or as reversions will affect their perceptions of the novel's end as revelatory or horrifying.

Bedford, K. A.

⇒ *Time Machines Repaired While-U-Wait.* 2008. Edge, ISBN: 1894063422, 9781894063425, 324p.

Aloysius "Spider" Web used to be a police investigator. Bitter over his dismissal and unsatisfied with his relationships, he repairs time travel devices for a living in a world where such jaunts are mundane. Webb discovers a woman's murdered corpse in a time machine, but the Department of Time and Space closes the investigation without explanation. Determined to know the truth of the matter, Webb uncovers a vast conspiracy that leads to the End of Time. Bedford packs a lot into this Aurealis Award–winning novel, including a murder mystery and a Big Doom to be dealt with, but ultimately his exploration of time travel leads to some carefully considered, if uncomfortable, revelations about reality and determinism.

Brunner, John

Stand on Zanzibar. 1999 (1968). Millennium, ISBN: 1857988361, 9781857988369, 650p.

In 2010, the overpopulated Earth is swarming with more than seven billion people. Humans turn decision making over to insane computers. Genetic engineering is commonplace, corporations run entire countries, and the government legislates eugenics; citizens feel overwhelmed by information and drown in media and advertising but use widely available drugs to cope. This novel almost makes the reader believe that Brunner could see the future, as his jagged plot weaves in, around, and through a series of jump-cuts that give nightmarish glimpses into every aspect of his future world. The author's premonitory vision earned him a Hugo, the British Science Fiction Award, and the Prix Apollo.

Harrison, Harry

Make Room! Make Room! 2008 (1966). Orb, ISBN: 0765318857, 9780765318855, 284p.

Detective Andy Rusch is an overworked New York policeman in a world on the brink of madness due to overpopulation, overcrowding, and starvation. The corrupt authorities, concerned about the murder of gangster "Big Mike," demand Rusch apprehend the killer. But in a city of thirty-five million people, Rusch's task seems all but impossible. A bleak sense of hopelessness pervades this novel, as Harrison demonstrates how diminishing resources and unchecked population growth lead to increased poverty, horrific dehumanization, and unbridled corruption. The author set his novel in the last months of 1999, adding millennial fears to the sense of panicked hopelessness, and believed that a then-inconceivable population of seven billion would be enough to drive home his point. In the twenty-first century, with a world population estimated uncomfortably close to the author's staggering figure, Harrison's cautionary tale seems uncomfortably prophetic. For an equally shocking experience, see the classic movie *Soylent Green*, based on *Make Room! Make Room!*

Pohl, Frederik

Jem. 2001 (1979). Gollancz, ISBN: 1857987896, 9781857987896, 300p.

Humanity, divided into three major power blocs, wages war against itself before turning its eyes to the heavens and discovering a habitable planet that can be remade into a utopia. Jem is home to three races that, despite their tensions, manage to live with one another in peace. Their peace ends when humans, in a race to found colonies on Jem, enlist the natives in their conflict and give them the means to kill each other. Pohl demonstrates incredible talent at world-building while simultaneously delivering effective social commentary on colonialism.

Silverberg, Robert

Dying Inside. 2009 (1972). Orb, ISBN: 0765322307, 9780765322302, 302p.

David Selig is a telepath, able to read minds and know the innermost secrets of everyone around him, but he is emotionally unable to cope with this knowledge. His difference defines him in his relationships with others and forces him to distance himself. Even when mentored by another telepath, Selig only finds small and petty uses for his ability. Even worse, as Selig gets older, the power that defines his identity fades, and although it brought him little joy, he fears its loss as most would fear the loss of their sight or hearing. Silverberg believably creates an unusual "other" with whom readers can identify.

Womack, Jack

Elvissey. <u>Ambient/Dryco</u>. 1997 (1993). Grove, ISBN: 0802134955, 9780802134950, 319p.

The frighteningly manipulative and powerful Dryco Corporation rules in an alternate future. Dryco is having difficulty with a religion that worships Elvis as a god. The company sends Isabel and her husband back in their timeline to bring Elvis to the future, so that Dryco can use him as a pawn in their schemes to control the problematic worshippers. Unfortunately, Elvis turns out to be a murdering psychotic and a reluctant messiah, and the assignment leads to bitter betrayal between the married Dryco operatives. Womack depicts a dark future, in which a single corporation can retask anything and anyone for its own benefit.

Going Boldly: Small Steps, Giant Leaps

Neil Armstrong's first words when he (and through him, humanity) took his first steps on the moon are among the most momentous in all of history. The moon landing heralded humanity's first steps into the greater universe, expanded our perspective, and opened the stars to our species. The following books serve to remind readers of the sense of wonder at the possibilities space offers, the perseverance to endure the necessary hardships and overcome any obstacle, the intelligence to deal with any dangers, and the joy inherent to exploring and discovering the universe and its mysteries. They also demonstrate that humanity has a stake to claim in the universe at large, although doing so may be fraught with difficulty.

Ellis, Warren, et al.

Orbiter. 2004 (2003). DC Comics, ISBN: 1401202683, 9781401202682, 99p.
GN

After the space shuttle *Venture* disappeared with all hands on board, a discouraged humanity turned its back on space. Ten years later, the *Venture* returns to Kennedy Space Center, now a slum and shantytown. Of the seven original crew members, only the pilot, John Cost, is aboard. Three NASA scientists investigating the shuttle find it changed beyond understanding: a skin-like coating covers the ship, and a theoretical energy source powers the engines. The scientists interview Cost and learn that humanity is not alone in the universe and that our neighbors are anxious to meet us. Ellis delivers an intriguing mystery with characters molded after science fiction's Golden Age and exhorts us to return to space.

MacLeod, Ken

Cosmonaut Keep. Engines of Light. 2001. Tor, ISBN: 076530032X, 9780765300324, 300p.

Two storylines interweave and mesh into a story about humanity's journey to the stars. In the near future, Matt Cairns and secret agent Jadey discover that they possess plans for an interstellar ship, even as global society destabilizes when aliens contact a communist European Union. Much later, in a universe where much older alien races keep humanity from spreading among the stars, Matt's descendent Gregor Cairns keeps the dream of human interstellar travel alive. The first of a trilogy, this novel was nominated for the Hugo Award.

Wells, H. G.

The First Men in the Moon. 2005 (1901). Penguin, ISBN: 0141441089, 9780141441089, 213p.

Professor Cavor creates a substance, modestly dubbed Cavorite, which ignores the pull of gravity. Businessman Bedford sees potential profit in the discovery and accompanies Cavor in a spherical ship to the moon. There the pair of humans marvel at the strange native flora, but nothing could have prepared them for the insect-like alien Selenites. The Selenites capture the pair and take them to their underground civilization, a hive society where the aliens are engineered to their social roles. Bedford manages to escape, but Cavor is left behind. The scientist later manages to open radio communications to Earth, but Cavor's signal is mysteriously silenced after he relates humanity's warlike nature to the aliens. Wells's fascinating adventure of humanity's first steps off the planet Earth is enlivened by a touch of social criticism.

Young, Larry, et al.

Astronauts in Trouble: Master Flight Plan. Astronauts in Trouble. 2003. AiT/Planet Lar, ISBN: 1932051163, 9781932051162, 288p. **GN**

This omnibus collects Young's acclaimed series Astronauts in Trouble and includes the graphic novels *Live from the Moon* (1999), *Space: 1959* (2000), and *One Shot, One Beer* (2000), as well as the short tale "Cool Ed's." All three stories contain a mad, marvelous dedication to reinvigorating imaginations and redirecting our eyes to the universe beyond our skies. In the first part, an eccentric billionaire cooks up a mad scheme to return to the moon and lay claim to it. The second story features an astronaut's sacrifice to keep his Cold War counterpart from taking over a secret space flight. The book finishes off with tales from the Moon's best (and only) bar, Cool Ed's, where pioneers and prospectors join to drink, boast, and swap stories.

Yukimura, Makoto

⇒ *Planetes*, **Book 1.** Planetes. Translated by Yuki Nakamura. 2003. TokyoPop, ISBN: 1591822629, 9781591822622, 235p. **GN**

Humanity's idealistic expansion to the stars requires a reality check as we bring our bad habits with us. Space debris, defunct satellites, and pieces of damaged vessels litter Earth's orbit and require highly skilled, low-paid laborers like Hachimaki, Fee, Yuri, and Tanabe to clean up the mess. Worse, radical ecoterrorists object to humanity's pollution of the stars and regularly attempt to disrupt and destroy any efforts at exploration and colonization. Yukimura delivers a stunning series that should make every SF fan's reading list with his combination of political complexity, solid science, and blue-collar protagonists, idealists, and heroes. This entry is for the first *manga* collection; the English translation spans five volumes.

Tomorrow Is Another Day!: Hope for the Future

With all of the hostile alien empires, controlling dystopias, depressing postnuclear outposts, and despoiled ecologies, readers may entirely lose faith in humanity's future. But just as a previous list offered more depressing fare, this section serves as an antidote to despondency and boosts readers' hopes for tomorrow. When times are tough and prospects appear bleak, sometimes hope is all you have. And sometimes that's enough.

Brin, David

The Postman. 1997 (1985). Bantam, ISBN: 0553278746, 9780553278743, 336p.

> After the end of the world, a drifter named Gordon Krantz stumbles upon the uniform and letter bag of a U.S. mail carrier. Passing himself off as an employee of a revived U.S. government, Krantz inadvertently inspires hope in those he encounters and becomes a symbol for all that was lost and all that might be regained. However, with survivalists ravaging the country, undermining and destroying every attempt at government save their own twisted authority, it remains to be seen if hope can survive. This novel was nominated for Hugo and Nebula Awards and won John W. Campbell and Locus Awards.

Haldeman, Joe

Forever Peace. Forever War. 1998 (1997). Ace, ISBN: 0441005667, 9780441005666, 351p.

> Julian Class is a scientist and part-time soldier. For a portion of each month, he fights ongoing wars from safety in a bunker while neurally linked to a remote-controlled fighting robot called a soldierboy. Conflict rages between First World nations that have nanotechnology and the abundance their cornucopia machines provide, and Third World nations who lack this breakthrough. Julian also works on an experiment that may recreate the Big Bang, a project with potentially devastating consequences. But an application of the neural technology that links soldiers in combat may point to a permanent end to violence. Haldeman's insight into the minds of the soldiers that fight our battles was so impressive that this novel won the Hugo, Nebula, and John W. Campbell Awards for science fiction—quite an achievement!

James, P. D.

The Children of Men. 1993 (1992). Knopf, ISBN: 0679418733, 9780679418733, 241p.

> The last human being was born in 1995. As the birth rate suddenly hits zero for unknown reasons, society begins to suffer from a bizarre duality of panic and apathy. Britain's government becomes increasingly oppressive, and

its people become shadows of themselves, their spirits crushed by the loss of any future for the human race. In a world where the final tomorrow can be measured by a human life span, the last men and women on Earth need a miracle to revive their hope. That very promise of hope in bleak times will appeal to many readers.

Longyear, Barry

⇒ *Enemy Mine*. Enemy Papers. 2004 (1979). IUniverse, ISBN: 0595309763, 9780595309764, 90p.

Willis Davidge is a warrior taught to hate and trained to fight humanity's enemy, the reptilian Dracs. Stranded on a hostile planet with Drac soldier Jeriba Shigan, the two must cooperate to survive, especially because Shigan is pregnant. Davidge's unexpected parenting duties force him to explore his own humanity. Longyear's novella, in which empathy and respect replace hate and war, received the Hugo and Nebula Awards and may resonate with readers looking for a short introduction to SF or a story that provides a more peaceful answer to conflict.

Miyazaki, Hayao

Nausicaä of the Valley of the Wind, **Vol. 1.** Nausicaä of the Valley of the Wind. Translated by David Lewis and Toren Smith. 2004. Viz, ISBN: 1591164087, 9781591164081, 130p. **GN**

Long after the Seven Days of Fire ravaged the world, humanity exists in a variety of kingdoms hemmed in by the toxic forest called the Sea of Corruption and its giant insects. The tiny kingdom of the Valley of the Wind is protected from the spores by the sea winds but bound by oath to aid the Kingdom of Torumekia when it goes to war against the Dorok Principalities. Humanity's failure to live in harmony with itself and the planet once destroyed the land. Now, the Torumekian emperor longs to reclaim the dreaded weapons of the past. Nausicaä, drafted into the Torumekian forces, must find a way to bring peace between the kingdoms and between humanity and the beasts of the Sea of Corruption, otherwise the Seven Days of Fire may return. Acclaimed director Hayao Miyazaki, also known for his anime films *Princess Mononoke*, *Spirited Away*, and *Howl's Moving Castle*, wrote and drew this magnificent, prescient, and ecologically conscious science fiction manga serial. If you're familiar with his other works, then be sure not to miss this beautifully rendered and carefully translated graphic novel reprint series.

In Space, Everyone Can Hear You Scream: Horror SF

A lot of horror is about violation, particularly violation of the body, the mind, and reality. The books on this list meld horror with science fiction rather than the supernatural. A truly alien being may see humanity as a source of sustenance or as a means to an end, or we may simply have something it wants. Alternately, aliens (and thus, the universe at large) may be entirely indifferent to humanity—we may simply be in their way, an anthill to topple over, perhaps the most disturbing possibility.

Iwaaki, Hitoshi

Parasyte, **Vol. 1.** Parasyte. Translated by Andrew Cunningham. 2007 (1990). Del Rey/Ballantine, ISBN: 0345496248, 9780345496249, 277p. **GN**

Alien spores drift to Earth and become shape-changing parasites that devour and infest their hosts' brains and take over their bodies. At least, that's how it's supposed to work. Unfortunately for one parasite, its prospective host, Shinichi Izumi, is wearing headphones at the time of infestation, and the alien becomes rooted in his hand instead. The parasites typically hunt and kill humans for food, but Migi (which translates as "Righty") and Shinichi develop a bizarre symbiotic relationship in which they alternately annoy and bond with one another, as when Migi reads all night to learn more about our planet while Shinichi sleeps. This unusual humor serves as a counterpoint to grisly and gory violent scenes, as other parasites go on killing sprees and Shinichi tries to stop them, all the while attempting to maintain the semblance of a normal life. While definitely meant for older teens and adults, *Parasyte*'s bizarre meld—one part *Odd Couple*, one part Peter Parker, and one part John Carpenter's *The Thing*—is truly unique.

Lovecraft, H. P.

At the Mountains of Madness: The Definitive Edition. Cthulhu Mythos. 2005 (1936). Modern Library, ISBN: 0812974417, 9780812974416, 186p.

Miskatonic University academic Professor William Dyer writes about his terrible journey to the South Pole as a warning to the world. An expedition to Antarctica finds the frozen remains of strange, ancient, unknown life-forms. When the expedition fails to check in, Dyer and his colleagues journey to the camp and discover a massive city of alien architecture. Deciphering the strange hieroglyphics in the city, they learn that the creatures they found were part of an ancient civilization whose slave race eventually overthrew their masters' society. A horrifying discovery leads to a harried flight back to the surface world, and Dyer hopes to dissuade any further investigation. Lovecraft applies his materialist worldview and converts the supernatural aspects of horror to rational ones without rendering them any less alien or terrifying. He also pays subtle homage to Edgar Allan Poe and his tale, "The Narrative of Arthur Gordon Pym." While typically classified a horror writer (and horror is indeed the emotion Lovecraft sought to evoke), Lovecraft translated these horrors into the language of science fiction. This volume also includes his excellent treatise on horror stories titled *Supernatural Horror in Literature* (1927).

Stross, Charles

⇒ *The Atrocity Archives*. Laundry. 2009 (2004). Ace, ISBN: 0441016685, 9780441016686, 345p.

When Turing discovered the mathematical theorem that breaches dimensions, he changed the world forever. Bob Howard is a computer specialist and secret agent in Her Majesty's Occult Service, also known as the Laundry, empowered to take care of occult disturbances. Sadly, the job isn't as glamorous as it sounds, with red tape aplenty and forms that must be signed with blood and in triplicate. And don't ever ask about their spell checkers. Stross's gleeful blend of otherworldly horrors with esoteric mathematics and espionage is a fitting twenty-first-century update of Lovecraftian concepts.

Thomas, Jeffrey

Punktown. Punktown. 2009 (2000). Cosmos, ISBN: 0843962062, 9780843962062, 288p.

In this collection of short stories, Thomas sets a dark stage for many subsequent novels and works. The planet Oasis hosts the colony city of Paxton, referred to by its citizens as Punktown, a grotesque patchwork metropolis constructed from graphic violence, noir, horror, and science fiction. Readers who explore its streets will discover a futuristic Pygmalion who works in cloned flesh, an artist trapped by her own performance, murderous aliens, and the terrible curse of perfect memory. Punktown is a place where both Rick Deckard and Jake Gittes (of the films *Blade Runner* and *Chinatown*, respectively) would feel terribly at home and where humans are as alien to one another as anything we might find among the stars. Punktown is a brilliant obsidian gem of a setting, but only for tourists who are neither faint of heart nor weak of stomach.

Wolfe, Gene

An Evil Guest. 2008. Tor, ISBN: 0765321335, 9780765321336, 304p.

A century from now, Gideon Chase, investigator and supposed wizard, gets a job from the government to track down a very dangerous man: Bill Reis.

Reis, a very wealthy man, spent some years on the alien world of Woldercan learning unusual powers and is not a man to be trifled with. Chase hires actress Cassie Casey to get close to Reis and obtain information, but as the novel progresses, both men come to love Casey, and she returns their affections. This dangerous love triangle among hunter, bait, and hunted becomes more horrific when Casey learns Reis's true nature. Wolfe blends noir style, a science fiction setting, and underlying horror to keep his readers guessing.

Future Perfect: Retrofuture Nostalgia with Yesterday's Worlds of Tomorrow

H. G. Wells, Edgar Rice Burroughs, and the early pulp magazines helped to shape the public's vision of science, the future, and life on other planets. These visions of mad scientists, beast men, deserts, and prehistoric jungles fascinated readers with their potential for adventure, and still do despite their inaccuracy and impossibility. This list of books demonstrates some authors' nostalgia for those early visions, a continuing fascination and admiration that shapes current fiction.

Edginton, Ian, et al.

Scarlet Traces. Scarlet Traces. 2002. Dark Horse, ISBN: 1569719403, 9781569719404, 88p. **GN**

In the aftermath of the Martians' invasion of Earth, Great Britain adapts the aliens' advanced technology and uses it for the betterment of its citizens and to assert dominance over the rest of the globe. When exsanguinated women begin washing up along the Thames, staining scarlet the reputation of the empire, a retired soldier and his aide investigate and discover a horrifying secret in the halls of power. Edginton and artist D'Israeli craft a pulpy steampunk (Marspunk?) addendum to a foundational SF novel, and fans of Alan Moore's *League of Extraordinary Gentlemen* will discover a tale that similarly satisfies their appetite. This graphic novel follows the creators' comic book adaptation of H. G. Wells's classic, *The War of the Worlds*, and precedes *Scarlet Traces: The Great Game*.

Mesta, Gabriel (a.k.a. Kevin J. Anderson)

The Martian War. 2006 (2005). Pocket, ISBN: 0743446550, 9780743446556, 256p.

H. G. Wells fights the War of the Worlds and opposes the alien invasion of Earth! He teams up with a certain Dr. Moreau and the brilliant scientist Griffin (also known as the Invisible Man), and even travels from the Earth to the Moon to liberate the native Selenites. Anderson effectively evokes both the era of the late 1800s and the tone of Wells's novels as he places the famous author among his own creations.

Moore, Alan, et al.

⇒ *The League of Extraordinary Gentlemen*, **Vol. 1.** The League of Extraordinary Gentlemen. 2000. America's Best Comics, ISBN: 1563898586, 9781563898587, 176p. 🆖

When Great Britain faces threats too dire and bizarre for conventional forces, the empire calls upon the League of Extraordinary Gentlemen. Campion Bond, on behalf of the mysterious M, recruits leader Mina Murray (formerly Mina Harker of Bram Stoker's *Dracula*) and her team of uncanny operatives: Captain Nemo (of Jules Verne's *Twenty Thousand Leagues Under the Sea*), Henry Jekyll (and his infamous, savage alter ego, Edward Hyde), Hawley Griffin (*The Invisible Man*), and H. Rider Haggard's fictional legendary adventurer, Alan Quartermain. The group must investigate and foil the fiendish plot of Asian criminal mastermind Dr. Fu Manchu before he can destroy all of London. This pulpy hybrid of nineteenth-century fiction and comic book superhero team astounds and amazes with its literary allusions, sharp wit, clever use of source material, and outrageous exploits.

Roberson, Chris

Paragaea: A Planetary Romance. 2006. Pyr, ISBN: 1591024447, 9781591024446, 399p.

Soviet cosmonaut Akilina "Leena" Chirikova launches into space, only to have her rocket fall through a mysterious portal to another world. Leena crash-lands and soon meets swashbuckling swordsman Hieronymus Bonaventure and Balam, prince of the jaguar men. The trio scour the planet looking for information that might lead to a return portal for Leena and meet with a host of human-animal hybrid races (some more friendly than others) and an android named Benu, who leads them to the technology they seek and informs them of the strange world's origins. Roberson blends a bit of Edgar Rice Burroughs with Flash Gordon to create a planetary romance that will charm and excite readers nostalgic for exotic worlds and magnificent adventure.

Stirling, S. M.

The Sky People. 2006. Tor, ISBN: 0765314886, 9780765314888, 301p.

When space probes reveal that Venus is teeming with life, the United States and U.S.S.R. scramble to explore and colonize the solar system's second planet. Venus is teaming with prehistoric jungles, dinosaurs, and Neanderthals—in fact, its life-forms seem suspiciously too similar to Earth's.

In a clear homage to Edgar Rice Burroughs and the SF pulps of yesteryear, Stirling writes a cracking adventure story and reveals a mystery surrounding the planet next door.

Under Pressure!: Race against Time

The pressure to perform can put incredible stress on a person. Many people have experienced the need to write a book, make a sale, or complete a project in a short amount of time. But imagine the strain when the fates of entire industries, societies, races, even worlds rests upon your shoulders. Then add a deadline. Who could stand up under the burden of others' hopes and fears in the face of impending doom? Science fiction authors seem to take a wicked delight in putting their protagonists through just these kinds of paces. The next time you're feeling stressed out, put yourself in these characters' shoes and breathe a sigh of relief.

Edelman, David Louis

Infoquake. Jump 225. 2008 (2006). Solaris, ISBN: 1844165825, 9781844165827, 540p.

> The science of bio/logics permits nanotechnological modification to the human body and mind. Natch is the king of bio/logics, so it's no surprise when Margaret Surina approaches him with an offer to work with what promises to be the next technological revolution: MultiReal. Of course there's a catch: Natch and his team must develop, market, and prepare MultiReal for widespread release in a matter of days. Edelman exuberantly relates a tale of intrigue, corporate warfare, and extreme job stress in the far future.

Kenyon, Kay

A World Too Near. The Entire and the Rose. 2008. Pyr, ISBN: 1591026423, 9781591026426, 425p.

> Having warned Earth of the threat posed by the Tarig, Titus Quinn returns to the Entire to find his wife and daughter and to prevent the alien overlords from using our universe to fuel their own. However, conniving scientist Helice Maki joins Quinn in his journey with designs of her own on the Entire, and the corporation sending Quinn back to this new universe has supplied Quinn with a doomsday weapon. Kenyon manages to increase the tension and urgency in the second volume of The Entire and the Rose while maintaining the sense of wonder inherent in her exotic, beautiful setting.

MacKay, Scott

⇒ *Omega Sol.* 2008. Roc, ISBN: 0451462033, 9780451462039, 357p.

An alien artifact suddenly appears in the vicinity of Earth's moon and begins siphoning hydrogen from our sun, accelerating its aging process and endangering the Earth. Dr. Cameron Conrad is convinced that the unknown race, which he dubs the Builders, isn't any more aware of humanity than we might be of an insect mound. Conrad desperately tries to make contact with the Builders, convinced that if he does so they will cease their project. The military, however, considers a more direct and possibly disastrous response. MacKay's frantic first-contact situation will keep readers on the edge of their seats.

Mitchell, Syne

The Last Mortal Man. Deathless. 2006. Roc, ISBN: 0451460944, 9780451460943, 435p.

Lucius Sterling controls the key to immortality. His corporate-owned nanotechnology frees humanity from death and disease, literally grows cities, and makes him wealthy beyond imagining. Unfortunately, his own descendent, Jack, is allergic to the very nanotechnology that grants society's boons. When a mysterious counter-technology appears that disassembles anything and anyone affected by Sterling's nanotech, Lucius calls Jack out of retreat and beseeches him to investigate and end the threat. Syne's novel combines a tense plot with a convincing depiction of a world where the science of immortality defines the haves and have-nots and raises interesting questions about class and capitalism.

Stross, Charles

Iron Sunrise. 2004. Ace, ISBN: 0441011594, 9780441011599, 368p.

When a weapon destroys a sun and the colony world Moscow, the automatic defense system deploys against the perpetrators, New Dresden. Agent Rachel Mansour discovers a possible conspiracy against New Dresden and must convince the surviving Muscovite leaders to call off their retaliation. An unknown assailant assassinating Moscow's surviving ambassadors adds an unfortunate complication to Mansour's efforts toward détente. A thrilling piece of SF espionage, this worthy sequel to *Singularity Sky* received a Hugo nomination.

Sullivan, Tricia

Dreaming in Smoke. 1998. Bantam, ISBN: 0553577034, 9780553577037, 401p.

When colonists arrive at the world T'Nane, they find the planet's environment hostile and inimical to human life and extremely difficult to terraform. They live aboard their ship, run by the artificial intelligence Ganesh, and try to resolve their dilemma. Kalypso Deed acts as an intermediary between human scientists and Ganesh, who helps the researchers process information. When one of the scientists goes insane, Ganesh begins to fail, endangering the entire colony. As Kalypso strives to comprehend the situation, a life-form previously unrecognized by the humans makes its presence known. Sullivan won the Arthur C. Clarke Award for her novel of catastrophe and common understanding.

Willett, Edward

Terra Insegura. 2009. DAW, ISBN: 075640553X, 9780756405533, 391p.

Marseguro's water dwellers successfully defended themselves against the crusaders that Earth's theocratic government sent to eliminate the genetically "impure." But Earth's spy, infected with a genetic plague, is returning home. Marseguro's denizens feel morally obligated to pursue the spy with a vaccine, but will they reach Earth in time, and will Earth accept their help? Willett's sequel to *Marseguro* depicts a risky mission of mercy and a race against time.

Reality Is Merely an Illusion: Pulling the Rug Out from under the Reader

When Einstein opened up our scientific view of the universe, he revealed underpinnings that appeared mind-bending and strange when compared to the clockwork Newtonian view of the world. Humanity's perceptions of the universe were suddenly subjects of debate and suspicion. As science continues to expand our view of reality, it's only natural that some science fiction authors extrapolate from theories about the uncertainty principle, quantum physics, and the holographic principle and start to monkey about with reality itself. Then again, it's always possible that reality might be perfectly serviceable, but the characters' perceptions may be askew. The novels on this list are a tad unusual (in the same way that Sasquatch is a tad hairy) and give reviewers reasons to use words such as "surreal," "twisted," and "bizarre." One thing's for sure: you know you're in trouble when you can't tell which is more unreliable, a story's narrator or its universe.

Aldiss, Brian W.

HARM. 2007. Del Rey/Ballantine, ISBN: 034549671X, 9780345496713, 225p.

Britain's Hostile Activities Research Ministry pursues the war on terror with ruthless efficiency and arrests author Paul Fadhil Abbas Ali for writing a passage in which two characters converse about killing the prime minister. Paul's captors imprison and torture him mercilessly long after they realize he poses no threat. Overwhelmed by torment, Paul soon comes to identify himself with Fremant, a guard to dictator Astaroth on the planet Stygia, where humans who have forgotten their past eradicate the native life-forms and establish a new regime. Aldiss's controversial novel requires us to acknowledge the injustices perpetrated in the name of a war on terror, and readers may prefer the brutal conditions on Stygia to our own reality.

Burroughs, William S.

Naked Lunch: The Restored Text. 2001 (1959). Grove, ISBN: 0802140181, 9780802140180, 289p.

Bill Lee is on the run from the law. He enters the Interzone, a surreal, nightmarish parallel of Tangiers with its own bizarre political parties, religions, and addictive substances, including the secretions of a species known as mugwumps and the much sought-after Black Meat of the giant aquatic centipede. Because of its content, Burroughs's brilliant, satirical novel was the focus of a landmark trial on obscenity and censorship in the United States. Although controversial, the book indicts the medical, political, and religious institutions of society in its nonlinear "plot" and fun-house mirror settings.

Chapman, Stepan

The Troika. 1997. Ministry of Whimsey, ISBN: 1890464023, 9781890464028, 251p.

Three people, Alex, Eva, and Naomi, trudge for centuries across an endless desert under the light of three suns. Nothing is reliable, not even the characters' own bodies. Bizarre sandstorms transform one protagonist into a vehicle, another into a dinosaur, and a third into . . . well, best to discover that for yourself. But don't worry—this is a very therapeutic process. Their therapist Dr. Mazer says so. It will come as no surprise to learn that Chapman won the Philip K. Dick Award for this novel, because the word "surreal" seems inadequate to describe this book. Although *Troika* is neither an easy nor a fast read, it is a rewarding one, particularly for readers who enjoy the works of Philip K. Dick, William S. Burroughs, and Franz Kafka, so stick with it.

Dick, Philip K.

Flow My Tears, The Policeman Said. 1993 (1974). Vintage, ISBN: 067974066X, 9780679740667, 231p.

Jason Taverner, star of music and television, wakes up one morning to discover that nobody recognizes him. Worse, all record of his existence is gone. Fortunately for Jason, he is also a Six, genetically engineered for intelligence and charisma. Unfortunately, he's trapped in the totalitarian police state called America. Dick's surreal novels, with their atmosphere of conspiracy, paranoia, and displacement, appeal to the reader's disturbing sense of disquiet, the vague, thrilling, vicarious fear that something is very much not right with the world. This particular work earned a John W. Campbell Award, as well as nominations for the Hugo and Nebula Awards.

Ellis, Warren, et al.

Aetheric Mechanics. 2008. Avatar, ISBN: 1592910483, 9781592910489, 44p.

GN

In 1907, Britain continues its war with Ruritania. Britain's advanced technology, including interplanetary battleships and a Mars colony, defends its citizens against unusual enemy planes and immense steampunk mechs. Doctor Richard Watcham returns from the front lines and calls upon his good friend, the detective Sax Raker. Haunted by memories of violence, Watcham is happy to lose himself in Raker's latest endeavor, a case involving scientists kidnapped and murdered by a man who flickers in and out of reality. This short graphic novel incorporates alternate history, quantum mechanics, and an homage to Arthur Conan Doyle's famous sleuth in a small, entertaining package.

Grimwood, Jon Courtenay

End of the World Blues. 2007 (2006). Bantam Spectra, ISBN: 0553589962, 9780553589962, 348p.

Kit Nouveau, a bar owner with connections in near-future Tokyo, has a troubled past and unpleasant connections to Japanese and UK crime families. Kit meets Nijie, a young woman with $15 million in tow, when she saves Kit from a very unpleasant death. But Nijie is also Lady Neku, a far-future princess from a powerful clan orbiting the Earth with her own story to tell. Or is she? Grimwood's tale alternates between crime noir and science fictional world-building. The book's adrenaline rush, complemented by the faint echo of life at the end of the world, earned an Arthur C. Clarke Award nomination.

Hall, Steven

The Raw Shark Texts. 2007. Canongate, ISBN: 1847671748, 9781847671745, 448p.

Eric Sanderson has lost his memory, and is quickly running out of time. A bizarre conceptual entity, a Ludovician shark, is periodically attacking Eric and devouring his memories. Fortunately, Eric sent letters to himself as guides to help aid his comprehension. As Eric learns more about his past, he becomes determined to confront his enemy, but how do you hunt a purely conceptual beast? Hall's original and humorous novel is also playful. Like Mark Z.

Danielewski's *House of Leaves*, *The Raw Shark Texts* sometimes formats text into pictures on the page. The novel also exists as a concept outside the printed product, as various un-chapters can be found in different editions of the book, on the Internet, and in the real world. Happy hunting!

Lethem, Jonathan

Amnesia Moon. 2005 (1995). Harcourt, ISBN: 015603154X, 9780156031547, 247p.

Chaos lives in post-apocalyptic Wyoming, a wasteland complete with mutants and a tyrant-preacher named Kellogg. Except the bombs never fell. Not really, anyway. It turns out that reality is broken, and certain people called dreamers can alter it. Chaos, a.k.a. Everett, undertakes a journey to find out just what went wrong and encounters new derangements in each city he comes across, from mysterious green fogs to alien invasions. Lethem's fractured United States offers social commentary and an absorbing odyssey of weirdness for those who see the absurd fractures in our own world.

Priest, Christopher

The Extremes. 2000 (1998). Warner, ISBN: 0446676454, 9780446676458, 393p.

After a mass murderer goes on a spree in Kingwood, Texas, and kills her husband, FBI agent Teresa Simons travels home to England to come to terms with her loss. She learns that on the same day as the Kingwood massacre, a parallel incident occurred in the English town of Bulverton. Teresa is familiar with the virtual reality technology of Extreme Experience (ExEx) from her FBI training and is alarmed to discover that a virtual experience of the Bulverton massacre is available for entertainment purposes. As she uses ExEx to better understand the Bulverton incident, she notices too many similarities between the two crimes, and a rather disturbing connection between virtual and actual realities. Priest writes a thriller that turns the readers' perceptions of the world on its head.

Roberts, Adam

⇒ *Yellow Blue Tibia.* 2009. Gollancz, ISBN: 0575083573, 9780575083578, 326p.

After Hitler's defeat and the fall of Germany, Stalin seeks to unify the country with fear of an external enemy. Believing the United States to be too weak to represent a lasting threat, Stalin assigns science fiction writers to design a believable scenario to terrify the world, a threat of alien invasion. Just as the project gains momentum, Moscow inexplicably orders the writers to cease their work. But decades later, one of the writers realizes that the events of their story are actually happening.

Thomas, Scarlett

The End of Mr. Y. 2007 (2006). Canongate, ISBN: 1847671179, 9781847671172, 452p.

Thomas launches on a melding of metaphysics, quantum physics, pop culture, and literary theory in this engaging story. PhD student Ariel Manto discovers a rare book written by her research subject, Thomas Lumas. It tells the reader how to access the Troposphere, a dimension where one can enter the minds of others. Unfortunately for Ariel, she's not alone in her discovery, and the other Troponauts don't like to share.

Von Schlegell, Mark

Venusia. System. 2005. Semiotext(e), ISBN: 1584350261, 9781584350262, 244p.

Roger Collectibles lives in a totalitarian colony on Venus. The government requires that its citizens consume flowers that eliminate thoughts about the past and the future, and then manipulates their perceptions and memories. When Roger acquires a very rare book about the founding of the colony, he stops taking the flowers, and reality begins to unravel around him. Von Schlegell touches on issues of control, rebellion, and freedom, as his characters perceive more than the government-sanctioned consensus.

Revenge Is a Dish Best Served in Space: Tales of Future Vengeance

For better or worse, a desire for vengeance is extremely motivating. Whether the hatred burns red hot or leaves an ice cold void, it cannot be ignored. A great wrong, a betrayal, a murder: all leave emotional wounds that some characters can only heal with a fatal response. Regardless of whether the protagonists conceive of their revenge as well-deserved justice or simply acknowledge their rage, the overwhelming obsession ensures a visceral, powerful story that we can enjoy vicariously. (It's true! Aristotle says so!) For the budding avenger within each of you, I present the following list of lethal grudges.

Banks, Iain M.

Matter. Culture. 2008. Orbit, ISBN: 0316005363, 9780316005364, 593p.

The Shellworld of Sursamen consists of artificial planets nested one within another. On one of these more primitive worlds, trusted aide Loesp murders his ruler, King Hausk. Ferbin, Hausk's elder son, heads outward into the larger universe seeking aid in avenging his father. His sister, Djan, left their world long ago and joined the Culture. Now, as a posthuman Special Circumstances (i.e., black ops) agent, she joins her brother and discovers a plot by her species' mentors and a deeper, more sinister danger to her homeworld. Banks's modern space opera contains some of the most eye-popping future imagery available in science fiction, yet manages to elicit the maximum impact from macro- and micro-scale scenes, where one character's actions can have galactic repercussions.

Bester, Alfred

The Stars My Destination (a.k.a. *Tiger! Tiger!*). 1996 (1956). Vintage, ISBN: 0679767800, 9780679767800, 258p.

Gulliver "Gully" Foyle is a brutish, forgettable individual. He is also the only survivor of a terrible accident aboard his spacecraft. When the *Vorga* cruises nearby, Gully's relief is matched only by his hatred as the other ship passes him by. His fury gives him purpose, however, and motivates his survival during months in the lonely emptiness of space. Gully intends to find each and every member of the *Vorga*'s crew and exact a terrible vengeance. One of the best-known science fiction novels of all time, *The Stars My Destination* charts the path of a man from brute to monster to something akin to a messiah.

Moore, Alan, et al.

V for Vendetta. 2005 (1989). DC Comics, ISBN: 140120841X, 9781401208417, 288p. **GN**

After a limited nuclear exchange, a terrified English populace allows a radical fascist party to take power. The racist, homophobic regime inters and executes "undesirables"—minorities and gays. Citizens live meek, miserable existences, terrorized by their own government. In this volatile, poisonous environment, a person known only as V works to free his country from the grip of tyranny. Wearing a Guy Fawkes mask and acting as vigilante, freedom fighter, and terrorist, V takes vengeance on the people responsible for his suffering and executes a cunning and multifaceted plot to return power to the people. This morally complex and intricately plotted graphic novel poses difficult questions even as it entertains and is the source material for the 2006 film of the same name.

Piper, H. Beam

Space Viking. Terro-Human Future History. 2007 (1963). Wildside, ISBN: 1434400565, 9781434400567, 173p.

Chaos enters Lucas Trask's life when a rival murders Lucas's wife-to-be on his wedding day. Trask takes his spacecraft, *Nemesis*, and funds a space

Viking raiding party as he pursues the murderer. The fall of the intergalactic federation removed law and order from the spaceways and left many worlds open to plunder. But as Trask continues his raids, he realizes how little effort it requires to improve the lots of these worlds and begins efforts toward reestablishing trade. Although fewer readers today know H. Beam Piper's name, he was once hailed as one of the bright stars of science fiction. *Space Viking* is one of his classic stories, with a hero motivated by revenge who changes over the course of the story into a man who might build empires rather than pillage planets.

Reynolds, Alastair

Chasm City. Revelation Space. 2003 (2001). Ace, ISBN: 0441010644, 9780441010646, 694p.

Tanner Mirabel, while acting as a bodyguard for arms dealer Cahuella, fails in his duty. He pursues the assassin, Argent Reivich, to Chasm City and the Yellowstone colony. The bad news is that a nanotech virus corrupts and mutates the inhabitants. The worse news is that Tanner is experiencing memories that aren't his. As in *Revelation Space*, Reynolds nests stories within stories and plots within plots, and wraps them in the enigma and wonder of his incredible setting that showcases a host of well-considered, slowly unveiled big ideas—there's a reason the series is titled Revelation Space, after all!

Schroeder, Karl

Sun of Suns. Virga. 2007. Tor, ISBN: 0765354535, 9780765354532, 331p.

Virga is a giant balloon, a fullerene sphere drifting in space and populated with artificial suns, giant floating lakes, and towns that spin to create a semblance of gravity. Young Griffin Hayden lost his family when their attempt to create an artificial sun for their nation, Aerie, led to an attack from their conquerors, the more powerful floating nation of Slipstream. Griffin intends to assassinate the Slipstream admiral Chaison Channing, believing him responsible for the death of his parents, and infiltrates the retinue of Channing's wife, Venera. Soon enough, Griffin finds himself part of the Channings' expedition to the heart of Virga and the treasure hidden there. Schroeder fills his novel with exotic locales, memorable personalities, pirates and naval battles, and rollicking exploits, making Virga a perfect place to explore.

Vance, Jack

The Demon Princes

Vol. 1. 1997. Tor/Orb/Tom Doherty, ISBN: 0312853025, 9780312853020, 397p.

Vol. 2. 1997. Tor, ISBN: 0312853165, 9780312853167, 397p.

Five criminals, known as the Demon Princes, lead a raid on a peaceful colony, ever after known as the Mount Pleasant Massacre. Only two people escape the horrific slaughter: young Kirth Gersen and his grandfather. After a lifetime of training, Gersen sets out to avenge his home and family and kill the Demon Princes. This classic tale of revenge is augmented by Vance's linguistic playfulness and the unforgettably mad and megalomaniac antagonists. The first volume contains the novels *The Star King* (1964), *The Killing Machine* (1964), and *The Palace of Love* (1967); the second volume consists of the final two novels *The Face* (1979) and *The Book of Dreams* (1981).

Weber, David

⇒ *In Fury Born.* 2006. Baen, ISBN: 1416520546, 9781416520542, 846p.

Former commando Alicia DeVries comes out of retirement when a band of space pirates murders her family and razes her home planet. Because the empire seems unable to stop the pirates, she takes matters into her own hands and steals a ship with its own artificial intelligence. Now she has both the empire and the pirates gunning for her, but hell hath no fury like a woman hell-bent on revenge. This expansion of an earlier Weber novel, *Path of the Fury*, will appeal to fans of Weber's <u>Honor Harrington</u> series and readers who like strong female protagonists.

Star-Crossed Lovers: Romantic SF

If sales figures are anything to go by, romance is by far the most popular genre of fiction around. Recently, there's been a surge of crossover fiction coupling romance with fantasy, horror, dark fantasy, and, yes, even science fiction. It's win-win, really: the addition of SF tropes allows for an increasing variety of stories, whereas the greater inclusion of love and romance gives these crossover novels wide appeal. Besides, love and desire allow for all sorts of insanity in SF. In a sitcom, these would usually be embarrassing moments of touching hilarity. In science fiction, "insanity" usually entails breaking the object of your affection out of prison, threading a starship through an asteroid field, or fighting against a galactic empire. Add the tantalizing possibility of torrid passion to the wide panoramic universes and wild action, and you've got yourself a fantastic combination.

Aguirre, Ann

Grimspace. <u>Sirantha Jax</u>. 2008. Berkley, ISBN: 0441015999, 9780441015993, 312p.

> Sirantha Jax is a jumper, a person with the rare genetic ability to navigate a ship through grimspace. She's also the only survivor of a shipwreck. The Corp wants to know what happened, won't accept Jax's claim of amnesia, and is willing to torture her to find out. A telepath named March frees her from imprisonment, but there's a catch—she has to be his new jumper. The successful pairing of pilot and jumper requires a powerful bond that Jax may not be ready for, but with the Corp hot on their trail, she has little choice. Aguirre's work of romance, rebellion, and renewal treats readers to a thrilling ride.

Asaro, Catherine

The Quantum Rose. <u>Skolian Empire</u>. 2002 (2000). Tor, ISBN: 0812568834, 9780812568837, 419p.

> Kamoj Quanta Argali feels trapped in a situation forced upon her by political necessity as the betrothed to cruel Jax Ironbridge. However, handsome and virtuous Havyrl Lionstar outbids Ironbridge. As Kamoj and Havyrl begin to discover their feelings for one another, Lionstar's presence involves local politics with imperial matters as his identity as a scion of the Skolian Empire comes to light. He and Kamoj must navigate dangerous waters as her planet is exposed to a larger universe, even as Ironbridge seeks to reclaim Kamoj by every means at his disposal. Asaro skillfully blends space opera and romance, even as she offers some biting critique of gender roles and relationships. She prevailed over strong competition to win the Nebula Award.

Grant, Susan

Moonstruck. <u>Borderlands</u>. 2008. HQN, ISBN: 0373772599, 9780373772599, 378p.

> With the war between the Coalition and barbaric Drakken Horde ended, Admiral Brit Bandar finds herself promoted to pilot of the starship *Unity*. To her dismay, it is a symbol of peace cemented by the inclusion of Drakken crew, and her second-in-command is none other than her nemesis, the warleader and pirate Finn Rorkken. His resemblance to her dead husband shocks her, but not as much as her growing desire for him, and as his strength and intelligence complements her own, their partnership becomes far more than professional. But if hostilities renew between the factions, how will Rorkken respond? Grant's space opera romance earned a Rita Award nomination and is an excellent genre bridge.

Lee, Tanith

⇒ *The Silver Metal Lover*. <u>Silver</u>. 1999 (1981). Bantam, ISBN: 0553581279, 9780553581270, 291p.

Young, wealthy Jane lives in a world where pills mold people and lifelike robots act as artists, companions, and sexual partners. Jane falls deeply in love with an android minstrel, Silver, and runs away with him before his creators, Electronic Metals, can disassemble him. As Silver and Jane interact, Lee's lush prose masterfully evokes an atmosphere of first love and ensnares readers through her characters' transformations, as Jane comes to know herself and Silver slowly evolves in emotional sophistication and learns to love beyond his initial programming. Lee frames the tale in the form of Jane's journal, a record of every moment of her time with Silver from her initial infatuation to the tragic end of their romance.

Mancusi, Marianne

Razor Girl. 2008. Dorchester, ISBN: 0505527804, 9780505527806, 308p.

Molly Anderson lived in a sealed bunker built by her father as the world fell to a ghastly plague that either killed its victims or mutated them into zombies. Anderson, now gifted with nanotechnologically enhanced strength, speed, senses, and razor-sharp claws, intends to meet up with her father in Florida. On the way, she encounters her former flame, Chase Griffin. Chase had to grow up in the nightmare world of the virus and leads a band of survivors in a dangerous day-to-day existence. Molly and Chase must reconcile their feelings for one another even as they slay zombies and make their way to the Magic Kingdom. Mancusi's romantic SF novel incorporates fannish homage to William Gibson's original razor girl, Molly Millions, and a liberal dash of Richard Matheson and George Romero to produce a fast-paced, action-packed mash-up that will entertain her madly grinning readers until the last page is turned.

Palmer, Diana

The Morcai Battalion. <u>Morcai Battalion</u>. 2007. Luna, ISBN: 0373802897, 9780373802890, 314p.

Terramer was a trial colony with settlers from over a hundred worlds. The Rojok warriors reduced that symbol of peace to rubble with an unprovoked attack. Captured Captain Holt Stern aims to escape his enemy and forms an alliance around him—his Morcai Battalion—to take the war to the Rojok and reclaim peace for the embattled worlds. Although he hoped for victory, he may be surprised to find love as well. Although this book was originally published in 1980 under the nom de plume of Susan S. Kyle, popular romance author Palmer revised and updated the text.

Shinn, Sharon

Heart of Gold. 2000. Ace, ISBN: 0441008216, 9780441008216, 341p.

The matriarchal indigo and patriarchal gulden societies live in uneasy proximity. Although nascent reforms relaxed social restrictions and prejudices, recent violence escalates tensions. When Nolan, an indigo male with a penchant for medicine, discovers a horrifying facet to the war, he and the indigo high-caste woman Kitrini strive to avert disaster and the consequences of racial hatred. Shinn brings a touch of forbidden love and genuine hope to a world plagued by terrorism and apartheid.

Sinclair, Linnea

Gabriel's Ghost. <u>Dock Five</u>. 2005 (2002). Bantam, ISBN: 0553587978, 9780553587975, 447p.

Chasidah "Chaz" Bergren was a respected pilot, but an unjust court-martial landed her in prison. Imagine her surprise when Gabriel Sullivan, supposedly dead rogue, smuggler, and mercenary, offers Chaz a job. Somebody is illegally breeding jukors, vicious winged killing machines, and Sullivan needs Chaz's skill and expertise to track down the culprit. As they investigate, the danger they face and desire they share make for a heady read. Sinclair's novel, a Rita Award winner, is an excellent crossover point for fans of either the SF or romance genres.

Trust No One: Paranoia and Conspiracy SF

The *X-Files* told us that "The Truth Is Out There" and to "Trust No One." The following authors apparently took this advice to heart. (Some of them did so before the *X-Files* ever aired. Coincidence? Or diabolical conspiracy? You decide!) The books on this list feature a fantastic lineup of alphabet-salad agencies, aliens, bizarre technology, distraction, deception, mind control, conspiracies, and secret plots to rule humanity. Find the secret codes hidden in these novels, and you may decipher the truth behind the lies. Or you may end up sounding like a complete nutter. It could all be nonsense, but do you *really* want to take that chance?

Barnes, John

⇒ *Gaudeamus.* 2004. Tor, ISBN: 0765303299, 9780765303295, 320p.

The author's friend, a private investigator named Travis Bismarck, pays him several visits, each time elaborating on his current case and supplying more bizarre and unbelievable details. The author dutifully communicates stories of teleportation, time travel, and telepathy drugs, and their connection to an Internet cartoon, all with a straight face. Barnes spins a yarn that reads like the *X-Files* by way of your best friend's tall tale.

MacLeod, Ken

The Execution Channel. 2008 (2007). Tor, ISBN: 0765320673, 9780765320674, 285p.

Al Gore won the election in 2000, but 9/11 continued on schedule. The nations compete in an escalating disinformation war. The world's increasing fear, paranoia, and hatred is perfectly captured in broadcasts by the pirate station The Execution Channel, footage that displays people's executions by various governments worldwide. James Travis, horrified by the increasing repression of his country, spies on the United Kingdom for France. His daughter, Roisin, is a peace activist who saw something she shouldn't have. The authorities are closing in, as they think the two are involved in the recent explosion on an RAF military base. And behind everything is a secret that could change the balance of power permanently. Fans of techno-thrillers and spy fiction will stay up all night to finish this novel.

Osborn, Stephanie

Burnout: The Mystery of Space Shuttle STS-281. 2009. Twilight Times, ISBN: 1606192000, 9781606192009, 328p.

When a space shuttle suffers burnout upon reentry, two investigators, "Crash" Murphy and Mike Anders, discover several discrepancies between the facts and the official cover story. Soon, people important to both men begin disappearing or dying under mysterious circumstances, and the two end up on the run as a conspiracy closes in around them. As they pursue the truth at the end of this trail of deception and secrecy, they discover that the answer to their queries lies at the center of Area 51. Osborn, an accomplished scientist and former NASA employee, writes a tense, thrilling SF tale that readers won't want to put down until they've finished the last page.

Shea, Robert, and Robert Anton Wilson

<u>The Illuminatus Trilogy.</u> 1984 (1975). Dell, ISBN: 0440539811, 9780440539810, 805p.

Saul Goodman is a cop investigating an office bombing. He comes across a sheaf of memos and begins pursuing their contents for leads. Over time, he realizes that the papers point to a massive conspiracy in complete control of humanity: the Illuminati! The Discordian Society, promoters of chaos, change, and freedom of thought, are the only serious opposition to the diabolical world masters. The Discordian leader, Hagbard Celine, educates Saul, guides him to the truth, and teaches him to see the Fnords. This mammoth tome, comprising the ultimate conspiracy story, consists of the books *The Eye in the Pyramid*, *The Golden Apple*, and *Leviathan*; it won the Promethean Hall of Fame Award.

Strieber, Whitley

The Grays. 2006. Tor, ISBN: 0765313898, 9780765313898, 335p.

We've all heard conspiracy theories about Roswell, Area 51, UFOs, government cover-ups, and the alien Grays, but what if they were true? What if aliens mingled their DNA with humans, perhaps to create a very special child? And whose plans for this child would be more terrifying, the Grays' or the government's? Strieber takes themes from his famous book *Communion*, in which he relates his own experiences with aliens, and infuses this novel of conspiracy and possible salvation with that knowledge.

Watson, Ian

Mockymen. 2004 (2003). Immanion, ISBN: 1904853129, 9781904853129, 330p.

An old Norwegian man commissions the creation of a jigsaw puzzle and requires the image to include the Vigeland Park sculpture garden. The puzzle makers accept the commission and experience horrific nightmares of a Nazi occult ritual in that same area. Years later, the alien Mockymen arrive with wondrous technologies that head off global disaster. They also introduce the drug Bliss, a substance that renders some of its users into comatose vessels for the Mockymen. But detective Anna Sharman suspects the Mockymen of less-than-noble motivations and comes across a former Bliss user who recalls his life as an old Norwegian man. Watson melds alien agendas, humanity's folly, and horror into a creepy whole.

Who Are You?: Missing Memories and Uncertain Identities

Identity is a fragile thing, particularly in the worlds of science fiction. Aliens can change shape and assume your features and form. A mind that can be uploaded, saved, and downloaded can also be edited, and technology can help fool even the closest friends and acquaintances. Even a simple head injury can have you reinventing yourself. Ultimately, you might realize that you are the person you choose to be. Hope that no reactivated neural implants make you out to be a liar.

Buckell, Tobias

⇒ *Crystal Rain*. 2007 (2006). Tor, ISBN 0765350904, 9780765350909, 370p.

John deBrun found himself with no memory on the shores of Nanaganda, a land of steam technology. In the decades since, he made a new life for himself with his wife and child among folk who live alongside powerful beings called the Loa. But another culture, the Azteca, intend to conquer John's adopted people and sacrifice them to the Azteca's bloodthirsty gods, the Teotl. To complicate matters further, a man named Pepper just exited a machine that fell from the sky and is looking for a man named John. Buckell's tale of invasion, alien gods, and a people too long separated from the rest of the galaxy is packed with suspense, adventure, and mystery—a science fiction story for fans of *Pirates of the Caribbean*.

Budz, Mark

Idolon. 2006. Bantam Dell, ISBN: 0553588508, 9780553588507, 448p.

Philm, a substance that projects whatever image it's programmed to display, enjoys ubiquitous use throughout society. People use it to enwrap objects, buildings, and even themselves, allowing them to conceal, transform, and project the reality and identities they envision. Philm can even link its wearers together, promoting bonding, affiliation, and belonging. But someone is manipulating the philm industry, altering it to go beyond projecting identity to compelling it, forcing behaviors and responses from philm wearers. Philm lies at the heart of a web of smuggling, cult activity, conspiracy, murder, and virgin births and draws in a host of characters, from an impoverished test subject to an immigrant, a detective, and a man of wealth and taste. This postcyberpunk thriller envisions how the biotech industry can raise questions of identity and reality to a new level.

Dantec, Maurice G.

Cosmos Incorporated. 2008 (2005). Del Rey, ISBN: 034549993X, 9780345499936, 448p.

Most people come to Grand Junction hoping to start a new life in space. They want to escape an almost unrecognizable Earth, a planet so damaged that a computer entity had to take over before humanity utterly destroyed itself. Sergei Plotkin arrives in Grand Junction with most of his memory erased, because the authorities might take exception to his orders to assassinate an important official. But when Plotkin meets the dying Vivian McNellis, he decides to help her escape offworld and risks his employer's wrath. Dantec is considered one of France's premier cyberpunk writers, and this recent translation will certainly cement his reputation with Anglophone readers.

Dick, Philip K.

A Scanner Darkly. 2006 (1977). Vintage, ISBN: 1400096901, 9781400096909, 278p.

Substance D, a deadly and dangerous drug, slowly causes its users to lose contact with reality. Agent Fred goes deep undercover to discover the source of Substance D on the street, and infiltrates the home of Bob Arctor. But Fred has gone from agent to user to dealer and addict and only slowly comes to realize that he is Bob Arctor. Paranoia takes on a new dimension when he cannot trust his own mind, but Agent Fred's failure ensures his success at his mission, though at great cost to himself. Dick's novel of drug abuse and the police state is a window into the core of crumbling sanity.

Finney, Jack

Invasion of the Body Snatchers (a.k.a. *The Body Snatchers*). 1998 (1955). Scribner, ISBN: 0684852586, 9780684852584, 216p.

Quiet Mill Valley becomes ground zero for an eerie invasion. Dr. Miles Bennell receives several alarmed calls from citizens complaining that something is subtly and indescribably wrong with their neighbors and relatives. When the good doctor investigates, he discovers replicated humans being grown in strange pods! As the body snatchers slowly take over the town, Bennell tries to escape to warn the world. Four film adaptations, as well as the term "pod people," found their origins in this novel, and many a critic has written about reflections of Cold War paranoia and fear of the Red Menace in the book's pages.

Stross, Charles

Glasshouse. 2006. Ace, ISBN: 0441014038, 9780441014033, 352p.

After a devastating war, mindwipes are available to delete unpleasant memories. Robin volunteered for just such a procedure. He received a handwritten letter from himself that tells him so. Suspecting that he is being hunted for what he may have known, Robin escapes by agreeing to participate in a program designed to recreate the Dark Ages of humanity (circa 1950 to 2040). Robin, now transformed into a housewife named Reeve, is revolted by the societal norms in the Glasshouse, norms reinforced through bizarre scoring by the controllers. Worse, it appears that several of the other participants were also active in the war, and Robin's disturbing memories are starting to resurface. Set in the same universe as *Accelerando*, this paranoiac novel was nominated for the Hugo Award.

Wolfe, Gene

The Fifth Head of Cerberus. 1994 (1972). Orb, ISBN: 0312890206, 9780312890209, 252p.

Suspicion abounds on the colonized planets of Sainte Croix and Sainte Anne. The colonists believe that the aboriginals, alien mimicks and shapeshifters, are dead. One researcher, however, theorizes that the aboriginals may be replacing the colonists. Three linked novellas, "The Fifth Head of Cerberus," " 'A Story,' by John V. Marsch," and "V.R.T." explore the mystery of these twin planets.

Chapter Five

Language

When we consider language in science fiction, the obvious context is communication with others, whoever or whatever those others may be. We must also consider the language of science itself, because many science fiction novels contain passages of exposition and explanation that aid readers in understanding the scientific underpinnings of a story. And of course, authors' use of language, their style, their pace, their tone, and their verbosity, may determine which audiences will eagerly embrace their work. Each of these aspects presents a different facet to the appeal of language for a science fiction reader, and I hope that these lists will communicate new vistas to both new and longtime fans.

My Side of the Story: First-Person Futures

I discuss SF far more than most people would consider healthy, and one of the topics that comes up regularly in those discussions is the preference of perspective, usually the third-person versus first-person points of view. Others may disagree, but whenever I find first-person narration in a novel, my interest in that book increases. For me, the preference comes down to a simple thought experiment. If I want to learn the facts about World War II, I could read a bunch of history books with a lot of names and places and useful information. That kind of tale-telling is necessary and has its place. But if I want to know what World War II was *really like*, I need to read about it (or better yet, hear about it) from somebody who was there, somebody who fought it and lived that experience. I have to see it through their eyes. These books let you see the future through the eyes of those who live it.

Bethke, Bruce

Headcrash. 1995. Warner, ISBN: 0446602604, 9780446602600, 344p.

By day, Jack Burroughs is a computer guru and geeky nobody slaving away for corporate giant Monolithic Diversified Enterprises, but after hours, he inhabits a second life in virtual reality as MAX_KOOL, king of the cyber realm. When the company ousts Burroughs, he receives an unusual offer for a risky bit of hacking. Bethke's novel is a superb send-up of cyberpunk and balances nerd chic with corporate culture on a hilarious edge. If you think a mash-up of Scott Adams' *Dilbert* and William Gibson's *Neuromancer* would be your cup of tea, then this is the next book you need to read.

Judson, Theodore

Fitzpatrick's War. 2005 (2004). DAW, ISBN: 0756402719, 9780756402716, 548p.

Hundreds of years after the Storm Times devastated all electrical technology, the steam technology of the Yukon Confederacy gives it preeminent power over the rest of the world. Lord Isaac Prophet Fitzpatrick, in a manner reminiscent of Alexander the Great, leads his nation to war with the intention of conquering the globe—and succeeds! Although victorious, Fitzpatrick's fear of usurpation leads to profound paranoia and drives him to suspect and murder even his closest allies. Finally, even the heroic Brigadier General Sir Robert Mayfair Bruce, Fitzpatrick's closest advisor and friend, feels compelled to join a conspiracy that plots to assassinate the tyrant. This fictional autobiography actually contains two first-person voices. The primary point of view belongs to Bruce, but the footnotes give voice to a second perspective, a twenty-sixth-century scholar named Professor Van Buren, who seems intent on discrediting Bruce and buttressing the canonical view of Fitzpatrick as a virtuous leader. Judson relates a frighteningly plausible tale of power and corruption that calls history to account and questions the foundation of officially sanctioned narratives.

Lethem, Jonathan

Gun with Occasional Music. 2003 (1994). Harcourt, ISBN: 0156028972, 9780156028974, 271p.

Conrad Metcalf, private investigator, lives in a rather bizarre world. A detective's job is more difficult because only government inquisitors can ask questions with impunity, and people regularly dose themselves with a drug that erases memories. Bioengineered animals do most of the menial labor and form a permanent underclass. The government keeps track of its citizens' karma, a diminishing abstract quantifier of innocence tracked on a debit card; when your karma gets to zero, you get a prison stretch in cryogenic suspension. Metcalf finds himself on a new case that the inquisitors and the local criminal organization don't want solved. With a kangaroo gunning for him and a lot of questions to ask, Metcalf has to figure out a murder before he finds himself in deep freeze. Lethem's absurdist SF love letter to Chandler and Hammett is slyly funny and sharply cynical, with a bite like whiskey on the way down.

Morgan, Richard K.

Woken Furies. <u>Takeshi Kovacs</u>. 2007 (2005). Del Rey, ISBN: 0345499778, 9780345499776, 450p.

As Kovacs continues a personal vendetta against some religious extremists, he discovers that there's a second, younger version of him running around. Apparently, the ruling elite of Harlan's world downloaded the ex-Envoy into a new body and commissioned him to hunt down the reembodied consciousness of a former revolutionary, Quellcrist Falconer. The Harlans of Harlan's World and their associates do not want to see Falconer upset the status quo a second time. The problem is, Kovacs knows himself pretty well, and his younger self may not listen to reason. This follow-up to *Altered Carbon* and *Broken Angels* continues the noirish escapades of Morgan's cynical idealist and ronin operative, and readers who like their SF gritty, violent, and morally gray will hunt down every book in the series.

Niffenegger, Audrey

⇒*The Time Traveler's Wife.* 2004 (2003). Mariner, ISBN: 015602943X, 9780156029438, 560p.

Henry De Tamble works at the Newberry Library in Chicago. He seems relatively normal on the outside, but Henry suffers from Chrono-Displacement disorder: he involuntarily travels through time. Unable to take anything with him, arriving naked each time, Henry learns the various skills his unique condition requires to survive, including a secretiveness that only his love, Clare Abshire, can penetrate. Clare first met Henry when she was six and he an adult, and she's spent her entire life knowing that they will marry and love one another fully and completely all their lives. But Henry has another secret: he knows his own fate, and one day he'll disappear and never return. This unique novel incorporates science fiction and timeless love in an unforgettable romance told from the alternating individual perspectives of the two lovers.

Dwarf Stars: Short SF Novels

There was a time when writers, editors, and fans considered a two-hundred-page work of speculative fiction complete. (No, really, it's true!) Admittedly, many science fiction fans prefer longer novels, believing that the authors require the extra space to flesh out the world, characters, ideas, and themes. But there are times when a fan needs to read a short book, perhaps due to limited space in the backpack or to cleanse the palate between longer series. The below single-serving, single-sitting novels and individually published novellas are fantastically fast reads that hit the sweet spots of sudden immersion and swift resolution while communicating thoughtful and challenging ideas.

Abbott, Edwin A.

Flatland. 2008 (1884). NuVision, ISBN: 1595477322, 9781595477323, 100p.

Mr. A. Square lives on a two-dimensional geometrical plane where the number of sides a polygon has determines its social class; with only four sides, Square is relatively low on the totem pole. Square is astonished when an ambassador from the third-dimensional plane discourses with him on the directions of Up and Down, and takes him on a tour of other dimensions. When Square attempts to communicate his discovery, however, his society imprisons him. Abbott's contention that the universe is bigger than our perceptions seems incredible and prophetic in a Victorian work; his satirical jabs at Victorian social and class conventions add humor to astonishment.

Barjavel, René

The Ice People. 1971 (1968). Morrow, ISBN: N/A, 205p.

An Antarctic expedition uncovers evidence of a 900,000-year-old civilization. The scientists discover two survivors in suspended animation and learn of the previous society's downfall due to foolish war. Although the pair has much to offer in the way of advanced technology and knowledge, the powers that be prefer the status quo. Originally titled *La Nuit des Temps*, this short French novel questions humanity's ability to rise above its senseless hatred.

Doctorow, Cory

Eastern Standard Tribe. 2005. Tor, ISBN: 0765310457, 9780765310453, 223p.

Art Berry is an asylum patient wondering if it is better to be smart or happy. He lives at a time when social networking affinities are more important to people than geographical boundaries or nationalities. Berry is part of the Eastern Standard Tribe, a group bound by its preference for that time zone's circadian rhythms and cultural affectations. The tribe's flame wars have evolved into actual shadow wars and conspiracies against their enemies, the Greenwich Mean Time Tribe. But Berry's latest scheme to trump the G.M.T.s leads to betrayal and institutionalization, hence his dilemma. When allegiances and extreme behavior are increasingly based on the most arbitrary criteria, it highlights the importance humans place on distinctions of "us and them."

Hoffman, Nina Kiriki

Catalyst. 2006. Tachyon, ISBN: 1892391384, 9781892391384, 171p.

Kaslin is a teen on the planet Chuudoku. He grows up poor and develops a crush on wealthy, attractive Histly. Money buys a lot of augmentations, and Histly uses them to bully Kaslin. When fleeing Histly, Kaslin takes refuge in a cave and stumbles across a new alien life-form that traps, bonds with, and changes Kaslin. It uses Kaslin to explore humanity at a time when Kaslin himself is just discovering his own body and budding sexuality, leading to a very unusual first contact situation. Hoffman explores the strangeness of the teen years, including puberty, maturation, desire, and yes, alienation.

Mamatas, Nick

⇒*Under My Roof.* 2007. Soft Skull, ISBN: 1933368438, 9781933368436, 151p.

The world is in a terrible mess. America's xenophobia is out of control, and the President is discussing nuclear solutions. A frustrated and angry Daniel Weinberg decides that the only sane solution is to secede from the United States. He builds a nuclear weapon with the help of his telepathic son Herbert, hides the deterrent in a lawn gnome, and declares his home the free and sovereign nation of Weinbergia. Now all they have to do is tell Mom . . . Mamatas's uproarious book is a fast, fun political satire.

Stross, Charles

Missile Gap. 2006 (2005). Subterranean Press, ISBN: 1596060581, 9781596060586, 99p.

At the height of the Cuban Missile Crisis, the entire Earth was rendered flat and transported by unknown entities and means to a large disc in another galaxy. Both the United States and the Soviet Union, still embroiled in the Cold War, set out to explore and colonize the new surrounding lands. Humanity is not alone in the universe, however, and these pioneers will uncover horrifying secrets and terrible knowledge about our place in it. Fans leery of patriotic expansionism will enjoy this SF novella with its dashes of *Dr. Strangelove* and Lovecraftian terror.

Nuts and Bolts: The Language of Science

Some readers are simply adamant about the importance of having real science in science fiction. (Go figure!) The following books, in addition to being great reads, are chock full of information on a plethora of topics and incorporate impressive and astounding interludes on the science informing their stories. Fans who want education as well as entertainment will find their desires fulfilled!

Benford, Gregory

Timescape. 2000 (1980). Millennium, ISBN: 185798935X, 9781857989359, 416p.

In 1998, Earth is on the edge of ecological collapse. Scientists send a message backward in time to warn of their fate, hoping to encourage changes that won't cause a time paradox. Meanwhile, in 1962, physicist Gordon Bernstein discovers that the interference in his experiment that he cannot account for is actually Morse code! Benford spends considerable effort describing both the physics of tachyon communication and the actual life of research scientists, including scrabbling for grants and promotions while maintaining personal relationships. The fact that he was awarded both a Nebula and a John W. Campbell Award for this book testifies to his success.

Clarke, Arthur C.

The Fountains of Paradise. 2001 (1978). Warner/Aspect, ISBN: 0446677949, 9780446677943, 330p.

Engineer Vannevar Morgan needs a challenge. He proposes building a space elevator leading from the surface of the island of Taprobane to geostationary orbit, 36,000 kilometers above Earth. This massive skyhook would make access to space relatively cheaper and more commonplace and would permit transport of payloads without the need for expensive rockets. Morgan's accomplishment demonstrates another important step of humanity toward space, and Clarke's accomplishment comes about both in his development of the concept and his depiction of a life's work fulfilled.

Clement, Hal

Mission of Gravity. Mesklinite. 2005 (1954). Gollancz, ISBN: 0575077085, 9780575077089, 203p.

The disc-shaped planet of Mesklin spins incredibly fast and exerts a crushing force of gravity near its poles. When a human probe proves unable to escape Mesklin's pull, humans must bargain with Mesklinite captain Barlennan to retrieve it. As the alien captain, whose body resembles a centipede, travels across his unusual world, Clement explicates the unusual properties such a planet would possess.

Egan, Greg

Incandescence. 2008. Night Shade, ISBN: 9781597801283, 9781597801287, 256p.

Two plotlines converge in this novel of the scientific method. Two scientists from a technologically advanced society fixate on discovering the origin of DNA-based life. Meanwhile, insectoids that live on an artificial body called the Splinter seek to understand their environment and its place in the universe in order to save their world. This novel exalts curiosity and the thirst for knowledge and demonstrates how science works in practice, complete with elaborate descriptions of hypotheses, experiments, and outcomes, making it a perfect read for hard SF fans.

Flint, James

Habitus. 2000. St. Martin's, ISBN: 0312245459, 9780312245450, 415p.

Young Jennifer Several takes two lovers, the gifted gambler Judd Axelrod and the brilliant Joel Kluge, whose later experiments combine aspects of physics, advanced mathematics, and the Kabbalah. Their bizarre lovechild, Emma, is a new stage in evolution and has genetic material from all three parents. And above them all, orbiting the Earth, Laika, the first dog in space, puts everything into perspective. Flint manages to meld information from a variety of fields into a fuller and realistically messier whole, a gestalt that echoes the themes of this unusual novel.

Stephenson, Neal

Cryptonomicon. 2002 (1999). Avon, ISBN: 0060512806, 9780060512804, 1152p.

In World War II, an Allied codebreaking team consisting of Dr. Alan Turing, mathematician Lawrence Waterhouse, and marine Bobby Shaftoe, crack the Enigma code and use their intelligence to foil Axis operations. Fifty years later, Randy Waterhouse and Amy Shaftoe, grandchildren of the original team members, apply this same knowledge of cryptography and advanced mathematics to create a safe haven for data in the twentieth century. Touching both narratives is a hunt for the whereabouts of a secret cache of Nazi gold. *Cryptonomicon* is an excellent example of modern fiction infused with the language of science and demonstrates that SF isn't just about spaceships and aliens.

Verne, Jules

From the Earth to the Moon. <u>Voyages Extraordinaires</u>. Translated by Edward Roth. 2009 (1865). Dover, ISBN: 0486469646, 9780486469645, 240p.

Civil War veteran and president of the Baltimore Gun Club, Impey Barbicane, proposes to build a giant cannon to fire a crewed space bullet to the moon. Verne's novel, originally published as *De la Terre à la Lune*, demonstrates his scientific rigor; Verne was uncannily accurate in many respects, considering that he's writing nearly one hundred years before the U.S.'s Apollo program, from the dimensions of the "bullet" to the placement of the launch site. To find out what happens to the crew after they launch, read the sequel, *Round the Moon.*

Watts, Peter

⇒*Blindsight.* 2008 (2006). Tor, ISBN: 0765319640, 9780765319647, 383p.

Siri is a Synthesist, able to perceive patterns of complex information and interpret them for others. His purpose is to observe his crewmates and monitor their mission as they make first contact with an alien life-form and report back to Earth's government. Although the technical terminology can be a bit heavy, this novel is an excellent example of nontraditional hard SF that uses biology and neuroscience to drive the plot. Watts raises interesting questions about the nature of intelligence and consciousness and even has an extensive section of notes that discusses the real-world science his novel uses as its starting point. And if you need additional incentive to read this book, the ship's captain is a vampire.

Found in Translation: Fantastic Visions Translated to English

Although I am all too aware that this guide primarily contains English language works, I wanted to acknowledge a few more fantastic novels from outside the Anglophone world that may inspire a love of science fiction. Much as I would like to be able to read all of these works in their original languages, I am grateful for the tireless efforts of translators and publishers who bring these treasures of imagination to foreign tongues and foreign shores. Thanks to them, and to the authors whose words they carry, I and other readers and fans can find enjoyment, enrichment, and illumination in these pages.

Jodorowsky, Alexandro, et al.

The Metabarons, **Book 1:** *Othon & Honorata*. The Metabarons. Translated by Julia Solis and Justin Kelly. 2004. Humanoids and DC Comics, ISBN: 1401203620, 9781401203627, 132p. **GN**

Jodorowsky frames his internationally popular science fiction comic with one droid telling another the history of the greatest and proudest warrior lineage in the universe, the Metabarons. Each generation, a father mutilates his son, and the son completes his training by slaying his father. Jodorowsky and his artist, Juan Gimenez, fill each Metabaron's adventures and quests with some of the most unbridled and insane creativity ever to grace a comic book page and craft an epic space opera with Freudian overtones and echoes of Frank Herbert's *Dune* saga.

Lem, Stanislaw

Eden. Translated by Mark E. Heine. 1991 (1959). Mariner, ISBN: 0156278065, 9780156278065, 276p.

A spacecraft crash-lands on the planet Eden. As the six human crewmembers explore the planet, they discover alien life-forms utterly transformed by technology and a factory churning out items that are immediately disposed of. Contact with a native demonstrates just how much of the crew's assumptions and explanations are products of their limited perspective. Eden's seemingly incomprehensible civilization is enhanced by Lem's subtle criticism, as the most bizarre aspects of his alien civilization uncomfortably reflect human political, economic, and social institutions.

Ogawa, Issui

The Lord of the Sands of Time. Translated by Jim Hubbert. 2009 (2007). Viz, ISBN: 1421527626, 9781421527628, 199p.

Sent from a future where invading aliens devastate the Earth, the robot Orville journeys to different periods in Earth's past to save lives and alter the war's future outcome. As Orville sees the fruit of his successes and failures in the past and future, he contemplates love and considers his commitment to saving humanity. Viz, already well known for sparking the *manga* revolution in the United States, kicks off its new line of translated Japanese speculative fiction novels with Ogawa's thoughtful cross-time tale.

Sena, Hideaki

Parasite Eve. Translated by Tyran Grillo. 2008 (1995). Vertical, ISBN: 1932234209, 9781932234206, 314p.

Mitochondria develop a collective intelligence, dubbed Eve, and a desire to supplant all other life-forms on the planet. Eve's ability to manipulate mitochondria in humans allows it to force its current host, Kiyomi, into an automobile accident. It then manages to get Kiyomi's kidney implanted into a more suitable host, young Mariko, for the purpose of giving birth to a new creature that can manipulate its DNA at will. Sena's tale of Darwinian parasites that enslave their hosts is an interesting blend of horror and SF; it updates tales of ghostly possession with considerable biological theorizing.

Strugatsky, Arkady, and Boris Strugatsky

Roadside Picnic. Translated by Antonina W. Bouis. 2007 (1972). Gollancz, ISBN: 0575079789, 9780575079789, 145p.

Redrick "Red" Schuhart is a stalker: he ventures into the Zone, where alien visitors left remnant and castoff advanced technology. Forays into the Zone are extremely dangerous because the alien artifacts warp the dimensions of space and time within the area, but they are also extremely lucrative, as the technology nets top dollar on the black market. Expeditions into the Zone wear on Red's psyche, but when his daughter, Monkey, is born a mutant, he makes one last trip to search for the fabled golden ball, said to grant its finder's deepest wish. *Roadside Picnic*, thoughtful and poignant, is an excellent example of literary SF.

Verne, Jules

⇒*Twenty Thousand Leagues under the Sea.* Voyages Extraordinaires. Translated by Walter James Miller and Frederick Paul Walter. 1993 (1870). Naval Institute Press, ISBN: 0870216783, 9780870216787, 392p.

Convinced that a massive leviathan terrorizes the seas, marine biologist Professor Aronnax, accompanied by his faithful servant Conseil and the harpooner Ned Land, sets sail with an expedition to slay the beast. When their ship meets with disaster as well, they discover that the sea monster is actually a metal craft, a submarine named *Nautilus* and piloted by the enigmatic Captain Nemo. Nemo treats his prisoners as valued guests but refuses to release them lest they inform the world's governments about the captain and his activities. Even as the companions hope for an opportunity to escape, they are astounded by the wonders of the undersea world Nemo reveals to them. Verne was a master of science fiction and fills his novel with wondrous locales and visions of underwater forests, massive beasts, and even sunken Atlantis, all the while expounding on scientific theory, applied electronics, and marine biology—real science!

Zivkovic, Zoran

The Fourth Circle. Translated by Mary Popovic. 2004 (1993). Ministry of Whimsy, ISBN: 1892389657, 9781892389657, 240p.

Zivkovic brings together a variety of personalities from a dizzying array of times, places, and realities, including the scientists Archimedes, Nikola

Tesla, and Stephen Hawking; a Buddhist computer scientist, Srinavasa; a sentient female computer program impregnated by a monkey; a medieval painter's assistant; and Sherlock Holmes and Sir Arthur Conan Doyle. As Zivkovic gathers his cast and reveals the secret of the Fourth Circle, he reconciles physics and metaphysics into a grand unity.

The Future of Hip: SF for the Reader in the Know

The books on this list are for fans that want style with their substance. The following works have that indefinable something that draws attention to them. Some of these pages are filled with flamboyant panache. Others capture the zeitgeist of a particular time, whether a specific era or a stage of life. Arrange your photo op and dare to be seen reading these books—you won't regret it.

Doctorow, Cory

⇒*Down and Out in the Magic Kingdom.* 2003. Tor, ISBN: 0765304368, 9780765304368, 208p.

>Jules is a citizen of the Bitchun Society, where scarcity, want, and even death have been overcome, and the only currency is reputation. Jules does his best to help maintain the integrity of the twentieth century's greatest artistic achievement—Disney World—but when he awakens in a new body after being murdered, he's convinced that a rival faction is trying to usurp his place in the Magic Kingdom. This book is a fast, funny, and surprisingly thoughtful read, where reputation is everything and people kill over amusement park rides.

Farren, Mick

The DNA Cowboys Trilogy. 2002. Do Not Press, ISBN: 1899344942, 9781899344949, 567p.

>Billy Oblivion and his friend Reave leave dull and dreary Pleasant Gap in a bizarre quest for excitement across the universe and face the most surreal menaces imaginable. The novel's influences read like a list of 1970s pop culture, including everything from rock-and-roll to low-budget kung fu films, and spaghetti westerns to sci-fi, with touches of sex and illicit substances along the way. Fans of Michael Moorcock's books and Quentin Tarantino's stylish collage of homage in the *Kill Bill* movies will delight in this omnibus, which includes the novels *The Quest of the DNA Cowboys* (1976), *Synaptic Manhunt* (1976), and *The Neural Atrocity* (1977).

Moorcock, Michael

The Cornelius Quartet. Jerry Cornelius. 2001. Four Walls Eight Windows, ISBN: 1568581831, 9781568581835, 855p.

> Prodigy and Renaissance man Jerry Cornelius is a fashionista, a rock star, a scientist, and a time-travelling English spy and assassin. Counterculture music and pop art permeate this dark picaresque in which Jerry Cornelius acts as reality's aesthete and champion for change against authoritarianism. The collected novels *The Final Programme* (1968), *A Cure for Cancer* (1971), *The English Assassin* (1972), and *The Condition of Muzak* (1977) chronicle this trippy traipse across time.

Thomas, Scarlett

PopCo. 2004. Harcourt, ISBN: 015603137X, 9780156031370, 505p.

> Alice Butler is a cryptographer par excellence, a gift she seems to have inherited from her grandparents. She works for the company PopCo developing toys for children. PopCo wants her to brainstorm a hit product for girls. All the while, she receives strange codes from an unknown source, and works on a very old puzzle she received from her grandfather. When she discovers the key to PopCo's desires, she must decide whether to yield the secret or strike the ultimate blow against brand marketing. Thomas depicts a quirky, brilliant, and marvelously geeky female protagonist, and manages to incorporate a cake recipe and pirate treasure into her narrative while explaining complex math with aplomb.

Vaughan, Brian K., et al.

Runaways, Vol. 1. Runaways. 2005. Marvel Comics, ISBN: 0785118764, 9780785118763, 448p. **GN**

> Six teens assemble at their parents' annual meeting and discover that their mothers and fathers are actually supervillains! The youth use the skills, powers, and equipment that they inherited and stole from their parents to oppose them and inadvertently become superheroes (of a sort). This award-winning series was a key to winning some *manga* readers back to Anglophone comics.

Womack, Jack

Going, Going, Gone. Ambient/Dryco. 2002 (2000). Grove Press. ISBN: 0802138667, 9780802138668, 224p.

> It's 1968. The Velvet Underground plays its gigs, but little else is right in this twisted American time. The incumbent president, unhappy with the possibility of Robert Kennedy running for office, hires Walter Bullitt to put a stop to the Democrat's candidacy. Bullitt, who runs a sideline in psychoactive substances that he tests on others, is reluctant to clash with the Kennedy clan.

His stress only increases when he starts seeing ghosts and has to deal with his timeline merging with another. Womack deftly manipulates language, crafting a complete slang that permeates the novel and firmly establishes its tone and setting.

If a Picture's Worth a Thousand Words, How Much Is a Moving Picture Worth?: SF Beamed to and from the Silver Screen

The story of Hollywood's success is pure science fiction, in that the movie industry combines the technology of light and sound, film and computer with creativity and the stuff of dreams. It's only natural that moviemakers adapted some of science fiction's most interesting and exciting tales to the silver screen, and even more natural that a film or two found its way from the dark theater to the printed page as well. Movies have their own visual language of lighting and angle, symbol and shadow, which requires extensive translation and (to some fans' eternal enmity) alteration of the source material. Judge for yourself if the works on this list made the journey to or from Hollywood without being mangled.

Brooks, Terry, et al.

   Star Wars: The Prequel Trilogy. Star Wars. 2007. Del Rey, ISBN: 0345498704, 9780345498700, 993p.

   In the days of the Republic, the Jedi knights keep the peace across the galaxy. But the Republic suffers corruption and rot at its very core, where a hidden foe revives the ancient teachings of the Sith lords and uses treachery and deceit to acquire power and forge the beginnings of an evil Empire. Fans of the Star Wars film franchise will find the plots and characterizations expanded and fleshed out with additional connections to the vaster universe beyond the six movies. This omnibus contains the novelizations of *The Phantom Menace* (1999), *Attack of the Clones* (2002), and *Revenge of the Sith* (2005).

Clarke, Arthur C.

   2001: A Space Odyssey. Space Odyssey. 2000 (1968). Roc, ISBN: 0451457994, 9780451457998, 296p.

   In the distant past, a strange metal monolith appears and influences prehumans to make an intellectual and evolutionary leap. Millions of years later, humans discover a metal monolith on Earth's moon. Scientists discover that the monolith sends a strange radio signal to one of Saturn's moons. When Dr. David Bowman and his crew fly to Saturn to investigate, the ship's malfunctioning artificial intelligence, the HAL 9000, becomes unstable and murderous. Adapted from Clarke's short story "The Sentinel" and written alongside Stanley Kubrick's film of the same title, *2001: A Space Odyssey* includes themes of evolution and extraterrestrial life that will fascinate the SF aficionado.

Lem, Stanislaw

Solaris. Translated by Joanna Kilmartin and Steve Cox. 2002 (1961). Harcourt Brace & Co., ISBN: 0156027607, 9780156027601, 204p.

    The research team studying the vast ocean of the planet Solaris suspects that it is actually an intelligent alien being. Kris Kelvin, a psychologist, comes to the station and soon receives a visitor: his dead wife, Rheya. Is the crew hallucinating? Are the visitors who appear on the ship actually memories made flesh? Or is Solaris trying to make contact? As the crew and visitors come to terms with their experiences, the reader may wonder how humans could possibly understand a truly alien being if we do not even know ourselves and those closest to us.

Levin, Ira

⇒*The Stepford Wives*. 2004 (1972). Harper Torch, ISBN: 0060738197, 9780060738198, 195p.

    Walter and Joanna Eberhart move to the seemingly idyllic suburb of Stepford, Connecticut. The majority of Stepford's wives seem obsessively dedicated to meeting their husbands' every need and seek nothing for themselves outside of obedient servitude. As Joanna's more liberated friends begin inexplicably mimicking the wives' behavior, she investigates the reasons and comes to realize that it's only a matter of time before she is replaced by a "perfect" wife. Ira Levin's creepy tale is sharply critical of men's desires and views of women and manages to convey Joanna's mounting terror effectively as she realizes how isolated and alone she is in the midst of the Stepford circle.

Priest, Christopher

The Prestige. 2006 (1995). Tor, ISBN: 0765356171, 9780765356178, 360p.

    Rupert Angier and Alfred Borden are stage magicians, each trying to outdo the other. Desperate to develop an unequaled illusion, Angier appeals to scientist Nikola Tesla and acquires a fabulous machine that will secure his reputation. As the driven magicians compete, their professional rivalry turns terrifyingly bitter as their hatred corrupts them and leads them to destroy one another. Priest artfully elaborates on the theme of obsession and its ability to inevitably poison the soul.

The Power of Words

Language enables us to communicate with one another. It shapes and gives expression to our perceptions and thought processes. It helps us to establish our identities, both individually and as collectives. This tool and medium also enables us to move beyond the barrier of self and come to some understanding of others. The following novels emphasize the power language has over its users, to define, unite, and divide. Peruse the following list of novels at your leisure and enjoy the power that their words have over you.

Burgess, Anthony

A Clockwork Orange. 1986 (1962). Norton, ISBN: 0393312836, 9780393312836, 192p.

> Young Alex is a vicious malchick, a sociopathic juvenile delinquent who leads his gang of droogs through evenings of depravity, rape, and ultraviolence after sipping a bit of drugged milk. When the authorities finally capture him, Alex opts to undergo the Ludovico Technique, state-sanctioned behavioral conditioning. The process leaves him unable to defend himself and nearly drives him mad. Burgess ably demonstrates that a forced excision or aversion to evil is not the same as morality or rehabilitation. He communicates his tale through an invented futuristic slang called nadsat that is believable, wholly absorbing, and serves to immerse the reader in Alex's reality.

Delany, Samuel R.

Babel-17. 2001 (1966). Vintage, ISBN: 0375706690, 9780375706691, 311p.

> Telepath Rydra Wong discovers that the unique code used by enemy forces is actually an entirely new language. Babel-17 is weaponized communication: it alters the thought processes of those who learn it and grants them new perceptions of reality and unusual abilities, but also transforms its speakers into tools and traitors. As Rydra becomes fluent in order to learn her enemy's plans, she struggles to retain her mind, her loyalty, and her sense of self. Delany's novel of thought control won the Nebula Award.

Elgin, Suzette Haden

Native Tongue. Native Tongue. 2000 (1984). Feminist Press at the City University of New York, ISBN: 1558612467, 9781558612464, 327p.

> Several centuries from now, women are property and lack even the most basic civil rights. Humanity trades with beings across the stars, and the vaunted linguists control communication between planets. Nazareth Chornyak slaves daily to train the next generation of linguists and longs for the

companionship of the Barren House where women beyond childbearing age retire. The Barren House hides a powerful secret: within it, the women create a new language, a women's language called Laadan, that they can use to transform their society and free themselves from oppression. Fans of Margaret Atwood will find new delight in Elgin's novel. Elgin actually constructed Laadan, and readers interested in learning it can begin their education at http://www.laadanlanguage.org/pages.

Heinlein, Robert A.

Time Enough for Love. Future History. 1987 (1973). Ace, ISBN: 0441810764, 9780441810765, 589p.

Lazarus Long is the oldest living human, an immortal overwhelmed by ennui. On a strange whim, he decides to play Scheherazade and delays suicide while telling his tales. As he relates his stories, including vignettes from his own considerably long life span, Long regains his curiosity and travels through time to experience the past. Heinlein and his character wax eloquent and philosophical on government, sexuality, and the stuff of life, and the book even includes a section of wise and witty sayings from Lazarus Long's own lips!

Stephenson, Neal

⇒*Snow Crash.* 2000 (1992). Bantam, ISBN: 0553380958, 9780553380958, 440p.

Hiro Protagonist, freelance hacker, makes money by delivering pizza for the mafia in an anarchically capitalist United States broken into franchises and enclaves. Hiro's friend falls victim to Snow Crash, a bizarre virtual drug and virus that affects both avatars and their operators in the real world, and subsequent investigation uncovers alarming connections among the virus, ancient history, Sumerian myth, and glossolalia. Archaeology and biolinguistics collide with reality simulations and geek culture with a delightfully chaotic crash, a harmonious cacophony that will resonate with many readers.

Tevis, Walter

Mockingbird. 2007 (1980). Gollancz, ISBN: 0575079150, 9780575079151, 278p.

Tevis portrays a bleak future where machines run society, and humans seem irrelevant and obsolete. People feel no connection because the law discourages relationships, the population is dwindling, reading is illegal and forgotten, and humanity is drugged into apathy (although an occasional person, overwhelmed by despair, will escape by means of self-immolation). Even Spofforth, the perfect machine, wants to die. But one man, Bentley, dares to read and live with another, and teaches her how to unlock the mystery of words. These small, proscribed actions reawaken humanity and hope.

Vance, Jack

The Languages of Pao. 2004 (1958). Ibooks, ISBN: 0743487141, 9780743487146, 220p.

> The citizens of Pao are peaceful and passive, traits that put them at a military disadvantage. Their ruler, the Panarch, makes a deal with scientists from Breakness to transform the populace. Because language determines how people think, Breakness develops new languages to alter the population's minds and create new castes, including a warrior caste. When the Panarch's brother assassinates him, the successor, Beran Panasper, escapes to Breakness and learns all the languages intended for Pao. How will this gift to his people transform his home planet? Vance uses linguistics to model a social revolution in this classic SF story.

Watson, Ian

The Embedding. 2000 (1973). Gollancz, ISBN: 0575071338, 9780575071339, 254p.

> Chris Sole performs linguistic experiments on young children. He teaches them language using unusual and bizarre embedding structures to determine a universal grammar. When aliens contact Earth, the governments use Chris as an intermediary to communicate with the extraterrestrials. They offer a trade: important knowledge in exchange for insight into human language structures. The visitors place a premium on learning new languages and host a vast galactic reservoir of linguistic information. Similar to Chris's research, the aliens see language as a key to discovering how reality is perceived. All the aliens need are a few fresh human brains. Watson's cynical story demonstrates how researchers might exploit others to gain new insights.

Slowly Savoring Each Word

Science fiction is certainly noted for its breakneck action, but some novels require readers to cogitate and take their time. Sometimes authors set a slow pace to develop a world fully, discuss the science in their work, or wholly realize the culture of an alien race. Nearly as often, all this development requires a larger number of pages for sufficient elaboration, explication, and exploration. These selections are meant to be sipped, not chugged, and should be savored, not raced through. Take your time and read these books slowly, and they will reward your meditation and rumination.

Bear, Greg

City at the End of Time. 2008. Ballantine Books/Del Rey, ISBN: 0345448391, 9780345448392, 476p.

Kalpa, the last city on Earth, sits at the end of time holding back the forces of entropy and chaos. Two beings, Tiadba and Jebrassy, brave the chaos, hoping to find another living city. Meanwhile, far in the past, three newcomers to Seattle dream of a city at the end of time. Ginny, Jack, and Daniel carry stones called sum-runners that contain vital information as they flee from a nameless and mysterious menace. Packed with theoretical physics and seemingly fantastical elements that bring Clarke's Third Law to mind, this book is a slow, savory read.

Griffith, Nicola

⇒*Slow River*. 1996 (1995). Ballantine, ISBN: 0345395379, 9780345395375, 343p.

Slow River maps the riches-to-rags story of its protagonist, Lore, and her discovery of herself. Lore comes from a wealthy family who built an empire on dealing with humanity's waste. When Lore is kidnapped, she escapes, but instead of returning to her family, she takes up with street-smart Scanner, who teaches Lore how to survive. Eventually, Lore comes to work in a water recycling plant, the very business from which her family derives its wealth. Griffith's story of reclamation in science and in psyche won both the Nebula and the Lambda Literary Awards.

Rand, Ayn

Atlas Shrugged. 1997 (1992). Signet, ISBN: 0451191145, 9780451191144, 1075p.

The government's takeover of economy, society, and business continues at an increasingly dangerous pace. Meanwhile, Dagny Taggart, businesswoman and vice president of her family's railway company, notes that the leaders of business are inexplicably vanishing. As drivers of economy, producers of wealth, and innovators of industry like the enigmatic John Galt disappear, society grinds to a halt and threatens to collapse. Rand envisions a dystopian alternative to pure capitalism and the demise of modern civilization due to government interference.

Slonczewski, Joan

A Door into Ocean. Elysium Cycle. 2000 (1986). Orb, ISBN: 0312876521, 9780312876524, 403p.

The water moon of Shora hosts a society of evolved women; their pacifistic Sharer community practices highly advanced biological and life sciences and an egalitarian form of governance. By contrast, the planet

Valedon, which Shora orbits, is patriarchal, hierarchical, and militaristic. The Valans want to colonize Shora and exploit its resources, even as two Sharers seek to determine if the Valans, with their alien values, qualify as human. Slonczewski slowly develops the differences between Valan and Sharer culture, as well as the importance of the Sharers' mission. She effectively portrays a society whose ideals rest on harmonious coexistence, both between people and with their world, and emphasizes the importance of maintaining one's ideals even in the face of violence.

Stephenson, Neal

Anathem. 2008. William Morrow, ISBN: 0661474096, 9780061474095, 937p.

Arbre is a world dedicated to empirical thought, a cloistered society that considers science, knowledge, and inquiry sacred and protects them from the irrational secular world. Rules change, however, when disaster looms, and young scholar Erasmas undertakes a journey that leads across the world and into space. *Anathem* combines *bildungsroman,* scientific theory, and philosophical dialectic and includes a glossary of new terms for the reader to peruse when necessary. It is a heady and weighty novel that is well worth the reader's time to relish.

Traversing the Empyrean: Literary Science Fiction

"Literary" is a loaded term. Some consider a book literary when it is experimental in form, structure, or written style. Others believe that literary works build upon (and make frequent allusions to) other literary works that came before, a relationship between classics new and old that one may describe as standing on the shoulders of giants or an incestuous and tangled knotwork of prose, depending on the perspective of the observer. More than a few colleagues only ascribe the adjective to the best works ever written, usually by academic standards. I have heard, though, that literary works attempt to explore the fullness of human experience and answer humanity's deepest and oldest questions: Who am I? Why am I here? What is the meaning and purpose of life, of existence? Ultimately, only you can decide whether those questions are suitably addressed in the books on this list. (The rest of you will probably just go to the index and look up "Adams, Douglas" for the answer to those tricky questions.)

Delany, Samuel R.

Stars in My Pocket Like Grains of Sand. 2004 (1982). Wesleyan University Press, ISBN: 0819567140, 9780819567140, 356p.

A sprawling galactic civilization with two major divisions, the progressive Sygn and the more conservative Family, wrestles with the phenomenon of "cultural fugue," which is capable of destroying entire planets. Rat Korga survived one such disaster. A slave completely without worry or will, thanks to the Radical Anxiety Termination (RAT) procedure, Rat Korga requires a master to care for him, a role fulfilled by Marq Dyeth, an Industrial Diplomat investigating the destruction of Korga's planet. Delany takes great care and great delight challenging contemporary mores and cultural assumptions. The book hosts as wide a variety of sexual liaisons as is possible in science fiction, and Delany enjoys linguistic play, as some pronouns are used depending on the desire of the speaker for the one referred to rather than by gender of the latter. Delany even conceives of civilizations that shun eating animal flesh but enjoy cloned human meat. This bizarre and beautiful book will challenge and reward the selective, determined reader.

Harrison, M. John

Light. Kefahuchi Tract. 2004 (2002). Bantam, ISBN: 0553382950, 9780553382952, 310p.

This novel revolves around three characters: Michael Kearney, a scientist and serial killer; Seria Mau Genlicher, a young woman permanently bonded to her spaceship, the *White Cat*; and Ed Chianese, a virtual reality addict who is forced into the real world. As the novel progresses, the links between these characters cross time and space and reveal patterns between their fates and the future of the human race. Harrison is a first-rate wordsmith, and *Light* is a very dense novel; this exploration of despair, absurdity, and even providential redemption requires some work from the reader.

Le Guin, Ursula K.

The Dispossessed. 2003 (1974). Perennial Classics, ISBN: 006051275X, 9780060512750, 387p.

Anarres is an inhabited moon of Urras near Tau Ceti. Long ago, the governments of Urras gave the moon to workers as a settlement rather than face the laborers' rebellion. Anarres' anarchist utopia is showing some cracks, however, as bureaucracy and pressure to conform quash individual excellence and originality. Shevek, a physicist, devises a General Temporal Theory, a radical reconception of time that includes philosophy as well as physics that may revolutionize communication over long distances. The increasing resistance Shevek faces leads him to travel to Urras and visit its nations: propertarian (capitalist) A-Io and socialist Thu. Shevek hopes to propagate his theory and obtain the resources he needs to test and perfect it but soon learns that he is a pawn of nations hungry for the power and wealth they can gain by exploiting his knowledge. Le Guin's novel of innocence lost and self-discovery won both the Hugo and the Nebula Awards.

McHugh, Maureen F.

China Mountain Zhang. 1997 (1992). Tom Doherty, ISBN: 0312860986, 9780312860981, 313p.

The supremacy of Communist China shapes the society McHugh envisions. The author's focus narrows to the lives of individuals trying to eke out their existence in a less-than-perfect future, where society's prejudices against other nationalities, races, and unsanctioned sexual orientations complicate and endanger the characters. The reader's immersion in those lives evokes empathy as the protagonists try to carve out places for themselves within their culture. *China Mountain Zhang* won the James Tiptree, Jr. Award, the Lambda Literary Award, and the Locus Award for first novel.

Ryman, Geoff

The Child Garden. 2005 (1989). Gollancz, ISBN: 0575076909, 9780575076907, 388p.

The cure for cancer has the unexpected side effect of shortening the human lifespan. The Consensus, the ruling gestalt mind, programs photosynthetic people with viruses that communicate knowledge, function, and role, such that behavior becomes a matter of biology. Milena, however, is resistant to viruses. Her love for music coupled with her incurable nonconformity may lead the Consensus to humanity's next incarnation.

Silverberg, Robert

Son of Man. 2008 (1971). Pyr, ISBN: 1591026466, 9781591026464, 225p.

Clay awakens to discover that he has inexplicably traveled eons through time to the far future. The world is nearly unrecognizable, but a powerful entity, a Skimmer named Hanmer, comes to Clay's aid and takes him on a tour of this new Earth. Along the way, Clay encounters examples of humanity's descendents, a variety of diversely evolved branches that more closely resemble goats and squid and saurians. He even takes on their forms for a time and experiences the world in a variety of bodies. Clay's perspective experiences a shock as he realizes all he knew, all that he considered familiar and important, was simply a tiny moment in time, insignificant and easily forgotten. Silverberg explores what it means to call yourself human in a world that's moved beyond you.

Simmons, Dan

⇒*Hyperion*. <u>Hyperion Cantos</u>. 1990 (1989). Spectra, ISBN: 0553283685, 9780553283686, 481p.

In the far future, humanity is dependent on artificial intelligences to run society in the vast web of worlds known as the Hegemony. From this immense population, seven pilgrims have been chosen to travel to the world Hyperion. Set against the background of interstellar conflict, each pilgrim tells his or her deeply personal and startling story and reason for pilgrimage. These seven will ultimately present their petitions to a being known only as The Shrike, a killing machine with the power of a god. It is said that, of all these pilgrims, only one will be granted his or her wish; the rest will die. Touching on the poetry of John Keats and reminiscent of Chaucer's *Canterbury Tales*, *Hyperion* helped redefine science fiction and won the Hugo Award in 1989.

Winterson, Jeanette

The Stone Gods. 2007. Harcourt, ISBN: 0151014914, 9780151014910, 206p.

The artificially immortal people of the planet Orbus are slowly killing their world with pollution. Eager to colonize a new place to live, they ship troublesome scientist Billie Crusoe and her lover, the robot Spike, to the wonderfully lush and beautiful Planet Blue. Unfortunately, the new home is riddled with troubling dinosaur life, but a handy asteroid strike clears up that problem, although there are unfortunate side effects for the colonists. From there, the reader enjoys a stint on Captain Cook's ship to Easter Island, thence to a post-apocalyptic wasteland, a long journey punctuated by consideration of the mysteries of love, the condemnation of consumer culture, and thoughtless abuse of the environment.

Appendix
Interesting and Important Anthologies

Rather than epic series and massive novels, sometimes you want a good, short, sharp plot or an idea piece. You might be on the lookout for a new author but want to get a taste of the writer's style without committing to a long novel. You may need something shorter that won't strain your memory as you strive to read in the small moments between various other responsibilities. Or maybe you just want a bit of bathroom reading. A good deal of science fiction's popularity began with short stories printed in pulp magazines and serial publications. Despite the sadly diminishing number of venues for short fiction, the short form has been good to SF, a place for authors to make their mark and get noticed. To acknowledge the importance of the short story, this appendix lists a variety of anthologies containing works by an even wider variety of authors. I have organized these lists by the titles of the anthologies rather than the editors' names. (In case you're wondering why the order differs from previous lists, many libraries shelve anthologies by title, and many bookstores order anthologies by title in the end sections of the appropriate genre shelves.)

Sequentially Yours: Annual Science Fiction Anthologies

The Best Science Fiction and Fantasy of the Year, **Vol. 4.** Edited by Jonathan Strahan. 2010. Night Shade, ISBN: 1597801712, 9781597801713, 500p.

Eclipse Three: New Science Fiction and Fantasy. Edited by Jonathan Strahan. 2009. Night Shade, ISBN: 1597801623, 9781597801621, 289p.
This volume is preceded by *Eclipse One.*

Fast Forward 2. Edited by Lou Anders. 2008. Pyr, ISBN: 159102692X, 9781591026921, 360p.
This volume is preceded by *Fast Forward 1: Future Fiction from the Cutting Edge.*

The Hugo Award Showcase. Edited by Mary Robinette Kowal. 2010. Prime, ISBN: 1607012251, 9781607012252, 384p.

Nebula Awards Showcase 2010. Edited by Bill Fawcett. 2010. Roc, ISBN: 0451463161, 9780451463166, 432p.

The Solaris Book of New Science Fiction, Vol. 3. Edited by George Mann. 2009. Solaris, ISBN: 184416599X, 9781844165995, 406p.

The Year's Best Science Fiction: Twenty-Seventh Annual Collection. Edited by Gardner Dozois. 2010. St. Martin's Griffin, ISBN: 0312608977, 9780312608972, 688p.

    This anthology series is probably the best-known yearly collation of SF stories. If you only have time for one SF anthology per year, this volume is like one-stop shopping.

The Year's Best Science Fiction & Fantasy 2010. Edited by Rich Horton. 2010. Prime, ISBN: 1607012189, 9781607012184, 544p.

The Year's Best SF 15. Edited by David G. Hartwell and Kathryn Cramer. 2010. Eos, ISBN: 0061721751, 9780061721755, 512p.

SF Spotlights: Themed Anthologies

Science fiction is a big genre, so many SF anthologies zoom in on a particular topic and explore it in greater detail. The following anthologies all focus on specific tropes, many of which are indicated by the title. Chances are at least one of these themes will catch your interest.

A.I.s. Edited by Jack Dann and Gardner Dozois. 2004. Berkley, ISBN: 0441012167, 9780441012169, 294p.

Aliens among Us. Edited by Jack Dann and Gardner Dozois. 2000. Ace, ISBN: 044100704X, 9780441007042, 292p.

The Best Alternate History Stories of the 20th Century. Edited by Harry Turtledove and Martin H. Greenberg. 2001. Del Rey, ISBN: 0345439902, 9780345439901, 415p.

The Best Military Science Fiction of the 20th Century. Edited by Harry Turtledove and Martin H. Greenberg. 2001. Ballantine, ISBN: 0345439899, 9780345439895, 544p.

The Best Time Travel Stories of the 20th Century. Edited by Harry Turtledove and Martin H. Greenberg. 2005. Del Rey/Ballantine, ISBN: 0345460944, 9780345460943, 425p.

Beyond Armageddon. Edited by Walter M. Miller, Jr. and Martin H. Greenberg. 2006 (1985). University of Nebraska Press, ISBN: 0803283156, 9780803283152, 387p.

This collection features life (or a reasonable facsimile thereof) after nuclear war.

Beyond Flesh. Edited by Jack Dann and Gardner Dozois. 2002. Ace, ISBN: 0441009999, 9780441009992, 260p.

When a flesh-and-bone body isn't enough, where does humanity turn?

Beyond Singularity. Edited by Jack Dann and Gardner Dozois. 2005. Ace, ISBN: 0441013635, 9780441013630, 288p.

Ah, that beloved singularity point, beyond which intelligence evolves beyond our current comprehension. Give thanks to Vernor Vinge before reading.

Clones. Edited by Jack Dann and Gardner Dozois. 1998. Ace, ISBN: 0441005225, 9780441005222, 254p.

Dangerous Games. Edited by Jack Dann and Gardner Dozois. 2007. Ace, ISBN: 0441014909, 9780441014903, 276p.

Daughters of Earth: Feminist Science Fiction in the Twentieth Century. Edited by Justine Larbalestier. 2006. Weslyan University Press, ISBN: 0819566764, 9780819566768, 397p.

Escape from Earth: New Adventures in Space. Edited by Jack Dann and Gardner Dozois. 2008. Firebird, ISBN: 0142411973, 9780142411971, 420p.

Explorers: SF Adventures to Far Horizons. Edited by Gardner Dozois. 2000. St. Martin's Griffin, ISBN: 0312254628, 9780312254629, 481p.

Extraordinary Engines: The Definitive Steampunk Anthology. Edited by Nick Gevers. 2008. Solaris, ISBN: 1844166341, 9781844166343, 441p.

Federations: Vast, Epic, Interstellar. Edited by John Joseph Adams. 2009. Prime, ISBN: 1607012014, 9781607012016, 379p.

Forbidden Planets. Edited by Peter Crowther. 2006. Daw, ISBN: 0756403308, 9780756403300, 307p.

The Furthest Horizon: SF Adventures to the Far Future. Edited by Gardner Dozois. 2000. St. Martin's Griffin, ISBN: 0312263260, 9780312263263, 478p.

Future Americas. Edited by John Helfers and Martin H. Greenberg. 2008. Daw, ISBN: 0756405084, 9780756405083, 312p.

Future Crimes. Edited by Jack Dann and Gardner Dozois. 2003. Berkley Pub. Gr., ISBN: 0441011187, 9780441011186, 276p.

Future Sports. Edited by Jack Dann and Gardner Dozois. 2002. Ace, ISBN: 0441009611, 9780441009619, 257p.

The Future We Wish We Had. Edited by Martin H. Greenberg and Rebecca Lickiss. 2007. Daw, ISBN: 075640441X, 9780756404413, 306p.

Futures Past. Edited by Jack Dann and Gardner Dozois. 2006. Ace, ISBN: 0441014542, 9780441014545, 290p.

Genometry. Edited by Jack Dann and Gardner Dozois. 2001. Ace, ISBN: 044100797X, 9780441007974, 272p.

The Good New Stuff: Adventure SF in the Grand Tradition. Edited by Gardner Dozois. 1999. St. Martin's Griffin, ISBN: 0312198906, 9780312198909, 450p.

The Good Old Stuff: Adventure SF in the Grand Tradition. Edited by Gardner Dozois. 1998. St. Martin's Griffin, ISBN: 0312192754, 9780312192754, 434p.

Fantastic companion set of anthologies that focuses on the adventurous and wondrous science fiction stories that got younger readers excited about science and SF. *The Good Old Stuff* covers the Golden Age to the 1960s, and the second volume covers the 1970s to the 1990s.

The Hard SF Renaissance. Edited by David G. Hartwell and Kathryn Cramer. 2003 (2002). Orb, ISBN: 031287636X, 9780312876364, 960p.

Immortals. Edited by Jack Dann and Gardner Dozois. 1998. Ace, ISBN: 044100539X, 9780441005390, 255p.

The Mammoth Book of Extreme Science Fiction: New Generation Far-Future SF. Edited by Mike Ashley. 2006. Carroll & Graf, ISBN: 0786717270, 9780786717279, 562p.

Man vs. Machine. Edited by John Helfers and Martin H. Greenberg. 2007. Daw, ISBN: 0756404363, 9780756404369

Metatropolis. Edited by Lake, Jay, et al. 2009. Subterranean, ISBN: 159606238X, 9781596062382, 264p.

Authors Jay Lake, Elizabeth Bear, Tobias Buckell, John Scalzi, and Karl Schroeder consider the shape of cities in the future.

Mirrorshades: The Cyberpunk Anthology. Edited by Bruce Sterling. 1988. Ace Books/Berkley, ISBN: 0441533825, 9780441533824, 239p.

Granted, this anthology is more than two decades old and out of print. It's also one of the finest, most fondly remembered SF anthologies ever collated. If you can find it, read it.

Nanotech. Edited by Jack Dann and Gardner Dozois. 1998. Ace, ISBN: 0441005853, 9780441005857, 276p.

The New Space Opera 2. Edited by Gardner Dozois and Jonathan Strahan. 2009. Eos, ISBN: 0061562351, 9780061562358, 545p.

> This volume is preceded by *The New Space Opera.*

ReVisions. Edited by Julie E. Czerneda and Isaac Szpindel. 2004. Daw, ISBN: 0756402409, 9780756402402, 312p.

> Alternate histories to make history professors' heads go boom.

Rewired: The Post-Cyberpunk Anthology. James Patrick Kelly and John Kessel. 2007. Tachyon. ISBN: 1892391538, 9781892391537, 424p.

Robots. Edited by Jack Dann and Gardner Dozois. 2005. Ace, ISBN: 044101321X, 9780441013210, 305p.

Sideways in Crime. Edited by Lou Anders. 2008. Solaris, ISBN: 1844165663, 9781844165667, 363p.

> Apparently, alternate history is like ketchup and the color black: it goes with everything. These crime stories occur in pasts that never were, so enjoy this unique combination of whodunits and whendidits.

The Space Opera Renaissance. Edited by David G. Hartwell and Kathryn Cramer. 2007. Orb, ISBN: 0765306182, 9780765306180, 941p.

Space Soldiers. Edited by Jack Dann and Gardner Dozois. 2001. Ace, ISBN: 0441008240, 9780441008247, 280p.

The Starry Rift: Tales of New Tomorrows. Edited by Jonathan Strahan. 2008. Viking, ISBN: 0670060593, 9780670060597, 530p.

Steampunk. Edited by Ann and Jeff Vandermeer. 2008. Tachyon, ISBN: 1892391759, 9781892391759, 373p.

Supermen: Tales of the Posthuman Future. Edited by Gardner Dozois. 2002. St. Martin's Griffin, ISBN: 0312275692, 9780312275693, 450p.

This Is My Funniest: Leading Science Fiction Writers Present Their Funniest Stories Ever. Edited by Mike Resnick. 2006. BenBella, ISBN: 1932100954, 9781932100952, 427p.

Time Twisters. Edited by Jean Rabe and Martin H. Greenberg. 2007. Daw, ISBN: 0756404053, 9780756404055, 306p.

Wastelands: Stories of the Apocalypse. Edited by John Joseph Adams. 2008. Night Shade, ISBN: 1597801054, 9781597801058, 333p.

Worldmakers: SF Adventures in Terraforming. Edited by Gardner Dozois. 2001. St. Martin's Griffin, ISBN: 0312275706, 9780312275709, 446p.

Best of the Best: Iconic Anthologies

There are many fine SF short stories. These editors purport to have tested the mettle of each and every one until they've yielded up the best brief SF tales ever printed. If you're going to SF cocktail hour, then these are the works the cognoscenti will be talking about.

> ***The Best of the Best: 20 Years of the Year's Best Science Fiction.*** Edited by Gardner Dozois. 2005. St. Martin's Griffin, ISBN: 031233656X, 9780312336561, 655p.
>
> > Dozois, who edits the annual anthology *The Year's Best Science Fiction*, distills the finest works from twenty years' worth of anthologies into this excellent compilation. This volume is followed by *The Best of the Best Volume 2: 20 Years of the Best Short Science Fiction Novels.*
>
> ***Masterpieces: The Best Science Fiction of the Twentieth Century.*** Edited by Orson Scott Card. 2004 (2001). Ace, ISBN: 0441011330, 9780441011339, 422p.
>
> > The author of *Ender's Game*, one of the few science fiction titles to break out into popular culture, selects his choices for the best stories of the last century.
>
> ***The Oxford Book of Science Fiction Stories.*** Edited by Tom Shippey. 2003 (1992). Oxford University Press, ISBN: 0192803816, 9780192803818, 587p.
>
> > Come on, people—this is Oxford University we're talking about! If this ivory tower prints its science fiction picks, then the list is definitely worth taking a look at.
>
> ***The Science Fiction Hall of Fame, Volume One: 1929–1964.*** Edited by Robert Silverberg. 2005 (1970). Orb, ISBN: 0765305372, 9780765305374, 576p.
>
> > This volume is followed by *The Science Fiction Hall of Fame, Volume Two A: The Greatest Science Fiction Novellas of All Time* and *The Science Fiction Hall of Fame, Volume Two B: The Greatest Science Fiction Novellas of All Time*, both edited by Ben Bova. Now you know where to go when you've finished these stories!

Index of Authors, Titles, and Series

About the Author

Photograph by Karen Woodworth Roman

STEVEN TORRES-ROMAN is a longtime fan of science fiction, a joyous obsession that began with comics and *Star Wars* and continues to this day. He further infects others with love for the genre by working at Illinois's DeKalb Public Library where he leads a monthly speculative fiction book discussion and runs programs for teens that involve comics and animation. (Yes, he gets paid to do these things. Envy is a terrible emotion—don't let it destroy you.)

He wanted to write a completely ludicrous fictional bio, something involving being raised by radioactive buzzards in the arid wastelands of Gamma 7, but the publisher frowned on such an endeavor, mostly because encouraging people to visit nonexistent planets is considered both wasteful and fraudulent.

He hopes that you find this book useful.